Lifting the World

The Autobiography of a Serial Entrepreneur

Bill Parkinson

*To my friends Marilyn & Susie.
Thank you for allowing
me into your highly social
lives! Enjoy my modest story.*

Bill Parkinson

Published by Ladyhill House

Bill Parkinson

First Edition October 2015
Set in 12pt Garamond

ISBN: 978-0-9934552-0-9

Printed and bound in the USA by CreateSpace

Published by Ladyhill House,
Breeze Hill Road, Atherton, Manchester, M46 9HJ UK.

To Irene, my long suffering and loving wife of 54 years.

To our three wonderful children Ian, Lorraine and Steven

and our even more wonderful grandchildren

William, Bethany, James and Conor.

CONTENTS

Preface

As a 75 year old looking back over my life, I can see that there have been many key moments. Decisions were made which, although not appearing very significant at the time, had a dramatic effect on the way my life progressed. It was sometimes possible, though rarely, to appreciate that a decision about to be made was profoundly important and therefore to accord the process appropriate attention and careful consideration. But most of the time decisions would be made on the hoof and the consequences would not be known until much later.

The story which follows will show how a man possessed of average intelligence and talent, born to modest circumstances and with only a moderate appetite for hard work, could achieve phenomenal success in business and acquire considerable wealth. The significance of getting a lot of small decisions right will become apparent.

For the sake of completeness and in order to provide a background to the story, the first few chapters will be devoted to the formative years which led to the momentous day, 2nd March 1970, when I started my own business.

My main motivation for recording this story is to let future, as yet unborn, generations of my family know how it came about that they have a more comfortable than average existence. I hope it will encourage them to build on what has already been a remarkable achievement. It will also give me an opportunity to acknowledge and thank the many friends, family and colleagues who have made a massive contribution to the story. And finally, I have the hope that young entrepreneurs may take some inspiration from the story and will say, "If he can do it, there's no reason why I can't succeed too".

Acknowledgments

Running a business is very much a team exercise and as the business gets bigger then more and more teams are formed involving more and more people. During the past 45 years in which I've been in business thousands of men and women have touched my life - as friends, colleagues, customers, suppliers and professional advisors. It would be nice to be able to name each one of them and to acknowledge their individual contribution to this story but that would clearly be impractical. I've therefore only mentioned by name those individuals who featured prominently in my life or who had a significant part to play in a particular episode or anecdote. I'm sorry if I've offended anyone by not mentioning their individual contribution.

To write a book like this requires the recollection of a lifetime of incidents and stories relying on a memory which is not necessarily perfect. Many friends and colleagues have helped me to remember for which I'm very grateful. If my recollections are subsequently shown to be faulty, the mistakes are entirely mine.

Much of the motivation to start the writing process came from two friends who have themselves gone through the process of writing a book. Firstly my very funny, wise and lucid nonagenarian American pal Ray Pavlik and secondly my old Horwich Squash team buddy John England. Without your example it's doubtful that I would have had the nerve to start this process.

I'm grateful to David Kerr, a Canadian friend who has immense experience in business and was kind enough to read an early draft of my manuscript and make invaluable suggestions. I'm grateful also to Paul Eustice the editor who has helped to shape my clumsy prose into readable English.

Author's note.

During my time in the lifting equipment industry the units of measurement for weights in the UK has changed from Imperial to Metric. This means that we now refer to tonnes and kilograms rather than tons, hundredweights and pounds. For the sake of consistency and to avoid confusion for the lay reader I've stuck to Imperial notation throughout.

Bill Parkinson
Atherton
October 2015

Bill Parkinson

Chapter 1 - Childhood

My parents, Les and Elsie Parkinson, were Lancastrians from Ramsbottom in the Rossendale Valley. Dad was a joiner and mum was a weaver. They married at Shuttleworth Chapel in December 1937. Mum's elder sister Annie (Nan) and her husband Johnny Kay had been married a few years earlier and had moved to London. Their reports of the work opportunities and wonderful quality of life were irresistible to Les and Elsie, who set off for London immediately after their wedding. They rented a flat in Kingston-on-Thames and Dad got a job working on the restoration of Hampton Court Palace whilst mum worked at Kingston Swimming Baths. Life was wonderful for the young couple. Dad and Uncle Johnny tried their hands at being on-course bookmakers at a dog track. Unfortunately for them, virtually every favourite won on their first night and they were cleaned out at once. That was the end of their embryonic careers as bookies.

Much more worrying clouds were on the horizon though. I was conceived in August 1939 and war was declared on 1st September. Dad joined the RAF and, after I was born on 6th April 1940, the heavy German bombing raids on London - the Blitz - meant that staying in the South was a dangerous option, to be avoided if possible. So mum moved back to Ramsbottom with her infant son Billy to live with her father-in-law, my grandfather William Parkinson who, as a widower, lived alone in his own terraced house on Peel Brow.

I have virtually no memories of the war years but I do remember the occasional air raid sirens and the rush to the shelters. I went to Peel Brow infant school, whose headmaster was the quaintly named 'Dinky' Booth. My life was very happy at this time with plenty of young pals who played outside on the Rec all the time. My best friend was Colin Ingham, who lived in the next row of houses to us. Colin will figure quite conspicuously later in my story.

During the war my dad came home on leave from time to time and these conjugal visits ensured that our family grew by the addition of my brother John in 1943 and my sister Joan in 1947. After dad was demobbed in 1945 he resumed his work as a joiner working for local builders and supplemented his income by driving an ice cream van at week-ends. This was great, as we kids were given extra scoops in the jug which we took to be filled.

We lived at 117 Peel Brow and our next door neighbours at 115 were the Davenports, with a very pretty blonde daughter of my age called Betty. Most of the children in the area attended Sunday School at Patmos Methodist Chapel, at the bottom of Peel Brow. The Chapel held an annual pantomime and in December 1947 that year's event was *The Wedding of the Painted Doll.* The cast consisted of about fifty performers, adults and children. Betty was chosen to star as the Painted Doll and I was to be her groom. Betty had a beautiful lace wedding gown and head-dress and I was kitted out in a black tail-coat suit complete with a top hat. We looked splendid as a miniature bride and groom but I was mortified when I discovered that I'd have to kiss her in full view of the audience!

I lost touch with Betty after that and never saw her again but fifty years later our paths crossed once more. I was waiting in the reception area of Murbros Printers, who did all of my printing, and started talking to a paper salesman. When we introduced ourselves the salesman exclaimed, "Bill Parkinson! I know of you. You used to live in Ramsbottom next door to my cousin Betty". He was Ray Gardner, who I'd known slightly as a child, but I was thrilled to meet him again and agog to know what had happened to Betty. He told me that she was now the Registrar of Births, Marriages and Deaths in Cheltenham and was happily married.

This was a terrific coincidence as by this time I was a member of a small syndicate who owned a racehorse. We were hopeful that our horse, Chipped Out, would qualify to run in the Cheltenham National Hunt Festival that year and had arranged to attend the races there. Ray gave me Betty's 'phone number and I telephoned her that evening. A man answered the 'phone and when I asked for Betty he said, "Who shall I say is calling?" I replied, "Tell her it's her first husband". He nearly went apoplectic but I asked him to just go along with the joke. He shouted for Betty and told her what I'd asked him to say and she immediately said, "Is it Billy Parkinson?" I couldn't believe it. She'd remembered me after fifty years and had immediately grasped the joke. We had a lovely chat and I promised to call to see her when we were in Cheltenham if time permitted, but in the event it proved to be impossible for me to call.

Then, in 1948, came the dramatic news which was to have a life changing effect for us all. My parents had bought a fish and chip shop in Padiham, near Burnley. I found out later that my grandfather (Pop to us) had lent them enough money to achieve this. We had to move thirteen miles, which might not seem to be very far by today's standards but to an eight year old boy it might as well have been the other side of the world. I had to leave all my pals, start a new school and live with my parents, grandfather, brother and sister in a two bedroom terraced house which doubled as a chip shop. Life was suddenly not as pleasant as it had been. Every town in Lancashire has its own distinctive dialect and the kids at my new school at Padiham Green mercilessly mocked this new kid who spoke with a 'funny' accent. I suppose this lasted for only a few weeks but it seemed like an eternity to me at the time. I was gradually accepted into the close-knit community and made some good friends.

By 1950 the chip shop business was doing well. Dad had bought a 1937 Ford 8 car and we had a telephone. Rationing was still in force and a fish and chip meal represented a tasty and nourishing family feast which most could afford. I was doing quite well at school and was entered for the Eleven Plus exam which was called the Scholarship exam in those days. My dad was obviously very keen for me to pass this exam as he arranged for me to have private tuition in addition to my school lessons. This clearly helped - I passed and subsequently took my place at Clitheroe Royal Grammar School.

Looking back on my five years at Clitheroe, I have mixed feelings. I was an unremarkable student with no particular ability in any subject or sport. Although I mixed well with my fellow pupils and maintained my place in the A stream, I gained only three passes at O level - Maths, Biology and English Language. However, a good education is one of the most vital assets that anyone can possess, even without a collection of exam passes, and the benefits I believe were of great significance for the rest of my life.

I guess that we all have memories of our schooldays and usually one teacher stands out as having been of special influence. In my case that teacher was undoubtedly Lewis Coles. For most of my time at Clitheroe he was my English teacher and I was terrified of him. In my first week at school he addressed me as Bunnockson, which I didn't understand until he explained that a Bunnock was a kind of Scottish Parkin cake. The name stuck and for the rest of my schooldays my nickname was Bunnocks. Mr. Coles was a very hard taskmaster who gave out more homework assignments than any other teacher. We'd have to learn long passages of Shakespeare, especially from Merchant of Venice, our set play for GCE English Literature. We then had to write out in class the passage which we'd learned, complete with punctuation. Typically, we'd have twelve or sixteen lines to write for which we were awarded twenty marks. Every mistake, however slight, caused one point to be deducted from the maximum twenty and a score of less than twelve resulted in detention. Needless to say I spent a lot of time in detention. It wouldn't have been surprising if this forced medicine had caused me to hate Shakespeare but the opposite was true. Although I am not a Shakespeare scholar, I came to appreciate his work very much. The same was true of Edward Fitzgerald's translation of the epic Persian poem, The *Rubaiyat of Omar Khayam,* which I have always thought was one of the most profound and beautiful works of literature that I'd ever read. Who could not be moved by verses such as:-

The moving finger writes and having writ,
Moves on. Nor all thy piety nor wit
Shall lure it back to cancel half a line
Nor all thy tears wash out a word of it.

Or:-

Life is but a chequer board of nights and days
Where destiny with man for pieces plays
And hither and thither moves and mates and slays
And one by one back in the closet lays.

I also discovered the writing of Somerset Maugham during my last year or so at school. Reading his short stories, set in the exotic locations of the far-flung outposts of the British Empire, used to set my pulse racing and had me fantasising about far Eastern exploring. The school library had a volume of Maugham's collected short stories which I inadvertently failed to return when I left school. It was a book which I would read and re-read many times over during the next twenty years, after which it played a very important part in an episode in my life which I'll recall later. Future circumstances were to dictate that none of my grammar school friends played a significant part in my subsequent life. It seemed obvious at the time that I was not suited to the demands of further education and I would have to leave school and find a job.

won 4-3 to secure the legendary Stanley Matthews his only winner's medal at the third time of asking.

This was in the early days of television and dad was persuaded to buy us a TV set. It had a twelve inch screen which showed pictures in black and white on one channel only. We were one of the first households in the neighbourhood to have a 'telly' and we had a full house to watch the cup final.

We tried desperately in vain to see Pop at the match. Programme scheduling was a bit haphazard in those days and there were often gaps between programmes. Rather than leave a blank screen the BBC would fill these gaps with what were called 'Interludes'. These consisted of several minutes of film and I clearly remember a speeded up film of the London to Brighton train making the journey in one minute. There was also a potter working at his wheel making a vase and later we were regularly treated to a film of Roger Bannister running the first four minute mile.

The other justification for buying a TV set at that time was the forthcoming Coronation of our new Queen, which was scheduled for the following month and proved to be the catalyst for many families to become owners of this new-fangled technology. Pop died a few weeks later and it was only when it was too late, as frequently happens, that I realised how much he meant to me.

I'd been smoking cigarettes since I was ten years old. As kids, a small group of us kept white mice in a shed on the allotment of the dad of one of my friends. We used to meet in the shed every day to look after the mice which multiplied at an alarming rate. One of the lads had a machine for rolling cigarettes and we'd go round the streets picking up discarded 'dockers' or dog ends. We'd take these back to the shed and remove the unused tobacco which would then be recycled into new cigarettes. Sometimes we would pad out the tobacco with crushed dried nettle leaves. I remained a smoker for over fifty years before finally quitting in my mid-sixties.

Chapter 2 - As a Youth

I decided I'd like to be an engineer, without really knowing what that entailed. I applied for an apprenticeship with each of the three biggest engineering companies in the area - Joseph Lucas, English Electric and Mullard. Their test procedures were very rigorous with a searching interview for all candidates. All had IQ tests, in which I had a certain ability, as well as a practical test. The Lucas and EE practical tests were very difficult for me, involving the re-assembling of bicycle bells and similar tasks requiring manual dexterity. However, the Mullard tests involved various series of levers and gear wheels and pulleys, which required logic rather than dexterity, and I found them much more suited to my abilities. I passed the Mullard tests and was rejected by the other two.

Mullard was a very modern plant, built at Simonstone just a couple of miles from Padiham, to make cathode ray tubes for the parent company Philips. There was a two-tier structure for apprentices. About a dozen trade apprentices were taken on each year to train in mechanical or electrical engineering and, in addition, two or three student apprentices were engaged to train in the same disciplines. The students were classed as staff and were paid more than their craft colleagues. They were expected to become technicians rather than tradesmen. I was offered a Student Apprenticeship in Mechanical Engineering before the 'O' level results were known. I went to see the local Youth Employment Officer to tell him the good news and he completely deflated my excitement by telling me that I shouldn't take the job as it was clear from my school reports that I was not good enough for such a job. Despite his misgivings I took the job which turned out to be a great decision.

All new apprentices went through a twelve month initial training period in the dedicated training school. There we were taught by the Apprentice Training Officer, Arthur Neal, and his assistant Jack Saul, covering all the basic manual skills such as filing and sawing. We also were taught how to use the standard machine tools such as drills, lathes, shapers, surface grinders and milling machines. We made various tools and equipment which would later become part of our professional tool kit, such as a vee block, tool clamps, calipers and, of course, a tool box, which taught us the fundamentals of sheet metal work. Mullard was a very enlightened employer and we were required to attend technical college to study for our Ordinary National Certificate (ONC) and Higher National Certificate (HNC). We were granted one day release per week for these studies.

Before I enrolled for my first year on the ONC Mech Eng course at Burnley Technical College the GCE results were published. Coincidentally, a lad called Frank Sherburn, with whom I'd gone to school as a junior at Padiham Green School and who had also been in my class at Clitheroe RGS, was also a Student Apprentice at Mullard. The Senior Training Officer received our exam results and called us into his office to deliver the news. I was terrified that I'd failed all subjects and when he opened up by saying to Frank and I, "One of you has done extremely well and the other one very poorly". my worst fears were confirmed. "You Frank have passed all eight of the subjects which you took. Very well done. Whilst you Parkinson have only passed three, Maths, English Language and Biology." Three! What a relief, and the three I would have chosen if I could. The Training Officer was not impressed but I was elated. He delivered a stern lecture that this standard was well below that expected of Student Apprentices and I would have to demonstrate considerable improvement if I was to continue my training at Mullard.

Suitably chastened, I started my first year of classes at Tech. This was called S1 and comprised three subjects, Maths, Mechanics and Strength of Materials. In order to progress to the second year, S2, it was necessary to pass all three subjects. Most of the other lads in S1 -

and they were all lads in those days - had been to regular secondary schools and found the course quite demanding. One of these was a fellow Mullard craft apprentice, Peter Beck, who also lived in Padiham. Having been to Grammar School, I was finding the course relatively comfortable and found that Peter was increasingly turning to me for help with homework. I didn't mind that and we gradually formed a close friendship based on our studies. The S1 exams were tough for Peter and he just scraped through with three passes whereas I sailed through with two distinctions and a credit.

During the S2 year we were introduced to Calculus, the branch of Mathematics which had been developed by Sir Isaac Newton. We were fired up by this and if Sir Isaac had seen further because he had been 'standing on the shoulders of giants', why couldn't we? Peter struggled again that year and just made it through again with three passes. I slipped back a little to one distinction, a credit and a pass.

By year three, S3, we were getting quite intellectual. We discussed all sorts of subjects, mainly of a scientific nature such as the origin of the universe, Einstein's theory of relativity and such mind blowing philosophical questions. I remember that we spent a long time trying to devise a way of accurately measuring the speed of light. The S3 year was of particular significance because a pass would mean the award of the Ordinary National Certificate in Mechanical Engineering, a very important milestone for a young trainee engineer. Peter and I worked hard that year, although there were plenty of other distractions making demands on our time. Peter just did well enough to gain passes in each subject whilst I got through with one credit and two passes. We were elated. After three years of part-time study we could proudly put the letters ONC (Mech Eng) after our names.

Student apprentices were moved about the various departments in the huge factory in order to give them experience in not only the engineering workshops but also in the production departments. The most popular of the departments for young apprentices to be posted to was Gun Assembly, where the electron guns were assembled before being fitted into the neck of the cathode ray tube. The assembly involved intricate, highly skilled high speed work carried out exclusively by young women of whom there must have been over two hundred. To be thrust into such an atmosphere as a shy young man was wonderful but at the same time very nerve-wracking. Some of the older women would mercilessly tease the young men who passed through their department, but it was all good fun and a great learning experience. It was here that I met a very pretty slim girl called Irene Lowe, from Padiham, who was only fifteen years old and had only recently left school. She had wonderful brown eyes and a shy smile which completely captivated me. The company hosted an Annual Christmas Dance at Padiham Town Hall which was coming up shortly. I would keep finding excuses to be near Irene's work-station but it still took several days for me to pick up the nerve to ask her to be my 'date' for the dance, but she amazed me by agreeing.

For the next three years we had a very on/off courting relationship, as I would get cold feet because I thought we were too young to be making a long-term commitment. Irene was the youngest of four sisters (it was actually five sisters but Irene's twin had died in infancy). Her mother and father, Gertrude and Billy Lowe, were quite elderly compared to my parents as Irene had been born when her mother had turned forty and her father must have been fifty at the time. They lived in a very small terraced cottage on the very steep Alma Street. They had an outside toilet, no bathroom and no running hot water. Baths were taken in the kitchen in a tin tub which was filled from pans of hot water which had been heated on the coal fire. The front door entrance from the street came directly into the living room with no vestibule, allowing icy blasts to enter the house during winter.

Alma Street was located on the opposite side of town to Hapton Road where I lived so I was faced with plenty of longish walks home if, as was usual, I missed the last bus. The first time I took her home to meet my parents she was absolutely petrified. We had a good meal which my mother had made - not fish and chips - and finished off with jelly and ice cream. Irene said she'd just have the ice cream as she didn't like jelly. My younger brother John and even younger sister Joan were incredulous. They'd never known anyone who didn't like jelly and kept teasing her about it. Irene told me later that she'd been very embarrassed and would have given anything at that moment to have liked jelly. But that wasn't as embarrassing as it had been for an earlier girl friend called Brenda who, on meeting my parents for the first time, volunteered to pour the tea after the meal and promptly dropped the tea-pot.

Apart from courting Irene and learning to play the Tenor Saxophone, another complication was that my mother had bought me a small printing press called an 'Adana'. This was manually operated and was suitable for printing letter headings and business cards. I solicited orders from family and friends and was soon supplementing my income significantly. I now wonder, looking back, if my mother deliberately did this in order to encourage me down the path of running my own business.

After I'd been printing for a few months I met a chap called Eric at work. He was also a part time 'hobby' printer who wanted to sell all of his equipment and stock. His set-up was much bigger than mine and he had an electrically driven press and a large stock of fonts of metal type of different sizes and typefaces. He called his business 'Mailsales' and he specialised in printing ladies hairdressers' appointment cards by mail order. For £100 it could be mine, but where could I raise that kind of money? I was earning about £5 per week at the time, which I had to hand over to my mother, but I reckoned that if he'd give me six months to pay I could make enough from the printing to cover it. He agreed to this but my troubles weren't over. Where could I set up all the equipment for my new business? As it happened, my parents had bought a three bed-roomed terraced house diagonally opposite the chip shop. The house had been owned by an old lady who'd died and it was in a very poor state. My dad bought it for £100 at auction and set about modernising it, which took a year or so. We moved in during 1957 so this freed up a room behind the chip shop which had previously been our living room. My dad allowed me to use this for my printing business. Problem solved!

The embryonic business went pretty well and I was able to keep up my weekly payments to Eric. Life was fairly hectic at this time as I juggled with trying to cope with work, technical college, courting, printing and saxophone lessons, which were all very time consuming. I also played club tennis during the summer and team table tennis in winter. Irene and I used to go to Accrington Conservative Club every Saturday night to the dance. Eddie McGarry's band played the music and Eddie junior, who played in the band, was my tenor saxophone teacher. I'd go to the dance an hour earlier than everyone else and have my lesson in a small room behind the stage before the dance started. I loved the sax and Stan Getz was my hero and inspiration. I aspired to produce those beautiful mellow notes that seemed effortless to him. Sadly, after many years of trying and practicing scales I had to reluctantly admit to myself that I had absolutely no talent for performing music and eventually I sold my sax.

Running this small printing business was a great experience for a young man. I learned about such complexities as cost estimating and making written quotations, preparing invoices, keeping sales and purchase ledgers, controlling stock levels, managing a bank account and, most importantly, juggling the cash flow. The ladies hairdressers' appointment cards side of the business provided a steady stream of orders and I also developed a nice line in Wedding Invitation cards.

My girlfriend Irene also worked at Mullard, in the electron gun assembly department, along with a couple of hundred other girls. They were all potential customers for my cards.

The girls had also helped me to make my first financial 'killing' a year or so earlier. Philips changed the design of their iconic Philishave and let it be known that employees could buy the old model, which had just been superseded, for the bargain price of £2-10s each, subject to a maximum of two shavers per employee. I bought two and paid three of the girls in the gun assembly department to buy their 'rations', which they didn't want or need. I kept one for myself as I'd just started shaving and sold the other seven to friends and relatives for £5 each. A profit of over £17 was not to be sniffed at when my wages were under £5 per week!

I was enjoying the whole experience of the printing business. It was very satisfying, of course, to make a profit through one's own initiative, but the actual process of printing from the design of the layout to the assembly of the type and finally the production of the printed matter were all aesthetically pleasing to me. I developed my skills as a proof reader, which was particularly important as it was very costly to produce printed work which contained errors. So the business was doing well and all the signs were good that it was going to continue to progress, but I was about to get a timely reminder that things can suddenly and unexpectedly go badly wrong in business just when you thought you were fireproof.

Ironically, I met my Waterloo as a printer as a direct result of receiving my largest ever order. The local elections were coming up in Padiham in a few weeks' time and the local Conservative party asked me to quote for producing their campaign leaflets, which would be posted through every door in town. I saw this as a massive opportunity to raise the profile of my business and quoted a keen price which ensured that I was successful in winning the order. I had only a few days to print several thousand leaflets, which meant working literally night and day to meet the delivery schedule. And that is what caused the problem. After coming home from my regular day job at 5.00 pm I had to start setting type, then at about 9.00 pm I'd be ready to start printing. My electric press was hand fed and wasn't too quick but once I'd got into a good rhythm the piles of finished product mounted very satisfactorily and the hours seemed to fly by. Then at about 1.00 am there was a hammering at the back door and my very irate next door neighbour, Mr. Howcroft, was standing there in his dressing gown. He threatened to kill me if I didn't stop this terrible racket immediately. I hadn't realised that he'd be able to hear the dull thump, thump, thump of my press through the walls of our adjacent houses,. Of course, I stopped the press immediately, but the damage was done and the following day Mr. Howcroft reported my activities to the local council, stating that I was causing a terrible nuisance. The council realised that I didn't have planning permission to carry on business as a printer in premises designated as a Fish and Chip shop and told me that I must stop printing immediately and apply for planning consent. Fortunately I'd nearly finished the big order and was able to complete it before closing down my press, temporarily, as I thought.

A ridiculous saga then ensued. I applied for planning permission which, to my horror and amazement, was refused after weeks of waiting. This was purely on nuisance grounds even though I'd undertaken that I would only operate the press between defined, reasonable hours. Health and Safety issues or food hygiene matters never came into consideration, which no doubt they would today. I was incensed. My Mailsales customers were being turned away and I was refusing wedding invitation commissions. What could I do?

I spoke to the planning officials to see what options were open to me and they said I could appeal against the decision. This seemed like a good idea so I appealed. I didn't know what I was letting myself in for. The wheels were set in motion and I was told that an inspector would be coming from London to hear my appeal in a public meeting to be held at the Town Hall. I was only about eighteen years old at the time with absolutely no knowledge or experience of these matters, but I was determined to try to show the Inspector that our neighbourhood could support a small printing business and that it could and would be run without inconvenience to others.

I drew a map of the area around the chip shop showing every house in a hundred yard radius. I then prepared a petition of support for my application and took it to every house shown on my map. Not one neighbour refused to sign my petition. It helped my cause that by now Mr. Howcroft had moved away and my new next-door neighbours were sympathetic to my cause, providing I didn't keep them awake at night. I also enlisted the help of a few elderly neighbours who would stand witness to the fact that I was a hard working, decent young man who was just trying to make his way in the world despite the efforts of the evil council who were trying to stifle this commendable initiative.

The day of the Public hearing arrived and I was astounded to find that it was an extremely formal affair being conducted in the manner of a court case in a room which resembled a Court with public galleries holding quite a few spectators. The Inspector opened proceedings and asked me who would be professionally representing me in the presentation of my case. When I told him that I'd be presenting the case myself his eyebrows arched in disbelief that a young whippersnapper would have the audacity to waste his time after he'd made the long journey from London. The hearing proceeded. The Council presented their case and I presented mine. My petition showing 100% support from the community, coupled with my passionate witnesses, proved to be irresistible and at the end the Inspector commended me on my presentation of the case saying that he'd rarely heard anything better. He granted my appeal with a limitation on the hours that I could operate the press. The local newspapers carried the story then the national dailies picked it up, with the Daily Express comparing the result to a David and Goliath encounter. It was very satisfying to gain the victory and great fun for a teenager to make the newspapers but in the end it was a hollow victory. The whole process took several months and through the enforced suspension of my activities I'd lost all my customers. My business no longer existed and I didn't have the heart to start again from scratch. I managed to sell all of my equipment and stock and called it quits. That would be my last business venture for more than ten years.

Life went on and Irene and I were courting strongly. My work at Mullard was proving very interesting. Student apprentices were moved every six months to a new department to ensure that they were familiar with every aspect of the complex process of making two and a half million television tubes per year. I was very active with our Apprentice Association and I became Secretary, which meant that I had to organise trips which would be of interest to the general body of apprentices - of whom there were about about fifty in total. I remember that we went to the Farnborough Air Show and to Cammel Laird's Shipyard in Birkenhead and also to Calder Hall (now Sellafield) Atomic Power Station. My abiding memory of Cammel Laird is of seeing a lathe which was so long that the operator used to cycle from the headstock to the tailstock. The biggest lathe we had at Mullard was about thirty feet long. The turner operating the lathe was cutting a shaft made of phosphor bronze. Even small pieces of this valuable metal were kept under lock and key in our tool-room at Mullard and when I asked the turner what the shaft was worth he told me that if I owned it I'd never have to work again!

In those days there was an annual national Apprentice of the Year competition. Both Peter Beck and I were selected to represent our company and we were very excited at this. We were given a series of practice interviews by senior managers, who would then give constructive criticism of our performance. In one of these interviews the manager asked me what I knew of the domestic hot water heating system of the average terraced house, which used a 'back' boiler behind the fire. I knew absolutely nothing about this subject but I thought I could bluff my way through. As I started waffling, my interviewer gently asked ever more probing questions until I'd dug myself into a deep hole of stupidity and ignorance. The lesson here, he pointed out, was that you shouldn't be afraid to admit a lack of knowledge. Honesty and frankness were always better than bluffing.

Peter and I headed for Manchester, where the North West regional round took place. There appeared to be about a hundred other lads from around the region from a wide variety of backgrounds, including the construction and mining industries. Only four candidates would be chosen to go forward to the National Finals to be held in London so we felt under considerable pressure, as we were representing our colleagues and our company. In the event I was chosen as one of the four to go forward to London in a few weeks' time.

When I turned up in London for the final series of interviews there were about twenty other finalists. We were able to meet and chat as we were waiting our turn to be called for our interviews. They all seemed pleasant lads but with an air of confidence about them, so I began to fear for my adequacy. One lad in particular seemed to dominate the conversation through strength of character without being overbearing or boorish. This was the lad who went on to win the competition and was declared 'Apprentice of the Year'. A brilliant achievement. For me the experience was extremely valuable in showing me that there were many qualities which went towards making a complete individual, not just academic competence. More importantly, it gave me the confidence to believe that it was possible for me to hold my own against the best.

Technical College studies resumed again to an air of excited anticipation. Peter and I were now in our first year, A1, of the two year course leading, if we were successful, to the award of the Higher National Certificate. It was September 1959 and the course continued to involve one day release and one night per week evening class. We got plenty of homework too and we both had to work hard to keep up with the pace. This was in the days before the Clean Air Act and the autumn nights would frequently be misty and sometimes very foggy. I always took the bus trip to Burnley with a strange mixture of anticipation and excitement. My dad had generously sold me his car for £15. It was a 1947 six cylinder 14hp Vauxhall J Type saloon. Quite a few of my friends and colleagues had motorbikes and I was hankering after one too. I think my dad sold me his car because he expected that I'd kill myself if I had a motorbike and, on reflection, he was probably right.

When I was learning to drive the country became embroiled in what was known as the Suez Crisis. The President of Egypt, Col. Nasser, seized the Suez Canal, which at the time was controlled by Britain. Our Prime Minister, Anthony Eden, threatened all sorts of reprisals including military and, for a while, the canal was closed. As it was a vital route for tankers carrying oil to Western Europe, including Britain, we found ourselves short of petrol and rationing was imposed. Also, a special temporary dispensation was granted to learner drivers, who were allowed to drive without being accompanied by a qualified driver. This was a great benefit to me and I was able to get plenty of driving practice in without bothering my dad or anyone else to accompany me.

Peter and I went to Tech one day in my car and at lunch-time, as was our usual practice, we'd drive from the College on Ormerod Road into the town centre for a quick lunch and a game of snooker in the local Billiard Hall. I'd parked the car on a very steep side street and had left it in gear with the handbrake on. When we came back to the car after lunch it wasn't there. It must have been stolen. We asked the shopkeeper nearby if he'd seen anything and he told us that the police had towed it away because it had 'crept' down the hill till it came to rest against another parked car. I'd known the handbrake wasn't brilliant but I hadn't expected this. I should have parked in reverse gear. We went to the Police Station to reclaim the car and the desk sergeant nodded at Peter who was tall and distinguished looking and said to me, 'Is this your Solicitor?' I thought I must be in serious trouble. In the end he sanctioned the release of my car from the compound after giving me a stern lecture on maintenance standards and let us go.

June 1960 saw the end of the academic year, which meant exam time. I'd struggled all year and was finding the course difficult. Peter, on the other hand, was benefitting from his hard work during the previous three years and was relishing the challenge. In the end I just scraped through A1 with three passes whilst Peter gained two credits and a pass. What a reversal of fortunes. Irene and I became engaged to be married at about this time though we weren't sure how we could afford it. Mum agreed that I didn't have to hand over my wages, but could pay her a nominal 'lodging' allowance. Also, we were very fortunate that the back and upstairs of the chip shop premises were now empty, as it was used as a lock-up shop. My parents agreed that if we would convert the premises into a self-contained apartment we could have it for 12/6 per week including use of electricity once we were married. This was an offer we couldn't refuse and we put a lot of effort into completing this work during the next twelve months.

I was twenty, a new academic year was about to start and it was the final year of my apprenticeship. This was the year when exam success would be rewarded with a Higher National Certificate (HNC). I continued to struggle in A2 in all subjects. I had opted to take the course for Mechanical Engineering with a Production bias. This meant that if I passed the exams at the end of term, with only one year's extra study I could also gain an HNC in production engineering, which appealed to me. The bias meant the introduction of new subjects such as Metrology, Metallurgy and Machine Tools. This became hypothetical as I failed in one subject and my low pass marks in the other subjects dragged my average down below the required standard. This was a disaster for me, made harder to bear by the fact that Peter had passed with excellent grades after having really struggled in the earlier years. He proved that if you're determined and ambitious and are prepared to work hard, anything is possible.

Chapter 3 - As a Young Married Man

Irene and I were married in September of 1961 and I was now 'out of my time' as an apprentice. After a short honeymoon in Torquay we moved into our newly refurbished apartment above the Fish and Chip shop. I couldn't afford a wife and a car so my beloved old Vauxhall had to go. Irene earned more than I did at the time and we'd bought our small amount of furniture from the local Co-op on HP. The deal was that if you paid off the full amount within six months you weren't charged interest. We managed to live off my wage and every penny of Irene's pay went to pay off the HP debt to make sure we met the interest free deadline.

The Mullard plant at Simonstone produced more Cathode Ray Tubes (CRTs) than anywhere else in the country, but Mullard didn't produce the glass components - the screen, the cone and the neck. For these we were reliant on supplies from Pilkington Brothers of St Helens, who were the pre-eminent glass manufacturers in the country and one of the largest in the world. We'd heard that our company had been in dispute with Pilkingtons over price. After all, Pilks were in a monopoly position. Mullard would just have to pay up or else. Or else what? Or else we'll build our own glass factory, that's what! The Philips Group were one of the largest industrial corporations in the world and could afford the massive capital cost of building a brand new glass factory on a green field site adjacent to the CRT works. A brilliant and audacious response.

As I turned twenty-one the glass factory had been recently commissioned and was now producing all of the glass components for the tube works. My first job after my apprenticeship was as a junior technician in the Batch House of the glass factory. This was where the sand and other various raw materials were meticulously weighed and thoroughly mixed in batches before being delivered through conveyors into the glass melting tank. There were some interesting technical problems to address from time to time but the work, by its nature, was largely repetitive. For five years I'd been used to moving to a new department every six months and facing new challenges and experiences. After six months in the Batch House I was ready to move on.

I did get a chance to work in the more demanding Tank Department, which was responsible for the operation of the glass melting tank. This is where I went through one of the most traumatic experiences of my life. The glass melting tank held hundreds of tons of molten glass at around 1500 degrees C. It was heated by a number of oil-fired burners above the surface of the molten glass. In order to prevent stagnant cooler areas under the surface, the burners were supplemented by electrodes inserted through the bottom of the tank. These electrodes were held in place by water cooled jackets which 'froze' the glass around the electrode. Very high electrical currents were passed between adjacent electrodes which provided extra heat for the melting process. However, the tips of the electrodes would erode causing them to lose height and efficiency. One of my jobs was to monitor the changes in the current flow characteristics and determine when remedial action was necessary.

This involved turning off the water supply to the cooling jacket and waiting for a certain time to allow the 'frozen' glass surrounding the electrode to melt. Using a powerful hydraulic jack and the help of three or four labourers the faulty electrode could be pushed up through the base of the tank to its rightful position. This was a task which was only required every few weeks and there were about twelve electrodes which needed pushing on this fateful day. Working on platforms in the considerable space under this mad hot tank was sticky and physically exhausting work. We gradually worked our way successfully through each of the electrodes and were about half way through our task when something went wrong. As the jack was pushing the electrode the noise of a crack was heard. Then we could see it. One of the thermal bricks which made up the base of the tank had broken. The weight of hundreds of tons of glass above was pushing at this now unstable weak point and it was bulging alarmingly. I dashed to report the problem immediately to the Tank Manager, Mr. Coates, who quickly assessed that the situation was very serious. Soon, molten glass started seeping through the crack, which was getting bigger all the time.

The most senior management then started to arrive on the scene and all sorts of solutions were tried to stem the flow. High pressure water pumps were used to flood the fissure with jets of water, all to no avail. The glass kept flowing. A growing mountain of semi-molten glass had now formed between the factory floor and the bottom of the tank. This void was about thirty feet high and was full of steel gantries and plant. The local fire engine arrived to add more pumping capacity but still the leak continued. By this time the crisis had been developing for about two hours, which seemed like a lifetime to me, as I contemplated that I would be held responsible for the disaster.

Unknown to me, sometime earlier the engineering department had been asked to quickly make a 12" diameter water cooled stainless steel cone on a long shaft. This arrived at the scene and in an act of the most incredible bravery I'd ever seen, Mr. Bird, the Production Director, donned an asbestos suit and, dodging the flow of leaking molten glass, climbed up the gantry and rammed the cone into the void through which the glass was escaping. It worked! The cone plugged the flow for long enough for the cooling water to 'freeze' the glass and stop it from flowing. I still don't know to this day what, if anything, I did wrong. Was there anything I could have done differently? The question has haunted me for years. The cost to the company in lost production and remedial work was immense. I never received a single admonishment for what happened but neither was I ever asked to jack the electrodes again.

Chapter 4 - Time to Move On

I had to deal with my failure to gain my HNC qualification and pick myself up to have another go. This time, I wasn't lifted by the anticipation of new challenges earned by successfully completing the previous year's course of study. The year of hard work which faced me was brought about by my own inadequacies. A further downside was that, as I'd completed my apprenticeship, I no longer qualified for day release and I'd have to go to night school for three nights a week. Not only that, but I'd lost my study companion, Peter, who was now a year ahead of me taking his HNC (Prod Eng). If I wanted to gain professional qualifications I had no option but to get stuck in and make sure that there were no more failures. I managed to get a good pass at the second attempt and the following year enrolled at Accrington Technical College to take the Production Engineering HNC, which I also managed to pass.

Irene and I had settled down to an uneventful married life. We were saving hard to have the cash for a deposit on a house and rarely went out. We'd have our friends David and Judith Hindle round on a Friday night, when we played cards and other games including, would you believe, tiddlywinks at which we became quite adept. Irene had gone to school with Judith at St. Leonard's in Padiham and we'd done a lot of our courting as a foursome. They married just after us and lived a few doors away from the chip shop on Hapton Road.

David was a teller at Lloyds Bank. One day he came home from work to show me an envelope containing one hundred £1 bank notes, the like of which neither of us had seen before. They turned out to be notes from World War 1 which had been issued by the Treasury of the British Government rather than the Bank of England, the usual issuer of currency notes. An old farmer had brought four hundred of them into the Burnley Branch where David worked in order to change them into modern legal tender and David's manager gave him permission to take some home to show them to me. The manager also said that if I wanted any I could have as many as I wanted for face value.

I'd always been a collector and when I was younger had a good stamp collection and, I'm ashamed to confess now, an extensive collection of birds' eggs. I searched through the old notes and was able to identify four designs which were different from each other in small, subtle ways. I decided I'd have one of each of these and gave David four pounds to cover the cost. I wasn't to know it at that time but that small transaction sparked a lifelong interest in collecting old British bank notes. Fifty years later I had built up one of the most comprehensive collections in the country, which I sold at auction for over £500,000. We still remain friends with David and Judith and, after fifty years, still see them occasionally.

I was now considering myself an engineer specialising in glass production but I felt that my horizons were limited if I stayed at Mullard. I'd only ever worked at Mullard and didn't realise what an incredibly good company they were. I thought every business was housed in custom built premises with the most modern machinery and equipment, with every activity meticulously planned and executed by highly trained employees who were fairly rewarded for their contributions. I was soon to discover another parallel world where these assumptions were not necessarily true.

Pilkington Brothers was one of the biggest glass manufacturers in the world with interests in optical glass, bottle production, fibreglass, windscreens and flat glass for windows, such as sheet and plate. They'd be the company to satisfy my ambitions and it was rumoured that Pilkington's were working on a revolutionary new way to make flat glass, and they were advertising for engineers to work in their Development Department at Cowley Hill in St Helens on a new process called Float Glass. What an opportunity. I made my application and was offered a chance to join the small development team working on this revolutionary new method of making flat glass. Although my salary would only be increased by two pounds per week and it would be necessary to move nearer to St Helens, I took the job with a sense of great anticipation. I was still without a car at this time and I'd need transport to make the daily round trip from Padiham to St Helens, a total of about 60 miles per day. I enlisted the help of my car mechanic brother-in-law, Roy Atkin and we found a ten year old Ford Thames van which would do the job for about £60.

I started the daily grind of commuting, which was to last for six months. There were no motorways in those days and my journey took me through Blackburn, Chorley and Wigan. The boredom of the trip was relieved somewhat because this was 1962 and mini-skirts were everywhere. The drive through Wigan was like driving through a tunnel made of girls' thighs. There was a significant improvement after I'd been making this journey for about 3 months when Barbara Castle, the Labour Minister of Transport, opened Britain's first ever Motorway. At the time it was called the Preston By-Pass but it later became the M6 and, though my journey became somewhat longer, I was able to save quite a bit of time. What a great pity that the development of the country's road network hasn't kept pace with the growth of traffic volumes.

My first day working at Pilkington's was a real eye opener. Our Research & Development offices were in the attic of an old, large, ramshackle shed. It was uncomfortable, cramped, filthy and totally inadequate for housing the two dozen or so chemists, physicists and engineers who were supposed to be working to perfect the biggest breakthrough ever in the history of glass manufacture. What had I done? I'd swapped the clean well-organised efficiency of Mullard for this hell-hole. Well, it was too late now, I'd just have to make the most of it and see what happened.

Up until the advent of Float glass there were two basic types of flat glass - Sheet and Plate. Sheet was produced in a continuous vertical process and was used for domestic windows where high quality was not essential. It was relatively cheap and could be produced in large quantities in various thicknesses. Where high quality was needed with an absence of distortion and ripples, for large shop windows for instance, then Plate Glass was the only answer. Plate was made by casting molten glass into a flat horizontal mould and, when it had cooled and solidified, it would be ground and polished on both surfaces with ever finer abrasive particles, culminating in jewellers' rouge until a highly polished sheet of virtually perfect glass resulted. This was how every glass manufacturer in the world made high quality flat glass. It was laborious, time consuming, labour intensive and very expensive.

Oil floats on water because it is less dense than the water. Alastair Pilkington (who though he happened to be called Pilkington was not a member of the original Pilkington Brothers' family) had the thought that if a liquid could be found that was denser than molten glass then it might be possible to float the glass over the dense liquid in a continuous ribbon. This would eliminate the need for grinding and polishing, at least on the top surface. What an impossibly audacious idea. After various experiments and the construction of a small pilot plant, the perfect dense liquid was found - molten tin. It was liquid and stable at the right range of temperatures and its density meant that the molten glass would spread out when it floated to an equilibrium thickness of 1/4" (6mm). Perfect - that just happened to be the most popular thickness for Plate glass. At the time that I joined Pilkington's the process had progressed from the pilot plant stage to one full blown production line. Molten glass was continuously fed from the melting tank into a rectangular box like structure about 200' long called the 'Bath' which contained the molten tin. The 100" wide ribbon of molten glass would gradually cool and solidify as it progressed through the bath until it emerged onto the conveyor rollers of the Lehr, where it would continue to gradually cool and emerge into the cutting room as a perfect continuous sheet of 1/4" thick Plate quality glass.

One of the biggest customers for flat glass is the motor vehicle industry, which uses a colossal amount of glass. Their requirement, however, was for 3mm thick glass, half the thickness which could be made using the Float process. The main task at this time for the Research & Development Department was to devise and perfect a way of making high quality 3mm glass using the Float process. After much work and experimentation, a method was finally found to achieve this. Basically, the edges of the molten ribbon were held by rotating edge rollers and the Lehr was speeded up. This had the effect of stretching the ribbon, which made it thinner.

This sounds like a simple solution but the reality was that in practice there were hundreds of variables involved which had to be tried in various combinations and the results meticulously monitored. After thousands of hours and some very inspired work we finally started making 3mm Float glass which was of an acceptable quality for the motor industry. This was a massive breakthrough for the company and vindicated the huge capital investment which had been made in this technology.

During the work on the 3mm project the staff working in our department were called into our manager's office one by one. We were all told that we were to be offered a three year contract and would be given a 10/- per week rise for signing. The contract would mean that we couldn't work for another glass manufacturer for seven years, we were sworn to secrecy regarding our work on Float development and we couldn't leave until the end of the three year contract. I was appalled. We were told we had a week to either sign or leave the company. At this time I'd been with the company for a year and was a very junior member of the team. Though I was proud to be working on what I could see was ground breaking technology, I was still far from happy with the antiquated working conditions. I thought that it was unfair of the company to impose this type of contract unilaterally and tried to get my colleagues to collectively refuse to sign.

We had no Union representation and in the end we all meekly signed our lives away. Very shortly after this episode the company's motives became clear. Once the 3mm problem had been cracked the process was seen by the world's glass manufacturers as the way forward for flat glass production. Pilkington had protected every aspect of the process with patents and the massively lucrative commercial opportunity for licensing was opened up. A succession of the world's most famous glass manufacturers were queuing up to take licences - St Gobain, PPG, LOF, Asahi, Nippon and many more. For the next twenty years or more Pilkington would not only sell dozens of licences but would also earn royalties on virtually every square inch of flat glass produced in the world. What a brilliant achievement for a privately owned company from Lancashire in the North West of England.

Irene and I had bought our first house, a small semi in a village called Rainford which was 10 minute drive from St Helens, which meant that I was finished with the 60 miles a day commute. I was still going to night school at St Helens Tech in order to gain additional 'endorsement' subjects which I hoped would later allow me to gain membership of the Institutions of Mechanical and Production Engineering respectively and become, ultimately, a Chartered Engineer. Irene managed to get a transfer from Simonstone to a small Mullard valve assembly factory at Haydock. But even though we didn't go out much the burden of a mortgage meant that money was still tight.

I managed to get a job teaching at night school at St Helens Tech, which would significantly help the finances. I wanted to teach Maths but there were no vacancies in that subject. Instead I was offered the chance to teach a subject for a new Technicians course which had been introduced three years earlier. I was to teach Fourth Year 'Engineering Materials and Design' to mature students who had successfully completed their first three years of study. It was a daunting task for me as it was the first year that this subject had been taught and there were no text books yet for the course and no previous exam papers.

Although I'd spent six months in the Drawing Office at Mullard I couldn't claim any skills or experience in designing. I studied the syllabus meticulously and prepared the content of my first lesson as carefully and thoroughly as I could. I was very nervous turning up for my first class and mortified when I discovered that two of my dozen or so students were full time professional teachers themselves who were aiming to improve their own qualifications. The academic year progressed and, with great difficulty, I managed to keep one step ahead of my students. I was mightily relieved when the exam results were declared to see that every one of my students passed my subject. What a relief. Not only was I pleased for my students but it almost certainly meant that I would be retained to teach the subject again next year. After all, I was the only person in St Helens who had ever taught the subject. Our new affluence meant that the old Ford van could be replaced by a brand new Ford Anglia Super 1200cc car. Wow! Not just a common 1000cc model but a whopping high performance 1200cc.

Our lives were further lifted in late 1964 when we found that Irene was pregnant. We'd been hoping for this but it still came as a shock. Our son Ian was born in June 1965 and I can clearly remember 'phoning Ormskirk Hospital from work and receiving the news that we had a healthy baby boy. I could have walked on the ceiling, I was so happy. Seventeen months later we hit the jackpot again when our cute baby daughter Lorraine was born in the same hospital. Some of my work at Pilks involved photographing faults in the glass and sometimes I had to work shifts. I had access to a dark room and photographic processing equipment at night and after Ian was born I took hundreds of photos of my infant son and developed and printed them myself at work during quiet spells. By the time Lorraine was born I no longer had access to these facilities and the novelty of photographing babies had worn off. Consequently we have lots of photos of Ian as a baby but none of Lorraine. She winds me up by saying that this is conclusive proof that she was adopted!

In recognition of the vital contribution being made to the company's fortunes by the Research and Development Department we were finally rehoused in new office and workshop facilities which were more conducive to producing high quality work. Not only that but we were increasingly hosting visits from technicians from licensees from all over the world and it would have been impossible and highly embarrassing to have them visiting our scruffy and cramped old facilities. It was interesting to witness the different national characteristics of the foreign technicians who spent time in our department learning what they could of this mysterious new 'Float' process. The Americans gave the impression that they already knew it all. They seemed reluctant to admit that the Brits could teach them anything at all about making good glass and their grounding in the intricacies of the process suffered somewhat as a result I felt. The Japanese, on the other hand, despite language difficulties, asked hundreds of questions, made copious notes and took photographs. It was no surprise to our team that when the licensees started up their own Float plants in their own countries the Japanese had the most trouble-free experience and were the quickest to start making commercial quality Float glass.

I was determined that at the end of my contract I wouldn't be signing away another three years of my life at Pilks. My contract ran until April 1967 so I started to look for alternative jobs towards the end of 1966. My colleagues all knew that I was intent on leaving and one of them, Brian Swift, with whom I'd struck up a close friendship, showed me a job advert in the Daily Telegraph. The advert was under a Box Number and was looking for a manager for the Manchester Branch of a small engineering company. Brian thought it sounded perfect for me and I wrote off for an application form. The form duly arrived which showed that the company concerned was based in Liverpool and was called 'Maritime and Industrial Services', describing themselves as ships' riggers and lifting gear engineers with five branches including Manchester. I submitted the completed form and waited for the response. I was invited to go to Liverpool to be interviewed by the company's Managing Director, Douglas Reevel, in a few days' time. I was very excited and determined to give this my best shot. I really wanted this job which, for some reason I felt would be right up my street.

I'd never heard of Maritime and Industrial Services (Maritime) and, even more worryingly, knew nothing at all about lifting gear or ships' rigging. Pilkington's had a good Purchasing Department and the Chief Buyer Richard proved very helpful to me in supplying copies of Maritime's catalogues and sales literature. I studied these avidly so that I'd be familiar with the company's products and services and the trade nomenclature. I also contacted a stockbroker and obtained copies of their last three years' accounts which, under English Law, are a matter of public record even for private companies. I attended the interview armed with as much background information as I could muster. The fact that I'd never held a management position, never held a sales position, was only 26 years old and knew nothing about lifting equipment meant that the odds were massively stacked against me.

There were 46 applicants, I was told, and I'd have to give an exceptional performance to prevail. In the event I found that Mr. Reevel, who had an old- fashioned formal demeanour, seemed to be warming to me. My confidence surged and I started asking him all sorts of questions about the company and the job requirements to such an extent that in the end it seemed that I was interviewing him instead of the other way round. Mr. Reevel was trying to establish a short list of three to be interviewed again in the Manchester Branch in a few days' time. Cheekily, I suggested to Mr. Reevel that I presumed he'd want to see me again in Manchester. He did. I was elated and a week or so later was offered the job after the short list interview in what was to become my new office in the huge Trafford Park Industrial Estate. If I hadn't succeeded in securing this job, the rest of my life would have been totally different. This was a major landmark moment.

The job offer contained two conditions. The first required me to move nearer to Trafford Park and the second required me to start within a month by mid-January 1967. This would seem to be an insurmountable problem as my Pilkington contract didn't end until April. However, I was only a junior engineer and it couldn't hurt them to lose three months of my services could it? I handed my notice in to my section leader who told me I'd no chance of leaving before April. I then submitted it to the Departmental Head who gave me the same story. I was beginning to panic. All of the effort that I'd put in to secure this job offer would be wasted if I couldn't leave Pilks. I then wrote to the R & D Director George Dickinson, who was a brilliant scientist. He explained that it was not a question of retaining my services for another three months but rather it was about preserving the integrity of the legally binding contract. In the three years since these contracts had been drawn up not one of the many clauses had ever been breached by any member of staff. I was definitely up against it but not yet prepared to concede defeat.

I then wrote to the Personnel Manager to outline my case. I pointed out that I was an ambitious young engineer whose ambitions were being thwarted by the fact that there had not been a single promotion in our department during the previous four years. This turned out to be a quite a powerful argument which, at first, was refuted. After all, R & D Dept comprised a group of highly qualified men successfully working on the most advanced and commercially significant project in the company's history. There must have been promotions? Apparently not. This group activity was so vital to Pilks that we were kept in virtual isolation in order to keep the team together. Seeing the logic of my argument, the Personnel Manager agreed to refer my request to abbreviate my contract to the highest available authority, Alastair Pilkington himself. The message came back that he was minded to grant my release but only if my prospective new employer would write to him giving a compelling argument as to why it was so vital that I should start my new job in January rather than wait until April. Mr. Reevel kindly agreed to do this and my release was granted a few days later, signed by Alastair Pilkington. As far as I know this was the only employment contract of this type that Pilks ever released.

Chapter 5 - The Trafford Park Years

The vacancy at Maritime's Manchester Branch had arisen because the incumbent manager, Derek Hurleston had been promoted to run the much larger industrial side of the Liverpool Branch. Derek was to stay at Manchester for a week to induct me into the company and show me the ropes. I was full of trepidation as I was shown round the branch on the first day and introduced to my assorted staff. There was my secretary Carol, the workshop foreman, Bill, the office clerk Charlie, the sales rep Fred, the transport charge-hand Johnny, the rigging foreman Sam and various blacksmiths, fitters, welders and drivers numbering about fifteen in total. Derek was a highly confident and competent man in full control of the business. He was technically capable and commercially astute and he must have feared the worst when he realised how green and naive his successor was. The most thrilling aspect for me was that I was responsible for every aspect of the branch's activities, sales, quotations, hiring and firing staff, purchasing, stock levels, staffing levels, debtor control and ultimately, profit. My performance would be judged on how much growth we could achieve and how much profit could be generated. I felt that this was what I was born to do.

Every lunchtime Derek would take me down to Deansgate in the city centre, where we had lunch of chili con carne and two pints of Double Diamond at The Grapes. The food was fantastic but the beer knocked me out. I wasn't used to liquid lunches and I felt like falling asleep every afternoon. Once Derek left for Liverpool I was able to get into a good working routine. The first task was to become familiar with the technical aspects of the business so that I could talk on an equal level with customers and colleagues. There were all the machinery aspects with which I had to get familiar - chain blocks, Tirfors, Pul-lifts, hydraulic jacks, machinery moving skates, then the tackle side of the trade involving shackles, eyebolts, wire rope slings, chain slings, turnbuckles etc. It wasn't rocket science but it was important that I became familiar with every aspect of the trade as quickly as possible.

I was provided with my first ever company car, a Morris 1100cc saloon. I was commuting to Trafford Park every day from Rainford and we were about to start serious house hunting in South Manchester. One day, during my first week, my morning drive to work was made difficult by a blanket of fog which covered the East Lancs Road. At the Greyhound Hotel roundabout at Leigh the line of traffic slowed suddenly and I had to brake sharply to avoid a crash. The car behind me wasn't so quick and ploughed into me, pushing me into the vehicle in front. I was the meat in the sandwich, with extensive damage front and rear and none of it my fault. Fortunately, I still had my Ford Anglia which I used whilst the Morris was being repaired.

Our workshop and offices were located in a long terrace of old industrial units called 'The Hives' and we had two adjoining units adding up to no more than 3,000 sq. ft. in total. I began to get very involved with the industrial side of the business and would frequently join Fred Mills, the sales representative on visits to our bigger customers. We had three significant competitors in the Manchester area, Dale's, Wilcox Chains and Peter Cassidy's and we'd always find ourselves quoting against one or more of them to secure orders.

The other main aspect of Maritime's business was Marine based. The Manchester Ship Canal was still very active in those days and ships would make the journey up the canal from the Mersey estuary to Manchester's busy docks. Most of the ships were owned by Manchester Liners or Furness Withy and we had contracts with both ship owners, negotiated at Board level, to maintain their ships' rigging equipment. The Health & Safety legislation required that all of a ship's lifting equipment had to be examined every year and every four years the tackle had to be not only examined but tested as well. This involved all of the ship's derricks with their sheave blocks, turnbuckles and other running gear having to be stripped off the ship whilst it was in Dock and brought by the lorry load to our workshops. We employed casual labour to carry out this work as it was required. Every morning the registered riggers would congregate at the dock gates and Sammy Webb our rigging foreman would go and select the men he needed for the work in hand. We were always working against the clock to make sure that the rigging tackle was back in place by the time the ship sailed. Each piece of equipment had to have a test or examination certificate and an appropriate entry made in the ship's register. Many was the time that we had to chase a ship which had already sailed down the canal and throw the certificates, which I'd signed, onto the deck of the ship at Latchford Locks near Warrington.

I was very conscious of the need to comply with the job offer requirement to move nearer to my work and Irene and I started house-hunting in earnest. The obvious areas to search were around Sale, Altrincham and Wilmslow, which would give me a reasonable commuting journey into Trafford Park. These 'stockbroker belt' towns were all on the south side of Manchester in Cheshire and we were excited at the prospect of moving up-market. The reality was that the price of houses in that area was considerably more than comparable houses in Rainford. We weren't prepared to take a step down in size or quality so we had to admit that we couldn't afford Cheshire and we started looking elsewhere. The cost of houses in the old Lancashire mill towns north of Manchester was generally significantly lower, like for like, and we eventually found a small new housing development in a small Lancashire town called Atherton, just south of Bolton. There were less than twenty houses being built by Fred Eckersley, a local builder, in the form of a cul-de-sac. This new development was about 10 miles from Trafford Park and there was a junior school close by. We could get a mortgage for a brand new three bed roomed dormer bungalow with integral garage and a decent sized garden. It could be built and ready to move into within six months, just in time for Christmas. Perfect. We finalised the details with the builder and signed the contract.

A few weeks later as the footings were being prepared I visited the site and noticed that, because the site was sloping, the foundations for our house were quite deep. I asked Fred if it would be possible to leave voids as a potential future basement rather than building supporting walls every six feet. He said that this would be possible if he put steel beams in to support the floor and I'd have to meet the extra cost. I readily agreed to this as I was going to gain three extra rooms for our new house and this was to prove of great benefit in a few years' time. In the meantime I continued to make the daily journey along the East Lancs Road from Rainford to Trafford Park.

The marine work was highly stressed, physically difficult work always working against a tight time deadline. It was lucrative but, as far as Manchester was concerned, it was a slowly declining part of our business as the number of ships using the Canal diminished over time. Around 1968, a very serious incident caused great consternation. A young ship's officer was killed in a tragic accident on a Manchester Liners' ship in the Port of Manchester. The becket of a single sheave wire rope block snapped off as the derrick to which it was attached was loading cargo. The becket was attached to a length of wire rope which was being hauled by a steam winch, operated by a casual labourer employed by the shipowner. The steel becket and wire were under tremendous stress when the failure occurred and they snapped across the deck like the crack of a whip at tremendous speed.

The young officer who was supervising the loading operations from over 100 ft away never had a chance. The becket cut off the top of his head and he died instantly. The subsequent high level investigation initially suggested that my company was at fault as we had examined the failed wire rope block and I had signed the examination certificate. It looked bad for my company and especially for me as the responsible person. This is where my mechanical engineering studies became useful. I was able to prove by calculation that the amount of force necessary to cause the failure of the becket was far greater than would result from loading the cargo in question. I was further able to show that not one steam winch had been used but two. The only explanation was that the two winches had acted in tandem and had both been pulling at the same time instead of one pulling whilst the other released. At the subsequent inquest the Coroner accepted my assessment of the sequence of events and exonerated my company of any responsibility for this tragedy. This was a great relief for all concerned and a sharp reminder that our work was vitally important in securing the safety of everyone engaged in the use of lifting equipment.

The growth of the industrial side of the business more than compensated for the decline in marine activities and my first year in charge as Branch Manager showed a significant growth in turnover and a healthy profit. I was growing in confidence in my relationships with my staff and our customers, bolstered by the excellent results which we were achieving and the fact that I had developed a sound technical knowledge of the lifting industry. The growth of industrial revenue was based largely on securing orders for designing and making items such as overhead runway beams, jib cranes, spreader beams and the like which put increasing pressure on our workshop capability. I was able to persuade my Managing Director Mr. Reevel that if we carried on this rate of growth then the 'Hives' would be inadequate and would inevitably inhibit our growth. He agreed that we could have bigger and better premises and I was given the authority to negotiate with the Trafford Park Estate Co. a 20 year lease for a 10,000 sq. ft. custom designed new industrial unit. What an exciting opportunity for a young Branch Manager.

My old night school partner, Peter Beck, was by now a Management Consultant with McKinsey, the pre-eminent US company. I was still in touch with Peter and he offered to help me plan the layout of the new location using an advanced technique. This ensured that the proximity relationships of the various functions and departments were scientifically evaluated and the layout of the shop floor reflected these evaluations. Our move to the new premises was a time of great excitement for us all - a new beginning. We believed that we were the best lifting gear engineers in Manchester and now we had the high profile premises and superb facilities to establish a dominant share of the local market.

The supply of wire rope slings to both industrial and marine customers was an important part of our business but we could only make hand-spliced slings, which would be made by our riggers. This was a highly skilled, difficult job which had been largely superseded by mechanical splicing by using a powerful hydraulic press to swage an aluminium ferrule to 'clamp' the ends of the wire rope together to make a loop or eye at each end of the length of wire rope. This process was known as 'Talurit' and the presses and ancillary equipment were provided by a company called Cable Covers Ltd, (CCL). At that time we didn't have a Talurit press in Manchester and I was forced to outsource slings from competitors which I was very reluctant to do.

CCL's representative was Chris Dykins, who regularly called on me to try to get me to buy a press, which would set the company back a few thousand pounds. I finally convinced Mr. Reevell that this would prove to be a good investment and Chris was rewarded for his perseverance. During and after this transaction, Chris and I saw quite a bit of each other and we subsequently became close friends, a situation which endures to this day. Another sales representative who saw his perseverance rewarded was Harold Guest, who worked for Glovers, a locally based wire rope manufacturer. When Harold first called to see me, for some reason I didn't take to him and brusquely told him that there was no chance of doing any business with him as our directors had negotiated a national wire rope supply contract with John Shaw's Wire Rope, who were Glovers' competitor. I was bound by that agreement to procure all of my wire rope needs from Shaw's. Harold knew of this and told me that if ever Shaw's couldn't supply what I needed in time then he'd be happy to oblige. He'd call on me every two or three months with the same story and still I was in no mood to give him a try. I was on the point of asking him to stop calling when one day our conversation casually turned to cricket. It turned out that Harold played for his local village team and he recounted some amusing anecdotes. He wasn't a bad chap after all. Then one day we had a rush order for a large number of wire rope slings using a wire rope of unusual construction. Shaw's couldn't supply wire of this specification so this was Harold's big chance. Glovers came up trumps and supplied excellent quality wire at a reasonable price and from then on I gave Harold regular orders as a gesture of gratitude for helping me out in our hour of need.

One of the functions of the business was to offer a repair and test service for our customers' lifting equipment. If your chain-block, Tirfor, Pul-lift or hydraulic jack needed to be repaired and tested we'd give you a speedy and competitively priced service. Sometimes it was difficult for a customer to cope without their equipment while it was being repaired. We'd try to lend the customer something similar to cover the temporary loss of their own equipment. This was like a garage offering you a courtesy car whilst your own is being serviced. I became concerned that the equipment which we were lending out in this manner was not subject to the usual stringent quality control procedures and might not be perfectly suited to the customer's requirements. No conditions were attached to these loans and I felt that we'd be vulnerable if there was an accident or failure of the equipment for whatever reason. Also, we were doing the customer a favour but gaining no revenue for our business. I felt that it would be better for the customer if we were to buy new equipment as a basic stock for this purpose and make a small hire charge when the equipment was 'lent' out. I put this idea to my boss Mr. Reevell and he agreed that I could spend up to £400 on equipment for this purpose. This was the inauspicious start of a Hire Department which would subsequently change my life in a most dramatic fashion.

From a very slow beginning the new hire department began to develop in a promising way. The £400 seed capital didn't go very far and we were always under pressure for more equipment to hire out. I deliberately misinterpreted Mr. Reevell's budget of £400 and thought that it would be ok to spend the revenue earned as well on new plant. Soon this new department was making a contribution of £8,000 per annum to our bottom line which meant that I wasn't going to be reprimanded for exceeding the capital expenditure budget.

The move from 'The Hives' to Ashburton Road significantly increased our overheads. Higher rent and rates, greater heating and power costs and extra staff costs all meant that for a year or so, until the revenue grew as expected, then we'd struggle to make a profit. This was all planned and anticipated and fully reflected in the budget which I'd submitted and which had been agreed by the Board of Directors. Unfortunately for me, the Board of Directors wouldn't be around for much longer and I'd have to justify the move to new premises to less sympathetic ears. My employers, Maritime and Industrial Services Ltd were taken over by a London based company, Coubro and Scrutton Ltd, which also had five branches. My boss, Douglas Reevell, retired and I had a new boss, Dennis Tattoo, whose background was in the marine side of the business. Dennis came to see me in Manchester shortly after the acquisition and after I'd shown him round our new premises, of which I was immensely proud, he told me that he'd heard great things about my ability and expected me to be appointed to the company's Board of Directors sooner rather than later. I was elated and filled with motivation to continue my branch's growth.

The next time Dennis came to see me a few months later, however, the story was completely different. Dennis was an extrovert natural born leader who shouted at his subordinates and banged the desk with his fist to emphasise his points. I was just the opposite and preferred to ask my staff politely to do as I wished. Dennis interpreted my management style as weakness and wanted me to be more aggressive, which wasn't my style at all. I'd had to re-write and re-submit my budget in accordance with the new Coubro style and this was being reviewed by Dennis against a background which would be measuring Dennis's own competence as the MD of the enlarged group. Although I explained to him that our overheads had dramatically increased due to our move to larger premises, which would result in small trading losses until sales revenue grew proportionately, he refused to accept a budget which projected a loss. He also refused to sanction any capital expenditure on plant hire equipment, which made me livid.

I argued that hire was the fastest growing and potentially most profitable aspect of our Manchester Branch's business but he wasn't impressed. He told me that we were lifting gear engineers who used our skills and experience to design, manufacture, repair and test lifting equipment for a wide range of industrial and marine customers. If I wanted to run a hire operation he'd put me in a shed in the middle of a field. This was the start of an increasingly acrimonious relationship. He clearly didn't like me and, despite the fact that I was working as hard as I could for the company, he didn't feel that I was an effective Branch Manager. Then, the week before Christmas 1969, I received a letter from him giving me the devastating news that the Board required me to offer my resignation by giving two months' notice. I had two young children under five years old and a mortgage on my house. I was offered no compensation and this was before such recourse opportunities as Industrial Tribunals. What was I to do?

Chapter 6 - On My Own

I felt very hurt and deeply embarrassed at being sacked. It was a great professional stigma. After all, hard-working competent employees didn't get sacked did they? I was even too embarrassed to tell my wife, Irene that I'd been sacked. I told her that I'd resigned because I could no longer work with my MD. My first instinct was to start job hunting again in earnest. I was a well-qualified engineer and I shouldn't have too much trouble getting a job. But my heart wasn't in it. I never again wanted my livelihood to be subject to the whim of another man's opinion of me. During the first weeks of January I continued working my notice and kept my company car. The Hire Department continued to operate although, starved of capital investment, there were quite a few orders which had to be turned down because of a lack of available plant. This was my opportunity. If Dennis Tattoo and Coubro didn't want to operate a hire service for their customers then I'd do it. I decided there and then to start my own business to be called 'Lifting Gear Hire' which would exactly describe what I was offering.

I worked feverishly on preparing a budget for the first year of trading. A turnover of £13,200 was projected, producing a profit of £1800. Very encouraging. However, in order to achieve this I'd have to incur capital expenditure on plant for hire, transport and office equipment and I'd have expenditure on premises rent, staff salary, printing and stationery, not to mention my own salary. The monthly cash flow projections which I prepared showed that I'd need at least £7,200 to start the business and make it through the first year. As I only had about £50 in the bank at that time it seemed like an impossible dream.

My work in Manchester during the previous few years had enabled me to get to know a lot of people and companies working in the lifting equipment or plant hire fields. I felt that my new company plans were so wonderful and irresistible that they'd be queuing up to invest in it. I would offer a 50% stake to any individual or company who was prepared to provide the £7,200 initial capital. I made a list of about a dozen potential investors and made appointments to see them all, armed with photocopies of my budget and a short written presentation. After two or three weeks I was full of despair as one by one my potential investors turned me down. Some thought that the idea was unsound - you'd never build a business on such a narrow specialist service. Others thought that the investment was too great for the potential return. Finally, I came to the last name on the list, Greenham Tool Hire.

Greenham was a subsidiary of Taylor Woodrow, the construction giant, and Mr. Hill, the local director, was a very experienced hire executive. He heard me out patiently. He explained that, although he liked my ideas and was impressed by the thoroughness of my projections, he couldn't possibly ask the Taylor Woodrow Board for the investment of such a paltry sum. I would have more chance if I was asking for £720,000. He then stunned me by suggesting that I contact my bank manager. If I owned my own house he pointed out, even though subject to a mortgage, then there would be equity which could be used as security. I was very sceptical of this idea as, to me, the bank manager was the guy who wrote to me at the end of the month if I'd overdrawn my account. Borrowing over £7,000 was difficult to imagine. But it was a lifeline, my last chance to turn my ideas into reality, so I'd no alternative but to give it a go.

I'd never previously met my local NatWest bank manager, Alan Cowley, but he readily agreed to see me at short notice. He read my budget and presentation with interest and then he explained that he was about to retire. This was a stroke of luck for me as,, whatever arrangement we agreed, he wouldn't be around to stand the consequences so perhaps he could afford to be a little more generous than would ordinarily be the case. He told me that his discretionary limit was to grant secured overdrafts of no more than £2,500 and he said that, subject to the equity in my house being of reasonable value, then this is what he was prepared to offer. On the one hand I was very happy and relieved but on the other hand, the amount being offered fell well below what I'd calculated would be needed. I'd have to sharpen my pencil and see where I could make economies in my budget.

This exercise proved to be good practice in lateral thinking and I immediately saw that I could survive without a full-time fitter/driver if I could recruit some part time assistance. Did I need a full time clerk/typist/telephonist/accounts clerk? No, Irene could deal with telephone calls when I was out and I could do the typing of invoices and recording of account details at night. I could manage without a family car and instead of new I could buy a second hand van on HP, which would double as the family transport when it wasn't being used to deliver lifting tackle. I didn't need to rent a unit on an industrial estate. If I could find a small cheap warehouse/workshop that would suffice for now and the foresight of having Fred Eckersley provide a basement under my house would now prove to be invaluable as I could turn it into decent office accommodation. This was all looking promising and I was shaving considerable costs from my budget and the cash-flow forecast. But it wasn't enough.

The biggest drain on cash would be the capital spent on new lifting equipment, which would form my core stock of plant to hire out to my customers. I anticipated that it would take several months of hire revenue earning before the cash flow would be sufficient to pay for this so there was nothing for it but to stand the capital cost.

The items I'd be buying were individually of low value and it wasn't possible to get HP finance on them. The main dealers of new lifting equipment in Manchester were William Allen Machinery Ltd. They were agents/stockists for Felco chainblocks, Yale & Towne Pul-lifts,

Tirfors, Tangye Hydraulic Jacks and Verrolec Machinery Moving Skates. These comprised a very large proportion of the equipment which I would need to buy. I'd already met Mr. Tomlinson, their rather severe and formal Managing Director, a few weeks earlier when he'd turned down the opportunity to invest in my start-up business, so it was with hope rather than expectation that I arranged to see him again. I frankly explained my present position and told him that if his company would grant me 3 months credit I was convinced that I had a business plan which would work. I promised that I'd pay his bills spot on the due date and wouldn't let him down. Most of his customers were probably taking two to three months' credit anyway so he readily agreed to my proposal subject to an upper limit of £5,000 credit. This was virtually the last piece in the jig-saw as far as financing was concerned so I could now turn my attention with confidence to the detailed planning of how to turn my plans into reality.

I still needed a workshop/storeroom and scoured the area within a mile or so of my home - which would now be my office. A well-established local business was Jay's Transport, whose owner, Eric Jay, was a prominent and successful businessman. I'd been told that Mr. Jay owned a small modern brick built building known locally as The Dairy, which would be perfect for my needs. I went to see him, hoping to persuade him to let me rent the building for a modest sum. He quizzed me carefully about my plans then said, "Ay lad, it won't work! Tha must be mad. Get thissel a job and make sure't kids don't starve." I was shocked. Here was a respected and experienced business man giving my plans the thumbs down. He wouldn't rent me his property because he didn't believe I could make it work. Oh no? I'll show him. Not a hundred yards from Jays on Bolton Old Road was an old Co-op building which had been taken over by Arthur Ramsdale and John Wilson, sausage manufacturers, who occupied the large basement of the building. There were various other rooms including two rooms of about 1000 sq. ft. each with separate loading bays. One was occupied by a carpet stockist but the other one was empty. John and Arthur let me have it for £2 per week.

Whilst serving the last couple of weeks of my notice period I was virtually on 'gardening leave' and spent the time finalising the details of my business. I registered the business name and designed what I thought was a pretty impressive logo. All Felco chainblocks and Yale Pul-lifts were green when bought from the manufacturers and my van was green so it wasn't much of a decision to choose green as the house colour for Lifting Gear Hire. I designed the letter heading and a small catalogue/price list plus delivery notes, invoices, statements and business cards, which I arranged to be printed on the side by the cousin of my friend and neighbour, Ray Garside. Ray has remained a good friend to this day and will feature again in various episodes of my story.

I found a firm of accountants, Edward Ryan in Bolton, who advised me on what financial records would be necessary and found an insurance broker in Rochdale who arranged for the basic vehicle and liability insurance cover. I had a local sign-writer paint my van with my business name and 'phone number on the sides and rear, together with my splendid logo. It was tempting to try to get my new venture off to a flying start by calling on potential customers. However, though I was very bitter about the way I'd been treated and was determined to compete with Coubro as aggressively as I could, I felt that it would be unethical to start selling to their customers whilst they were still paying my salary. I also visited the Unemployment Office and signed on the 'dole' which meant that I'd be paid unemployment benefit. I explained to them that I was starting my own business but didn't expect to be earning any money for a month or so. They assured me that it was perfectly acceptable to sign on in those circumstances and the benefit payments certainly helped in those early days.

One of my most important tasks though at this time was to arrange for help on the practical, maintenance side. Although I was a qualified engineer and was competent with the theoretical aspects and technical specifications of lifting equipment, I'd never stripped down a chain block or a Tirfor in my life. Once my business was up and running I'd need someone to take care of this aspect. Fortunately, I'd met a young fitter some months earlier. His name was Dave Pasquill and he was a wiry, strong, fit ex-rigger who was not only very skilled and experienced with lifting tackle but a workaholic whose full time job was with a local Plant Hire company who also dealt in lifting equipment. He was keen to increase his earnings by moonlighting for me and we came to a mutually satisfactory agreement. I promised Dave that if my business prospered he'd be my first employee.

Chapter 7 - In Business

Monday 2nd March 1970 was a date which became etched into my consciousness forever. It was the date that my business officially opened its doors and I'd finally become my own boss. However, I still didn't have any customers so I was keen to get on the road and spread the word about my unique new offering. From my Coubro days, I knew of about twenty companies who regularly or intermittently would hire lifting equipment and, of course, these were my first targets. I've never considered myself to be a good salesman and I very much admire the smooth confidence and affable manner which the true professional salesperson displays. I like to think that my exuberance and enthusiasm more than compensated for my lack of professional selling skills as I visited all of these potential customers in turn. The need to hire an item of lifting equipment doesn't arise every day for any given customer and it was unlikely that I'd ever be greeted with open arms as "just the person we've been hoping to see". Most were happy to listen to my presentation but usually let me know that they only needed to hire on rare occasions and, in any case, were satisfied with their present suppliers. A few said that they'd give me a try if the opportunity arose. My first week as a businessman ended without receiving a single enquiry. I wasn't too despondent but I was itching for some real action.

Then it happened! On the Tuesday of the second week I was in my office at home when I got a call from Alf Lewis of Capper Pipe Service Co. in Warrington. Cappers were plant and pipe work fabricators and installers for the petro-chemical industry. Widnes, Runcorn, Warrington and Ellesmere Port were a rich source of work and they had teams of men working on various contracts throughout the area. Alf was responsible for supporting the workers in the field by ensuring that all the plant and equipment which they needed to complete the contract was available when required. He had been one of my first calls the previous week and he'd promised to give me a chance sometime. He was as good as his word and he asked me to supply on hire a 1 ton chainblock, 20ft height of lift, and deliver it that afternoon to the Capper team working at ICI's Kestner Kellner Plant in Widnes. Quickly 'phoning William Allen to order a new Felco chainblock, I typed out my first delivery note, which doubled as a hire agreement, and jumped into my van heading for Manchester. I collected the chainblock and delivered this shiny new piece of equipment on time to Capper's team foreman in Widnes. The chainblock had cost £28-10s, for which I'd charge £2-17s per week. The government had announced that we would be converting to decimal currency later that year so my catalogue/price list showed prices in both Pounds, Shillings and Pence and decimal notation.

The following day Alf 'phoned again, this time to order two 1 ton chainblocks, 20ft h.o.l. (height of lift) for the same site. I followed the same procedure but was a bit concerned that my first three plant items were identical to each other. I wanted to develop a wide range of different lifting products and here I was sinking all my capital into the same items. I needn't have worried. The next few weeks saw a slow but steady increase in orders from an ever widening customer base wishing to hire a wide variety of products. Dave was having to spend an hour or two each night in the workshop checking over and cleaning equipment which had been returned and making sure it was safe and ready to be hired again. My time was spent in collecting new equipment from William Allen and delivering to customers all over the greater Manchester area.

Once I'd made a delivery it was my usual practice to look around for other potential customers in that locality and call to make my sales pitch and leave a catalogue. I remember driving past a commercial bakery in Leigh called Guest's Model Bakery. I wasn't in a hurry so, on a whim, I stopped to make my sales pitch without much expectation of winning any business. After all, this was a bakery and bakeries didn't use lifting tackle did they? I saw the engineer who was responsible for the maintenance of the mixing equipment, the ovens and the conveyors. He was thrilled to see me as he was responsible for completely changing the layout of the bakery and all of their machinery was to be moved around and re-located. He gave me a substantial order for a wide variety of equipment which would make his task much easier. This incident proved to be of great significance to me as I not only gained a decent order but it re-inforced my belief that the service which I was offering could be relevant to virtually any commercial operation. I gained a lot of confidence from this.

Right from day one I was a meticulous record keeper. I created a card index system and each new item of plant had its own record card. The full technical description was noted, together with capital cost, serial number, test certificate number, date of purchase, due date of examination and hire rate. Each hire transaction for that item would be recorded with the on-hire and off-hire dates noted and cumulative days hire recorded. In addition, I erected a large hardboard peg board on the wall behind my big metal second-hand desk. Each item of plant had a label stuck on the board which identified it and clearly showed the hire rate. I bought dozens of coloured plastic golf tees which perfectly fitted the holes in the peg board and inserted these against the appropriate labels to signify the status of an item at any given time. Red signified 'on hire', yellow indicated 'available' and white showed 'under repair'. Every Friday evening I would add up the weekly hire rates of all the labels which had a red peg and this would be a snapshot of the total weekly hire revenue being generated by LGH. I would plot this figure on a graph which I was encouraged to see was slowly but constantly rising. I clearly remember dashing up the steps from my basement office one Friday evening to excitedly announce to Irene, "We've hit £100 per week! We have a business".

Although things were going well, the budgeted first year's turnover of £13,000 appeared to be out of reach. It was October and construction and maintenance operations were less active than during the summer. Cash flow was a continuous struggle and I chased my customers to pay me quickly so that I could meet my promise to pay William Allen on time. Most businessmen will look back on their careers and point to significant moments which helped to shape their businesses. I was about to experience such a moment though the significance would not become apparent for quite a few months.

I received a 'phone call from Johnny Byrne, who'd been my transport charge-hand at Coubro. Johnny was now responsible for running the remnants of Coubro's hire department, though it was a struggle for him with the limited resources which were afforded to him. He asked me if I had any 1225 Hydralite Jacks available. This is a hydraulic jack of 25 ton capacity with a 12" stroke, made by Birmingham based Tangye. When I said that he could have as many as he wanted he said that he couldn't deal with me. Dennis Tattoo had told my old colleagues that I'd quickly go bankrupt and under no circumstances were they to deal with me or my new business. Johnny said he had a customer with an urgent need for two of these jacks at the massive construction site for Air Products at Carrington. The customer was Taylor Woodrow and the contact was John Acton-Brown.

Hydraulic jacks are susceptible to fluid leakage around the ram as the seals wear or the ram gets scored. Coubro had dozens of these jacks in stock but not one was in a fit state of repair to be hired out. Their failure to spend a few hours and the cost of a few hydraulic seals gave me an entrée into what was to become the biggest account in the first year's trading of my business and I believe it's no exaggeration to say, possibly made the difference between survival and failure. On such twists of fate are fortunes decided. I 'phoned Mr Acton-Brown, who was surprised that I knew of his requirement for the jacks until I told him that Coubro had referred his enquiry to me. He wasn't concerned who supplied his jacks so long as he got them on time and they were in good condition at a reasonable price. I didn't have any in stock but after my usual detour via William Allen I was able to deliver them in good time. Of course, I took the opportunity to meet Mr Acton-Brown, who was responsible for procuring all of the supplies for this huge contract. I was able to give him my full sales 'spiel' and offered to promptly and efficiently deal with all of his future lifting equipment needs. I was on and off that site dozens of times during the next few months and my revenue earnings got back on track to achieve the magic target of £13,200.

Another key account for that first year also materialised in a strange way. I received a 'phone call from the site manager working for Redman, Heenan and Froude, who were the contractors building a large new refuse incinerator plant for Bolton Corporation. He told me he had a requirement to hire a large quantity of lifting equipment and would like to see me. I'd never heard of his company and asked him how he'd heard of LGH. He told me that he'd "followed one of your vehicles" and made a note of the telephone number on the back of the van. He'd imagined that I had a fleet of such vehicles and didn't realise that this one van was my entire transport fleet. After I'd been to see him he gave me a very substantial order for a wide variety of equipment, including a 30cwt diesel winch. This put me in a quandary. The hire rate that I could achieve at the time for such a winch was about £20 per week. I could re-hire one from a local plant hirer for £16 including trade discount. I could make a turn of £4 per week for doing very little and incurring no capital expenditure. But hiring from a competitor was completely against my instinct. He'd be getting stronger whilst I was treading water and, although cash flow was very tight, I very much wanted to get into the winch hire business. A new Thompson winch would cost £800, which I didn't have, so I contacted Lombard North Central, the finance arm of NatWest who'd arranged the HP for my van. They agreed to finance the purchase of the winch over two years and I drove down to London to pick it up from Thompson's factory, driving back in the early hours of the morning to ensure I could meet the delivery promise I'd made to Redman's. I also took the opportunity to meet

Mr R.R.Thompson, the owner of the business, who kindly showed me round his premises. During the course of the next few months it was apparent that this was a good decision, as the customer kept it on hire for about twenty weeks, thus recovering 50% of the capital cost in the first hire. Not bad. And I was now in the winch business, which would prove to develop into a very lucrative part of my enterprise.

The end of my momentous first year's trading arrived and the audited accounts revealed that I'd achieved exactly the budgeted £13,200 turnover. The profit after my minimal drawings was £1600. I just managed to keep within my overdraft limit of £2,500 and I'd kept my promise to pay William Allen on time. I now had a reasonable stock of lifting equipment on racks in the workshop and had built up good relationships with a growing number of customers.

I'd always felt that achieving the budgeted figures was very important as it demonstrated to the bank that I knew what I was talking about and could be relied upon to deliver my promises. The value of this became obvious as I started to develop my plans for the second year's trading. My projections indicated that I could double turnover to £26,000, but I'd need help. Dave Pasquill would have to be engaged full-time and would double up as a delivery driver. This would free me to spend more time selling and also more time in the office, responding to customers' enquiries, which was where I was most comfortable. It was clear that I'd need a part-time accounts clerk too at some time during that summer of 1971. More plant would be needed to produce that level of revenue and the transport 'fleet' would have to be bolstered by the addition of a pick-up truck. My overdraft limit would have to be increased to cope with the growth.

On the domestic front, the move to the new cul-de-sac at Lancaster Avenue was working well. Among the sixteen or so new houses were a majority of young couples with young children. We made plenty of friends and so did our children, Ian and Lorraine, who had recently started school at Park Road Junior School. Two of our neighbouring couples became lasting close friends who would play significant parts in the developing story - Ray and Kath Garside and David and Carol Slane. Our next door neighbour, Keith Stringer, would become an extra driver on his day off if needed and so would shift worker Tom Seddon from across the road. Ray was a sales representative for Coates, the printing ink manufacturers. His territory extended all over the north-west. Although he knew nothing about lifting equipment, he agreed to drop my catalogues off at any promising looking companies that he happened to pass. I didn't pay him for this but agreed that if any of his calls resulted in business for my firm then I'd pay him a commission. One of Ray's speculative calls was to an Ellesmere Port company called Lakers Northern, who were similar to Cappers and became quite good customers. Ray was happy with his modest windfall.

Just a few hundred yards from our avenue was a kind of working men's club with a bar and two snooker tables, darts and dominoes, together with a bowling green. At the time keg beer had virtually taken over most of the pubs and bars in the UK but the Botanical Gardens Club still had Hydes Anvil Bitter, served as a cask conditioned beer. It was an exceptionally good beer, which was well kept by the stewards, John and Mary. It was here that I came to appreciate the difference between the bland gassy keg beer which was being thrust upon us and the exquisite, smooth, flavourful real ale. Now I understood what CAMRA were trying to preserve. Some of the men on our avenue, including me, made the Botanical Gardens our regular and I eventually played for their 'B' team at snooker every Tuesday night.

Ray and I, plus a few other neighbours, joined a beginners' badminton class on Monday night at St Mary's School, Leigh, in around 1969. We became fairly accomplished and very keen and continued the class into a second year. Then local authorities started building public Leisure Centres and six of us continued playing badminton every Monday night at a succession of venues. First there was Silverwell Street in Bolton, then a school in Westhoughton, followed by the new and very smart Horwich Leisure Centre. Here there were also squash courts and we all started playing squash too in addition to badminton. So we played an hour of men's doubles badminton 7.30 to 8.30 then we had two squash courts from 8.20 to 9.40. Then it was a quick shower and into the pub for a game of dominoes and a couple of pints. We transferred to a venue nearer home when Howe Bridge Leisure Centre was built and continued this very enjoyable routine until 1995, when our ageing bodies began to feel the strain. We might have stopped playing squash and badminton but we could still play dominoes and the six of us carried on meeting every Monday night. As I write this in 2015, we still do, making it 45 years of wonderful camaraderie.

Chapter 8 - Pushing On

My original bank manager, Alan Cowley, had retired and I had to get to know his replacement, Ron Gleave. During the first year I made sure that Ron was familiar with my triumphs and disasters and he seemed to take a close interest in my business. I think it's true that most business failures occur during the first two years so I was still in a vulnerable position as far as the bank was concerned. Ron was aware that the second half of my first year had seen some good growth, accompanied by high capital expenditure. When I went to see him to discuss my plans to double in size during the second year, he didn't seem concerned or incredulous. I was looking for a big increase in my overdraft facility to fund my ambitious growth plans and supported my proposals with detailed profit and loss account, capital expenditure and cash flow budgets. I had included amounts to cover contingencies in case things didn't go quite to plan and Ron agreed to meet my request for a larger overdraft but knocked 10% off what I was looking for, saying, "Sorry Bill, the bank doesn't deal in comfort money".

Armed with more funds, I offered Dave a full time job in April 1971 and he became my first full time employee. Then I bought a Ford Transit 1 ton pick-up truck on HP. Business was on track to deliver what I'd planned and I needed an accounts clerk. My friend and neighbour, Ray's wife Kath, had recently lost their first baby close to full term. She'd worked for a large local company, BICC, as a secretary and also had accounts experience but, because this was before the days of maternity leave, she'd lost her job. I offered Kath a part-time job as a general office factotum - typist, telephonist, accounts clerk. She would be working from the basement of my home, which was not a normal arrangement, but she readily accepted. Kath was particularly neat and precise in her work and had an excellent telephone manner, which I felt helped to improve our profile with our customers.

On Sunday nights it was usual for me to go for a drink and a game of dominoes to The Royal pub in Atherton with my next door neighbour, Keith Stringer. One Sunday, at 10pm, the landlord told me that I was wanted on the 'phone. It was Irene calling to tell me that Alf Lewis of Capper Pipe wanted to speak to me urgently. She gave me his home number and I called him from the pub. He explained that an emergency had arisen at a site in North Wales and he needed to hire two 10 ton chainblocks with 40' height of lift. They had to be on site by 6 a.m.! I told Alf we could do it and took down the delivery instructions. Then I 'phoned Dave and asked him to meet me at the workshop.

We only had two 10 tonners in the fleet and I knew that they were available but they had only 20' h.o.l. To achieve 40' h.o.l. requires a length of chain of 200' on five falls and a hand chain of 80' circumference. We had the chain available and Dave and I set about feverishly to chain up the blocks to the customer's requirements. We were done by 3 a.m. and loaded them onto the truck, which Dave took home every night and which he'd used to come to meet me. Dave set off for Wales and arrived on site by 5.30 a.m. Mission accomplished!

Although Capper were good customers, I knew that we were supplying less than half of their lifting equipment needs so, when Alf 'phoned me the following morning, I was ready for him. He was full of thanks for what was a remarkable achievement and asked me what premium we'd be charging for having worked through the night and saving his company a fortune in penalties. I explained that he'd be charged the usual hire rate for the equipment and the normal delivery charge on a mileage basis. When he protested that he wanted to pay us a bonus I refused but asked him to consider, next time he was procuring lifting equipment on hire, who else could he have called at 10 p.m. on Sunday and received such service. From that time onwards we became Cappers' main lifting equipment supplier and their account with us continued to grow for many years, peaking at £85,000 pa.

Dave was working hard and at times appeared hyper-active. We had the odd little disagreement and he'd go off in a huff for a while but he'd settle down for a few days before getting annoyed again. Then he hit me with a shocking ultimatum. He felt that he was doing all the work while I "sat in the office" and he wanted to be a partner in the business, otherwise he'd leave. Dave was very important to the business and it was true that he did much of the physical work, such as preparing and repairing the lifting gear and making deliveries and collections. It would be very difficult to keep my business going without him, or someone with similar talents. I explained to Dave that the business was my concept and it was my house which was offered as security to the bank. Giving him a share or a partnership was not an option. I would pay him well and he was sure to prosper as the business continued to grow. He immediately gave me his written notice to leave my employment in one month's time, as was required under his contract. This was a major unexpected blow for which I was totally unprepared and I'd no idea how to deal with the impending crisis.

That evening I told Irene what had happened and, after thinking about the problem for a while, she suggested that I might consider contacting John Williams to see if he could help. John and his wife Val had been friends of ours when we lived in Rainford whilst I was working at Pilkington's. Val and Irene had worked together at Mullard in Haydock and John and I shared an interest in snooker. John had worked for the CEGB at Bold Power Station for many years in an unskilled capacity. He wasn't a qualified time-served fitter and had no knowledge of lifting equipment so why would I consider him as a replacement for Dave? Well, he clearly had high personal standards of conduct and appearance. His garden and house were always immaculate, he spoke quietly but with authority, he maintained his car himself to a very high standard. He was big and strong and fit and he was a very pleasant, honest and dependable guy. He could soon pick up the rudiments of lifting equipment and, if Dave would stay long enough to train him, it could work. I telephoned John to put the idea to him and describe what the job would entail. After a brief discussion, during which we barely mentioned remuneration, John said he'd do it - much to my astonishment. Not only that, but John had two weeks of accumulated holiday leave due and would only have to give two weeks' notice. He took holidays in lieu of notice and was able to start the following Monday, only four days after Dave had resigned.

Dave was shocked that I'd found a replacement so quickly and the relationship between the two of them was quite strained at first. To be fair to Dave, however, he showed John all the basics of stripping down and reassembling all the various machinery which was our stock-in-trade. John was a quick learner. He had higher housekeeping standards than Dave and soon the workshop was looking immaculate. The end of Dave's notice period was rapidly approaching but I was confident that his departure wouldn't precipitate a crisis. Then Dave came to see me and said "Bill, I think we've made a big mistake". I said "No Dave, you've made a big mistake". He asked me if he could withdraw his notice. I explained that John had given up a steady job at a moment's notice to help me out in my hour of need and I couldn't possibly let him go. I didn't think I could justify or afford another fitter/driver so his notice would have to stay on the table. As it happened, we were very busy at the time so I agreed that Dave could stay as long as there was sufficient work and I could afford to pay him. The next few months were incredibly busy. It was clear that we couldn't have coped without the extra pair of hands and Dave and John worked well together as a team.

On one occasion, we had been asked to supply the equipment to move a heavy machine from A to B in a non-engineering workshop. We supplied jacks, skates, a Tirfor hand winch and assorted other tackle which we'd advised the customer would be needed. Dave delivered the equipment, but it was clear that the customer didn't have a clue how to set everything up to carry out the job. Dave ended up not only showing them how to use the equipment but actually moving the machine. We'd earned about £50 for the hire of the equipment, which was a fraction of the price the customer would have had to pay for a professional machinery moving contractor. This was clearly not fair and I decided that in future we would actively seek to carry out the work of machinery moving as a contractor. It made sense as we had all the lifting equipment we'd need and the skilled riggers too. We had to be careful, though, not to be seen as competitors to some of our customers who were also in that business.

One particularly memorable job in the machinery moving line happened at this time. Manchester Airport were having a new terminal built and Taylor Woodrow asked us to quote for installing an air conditioning unit, which weighed 40 tons. It was a tricky job and our successful bid was £2,000. The unit was about 20' long x 15' wide x 12' high and after unpacking the unit from its packing case it had to be moved inside the specially built room. Normally we'd have jacked up the unit and lowered it onto machinery moving skates before winching it into the building. On this occasion, though, this was not possible, as the skates were 3" deep and the door was only 12' 1" high. Virtually no headroom! Our solution was to buy two dozen 15' lengths of 1/2" diameter steel bar, which were placed under the unit to act as rollers. Once we managed to move the unit inside, we faced the really tricky part. It had to be lowered into a 10' deep pit with only about 24" clearance on each side. Inside the pit we built a latticework platform from railway sleepers and winched the unit over the platform. Using jacks, we were able gradually to lower the unit into the pit, removing one pair of sleepers at a time. The whole job had been planned meticulously by Dave and had been carried out by Dave, John and myself safely, without incident and without too much physical effort in a day. Two thousand pounds for a day's work for three of us. I was able to give Dave and John a generous bonus and still have the most profitable day of my life. The customer was happy, Dave and John were happy and I was happy - capitalism at its finest!

Two weeks later our landlord, John Wilson, spotted me in the workshop at Bolton Old Road and told me he'd bought a second hand meat mincer from a butcher in the neighbouring town of Westhoughton. Would I do him a favour and pick it up for him? "It only weighs 5 cwt", he said, so I confidently told him, "OK John, no problem, I'll do it this afternoon". After all, we'd just moved a 40 ton AC unit so a 1/4 ton mincer would be a piece of cake, yes? No. I took all the equipment I thought I'd need - soft slings, shackles, skates, a crow bar etc. - and set off to find the butcher's shop.

My truck had a 1 ton capacity hydraulic crane but I had a terrific problem manhandling the top-heavy mincer out of the shop and through the narrow shop door onto the pavement, where my crane could pick it up and load it onto the truck. The biggest problem, however, was back at the sausage works. Dave and John were both out so I was on my own. I had to negotiate a cobbled yard then get the.mincer down a flight of steps into the basement sausage factory. I sweated blood! When I saw John later he thanked me for doing the job for him and tentatively asked, "Do I owe you anything?". When I suggested that £25 would be about right he became apoplectic. "But I only paid £10 for the mincer," he exclaimed. The moral of this episode was not to mess about with the small stuff. Everyone knows that to move 40 tons is a difficult and potentially dangerous task, only to be undertaken by experienced professionals equipped with the most suitable equipment, who are expected to charge appropriately for their services. Moving a quarter of a ton? Forget it!

Machinery moving jobs were fairly infrequent at this time but they were very profitable when they came along, which enabled me to share the profit with Dave and John and this provided a useful enhancement to their earnings. I'd made the decision at the time of engaging Dave full time that I would only pay staff on a monthly basis. It seemed a big waste of time to me to be doing pay calculations four times a month when it could be done only once. If employees needed time to adjust from a weekly paid background then this could be arranged by providing salary advances for the first few months. Dave was never comfortable with this and would rather have seen cash in his hand every week rather than a cheque at the end of the month. He still had a chip on his shoulder about not being able to become a partner in the business and our disagreements became more frequent and intense. This culminated in Dave once again resigning and this time I accepted the situation without qualms. John had become very proficient and I trusted his workmanship implicitly. However, the business was still growing and it was clear that Dave would have to be replaced quickly.

I advertised for a skilled fitter in the local paper, stressing that applications were to be made in writing only to my office address, which was still my home address. On the night that the advert was published there was a knock on our front door. When I answered the knock a young man stood there saying his name was Trevor Lamprell and he'd come about the job vacancy. I was livid. I reminded him that the advert specifically asked for applications in writing only and if he couldn't follow a simple instruction like that then he was of no use to me. He apologised and explained that he'd understood that but he was so keen to get the job that he wanted to be ahead of the queue. I saw a little bit of the same cheekiness that I'd had when applying to Maritime a few years earlier and decided that as he was here I might as well give him an interview. He interviewed well and his engineering apprenticeship training with Gardner's Diesel Engines was entirely appropriate for this job with LGH. We agreed terms and I offered him the job.

As soon as that staff mini-crisis was resolved, another one came along. Kath announced one day, as young women are prone to, that she was pregnant. She had handled the office work very smoothly and efficiently but the fact that she worked in our house would make the choice of a successor more difficult. But it did give me a good opportunity to step up the hours from part-time to full-time to ensure that the office, and especially the 'phones, were manned at all times. Our neighbours across the road, David and Carol Slane, presented a possibility. David worked as a manager in the clothing industry. Carol had worked for British Rail in Manchester in an administrative role, before having a baby boy a year or so earlier. Like in Kath's case, there was no maternity leave available so she couldn't automatically resume her old job. When I approached her to suggest that she might care to join my little company she seemed keen, but when I said that I now needed someone full-time she told me that it wouldn't be possible as her mother could only look after her infant son, Mark, on a part-time basis. "But I have a sister-in-law, Muriel, who lives nearby who also recently had a baby and wants to get back to work part-time. If you're agreeable," she said, "I could ask her and we could double up, one working mornings and the other afternoons". I quickly saw that if one worked from 9 a.m. to 1 p.m. and the other from 1 p.m. to 5 p.m. then there'd be no lunch break and the 'phones would be covered continuously. These were talented and experienced young women who were keen to make a contribution to my business and earn a little more than pin money. In what would prove to be an inspired decision I offered them the jobs and they started on 1st March 1972, almost two years to the day after LGH had started.

Our financial year end had been set at 30th April and, as we approached the end of our second trading year, I was confident that I had a business which could support me and my family and pay the mortgage. Hiring lifting equipment, though, was a very narrow field of endeavour and I was thinking that it would be difficult to grow much more. Also, the growing stock of plant available for hire was putting a big strain on our capacity at the workshop and working from home, whilst convenient in some ways, would inevitably become a limiting factor. The audited accounts for our second year again almost exactly matched my budget. We'd doubled to £26,000 turnover and had again managed to keep within our enlarged overdraft facilities and kept on top of the William Allen agreement. Our auditors, Edward Ryan, suggested that I should consider giving up my status as a sole trader, trading as Lifting Gear Hire. It would have certain advantages if I were to form a limited liability company. My bank manager, Ron Gleave, agreed, after being suitably impressed with our recent results.

Chapter 9 - Accelerating

I applied to Companies House to register my new company, Lifting Gear Hire Ltd, and filled in all the appropriate forms. I would be Managing Director and Irene would be Company Secretary. I was staggered when the application was turned down by the Registrar because he believed that our name was too similar to an existing company called Lifting Gear Services Ltd. I'd never heard of them and when I searched at Companies House I discovered that it was a dormant company which hadn't traded for years. Further enquiries gave me the name and address of the owner, whom we'll call Mr. Smith-Jones. I managed to find his telephone number and called him. I explained to him that I'd been trading successfully for two years as Lifting Gear Hire and I now wanted to register as a company and it was vital to keep the same name. The existence of his dormant company was blocking my plans and I'd be grateful if he'd sell me the shell company.

He turned out to be a very pleasant man who was very amenable to the idea and said he wouldn't take any money provided I'd pay the legal fees. I was relieved and delighted until he called me back a few days later to explain that there was a snag. Some years earlier he'd had a particularly valuable employee whom he'd rewarded by giving him one share in the company out of a hundred issued. The employee had subsequently run off to Ireland with an air hostess and had never been seen since. For some reason which I now can't recall, this meant that Mr Smith-Jones couldn't sell me his company. However, his solicitor suggested a solution to the problem. I would set up a company called Smith-Jones Ltd which I would wholly own. The directors of the two companies would each hold General Meetings and resolve to swap names with each other. We did this and my new company (formerly Smith-Jones Ltd) became Lifting Gear Services Ltd. I then reapplied to Companies House to register Lifting Gear Hire Ltd and enclosed a letter from myself as owner of Lifting Gear

Services Ltd to the effect that I had no objection at all to the new registration.

I was feeling pretty smug at my clever ploy but the smile was wiped off my face when the Registrar again turned me down, this time on the grounds that the name was too generic and would give the impression that we were the only company offering this service - which was precisely what I was trying to achieve. I was very annoyed and felt cheated but thought I'd give it one more shot. I wrote to the Registrar to point out that I'd gone to great trouble and expense to overcome his original reason for refusing my application. It seemed grossly unfair that he had now produced a completely different reason. I think I must have worn him down as the application was granted without further debate. There were two lessons to be learned from this episode. The first and most important one was that perseverance in the face of adversity can often result in a successful outcome. The second one was to learn from Mr Smith-Jones' experience and never give away shares in a private company. Unless the company is being sold or is paying dividends, minority shareholdings are generally of no value. There are other more appropriate ways to reward valuable members of staff.

Trade was very brisk that summer of 1972 and I was having to revise my view of the potential of the business. It was clear from my surging graphs that we were going to double in size again. Everyone was working flat out and other new employees would have to be recruited. I'd been able to afford a new car, a 1600cc Ford Capri, and the van was released for delivery duties. My biggest priority was to find new premises to kick-start a new growth phase. There is an old adage in the industry that 'Plant should be hired from yards, not palaces' and, mindful of that, I was not too put off when I found Dan Lane Mill, close to the centre of our town of Atherton. The Mill had been partially destroyed by fire a few years earlier but sections of it were quite habitable and were rented from Leslie Fink, the owners, by a variety of small businesses. The largest section was about 3,000 sq. ft. with a big unpaved yard/car park fronting on to Hamilton Street. It had previously been occupied by sheet metal workers Hamilton Fabrications who had outgrown the property.

One unusual feature of the property was that the huge mill chimney had its base in one corner. At £400 per year it was a snip, though four times the rent I'd been paying. I agreed to a one year rolling lease and we moved in very quickly. British Aluminium had become regular customers and their chief engineer gave us a job one day to dismantle a large section of steel racking, made not of sheet metal but substantial steel joists. I offered to do the job for nothing if we could keep the racks we were dismantling. We re-erected the racks at Hamilton Street and they were perfect for hanging our ever growing stock of equipment neatly and safely. There were no offices in the building so I paid a local joinery firm to create offices out of wood. Myself and Muriel and Carol were able to move in to our new offices and leave Irene and the children in peace.

We found out that Irene was pregnant again in early 1972 and our third child and second son, Steven, was born in Bolton's Towneley Hospital in October. Just a few weeks earlier our friends and neighbours, Ray and Kath, had a baby girl, Estelle. Steven and Estelle were good playmates as they grew up on the avenue. Other neighbours were also producing children regularly and, being a cul-de-sac, it was relatively free of traffic so the children were able to play outside quite safely. It was a small, young and happy community with lots of children's laughter.

The range of Tangye Hydralite, Hydraclaw and Hydramite jacks were in great demand from our hire customers. The 5 ton Hydraclaw was especially popular particularly for machinery moving contractors. For some reason, Tangye struggled to meet demand, so they were always in short supply. Tangye had a small branch depot in a terraced row of houses just a few miles from us, on the way to Wigan. They offered a part exchange repair service for jacks which were faulty and I was a regular visitor to their premises.

I got to know their maintenance fitter, Bert Leigh, very well. He was not only very knowledgeable but also always most obliging. One day I was frustrated at not being able to buy new Hydraclaws to meet heavy demand and Bert said he could help out. He'd been taking scrap jacks out of the bin and taking them home to work on in his garage, using spares which he bought from the company. He offered to sell me these refurbished jacks for £10 each, at a time when the new price was £28 each. I could get £2 per week for a Hydraclaw and was achieving virtually 100% utilisation, so a £10 investment was yielding £100 per annum return. Not bad. This was the start of a long business relationship with Bert and I persuaded him to set up his own business with me as a 40% minority partner. He moved into LGH's old premises on Bolton Old Road with the promise of lots of hydraulic maintenance work from LGH. We called the new business Hydra Services.

It was fantastic to be a part of the accelerating exponential growth of the business. I think the few of us who were there at this time sensed that we were part of something special. The concept of hiring is beautifully simple and the potential for profitable returns on capital is massive. However, before money can be made from hire it has to be spent on plant, so growth produces negative cash flow. Rapid, exponential growth such as we were experiencing results in extreme negative cash flow. I would need to have a very understanding bank manager. Fortunately, Ron Gleave and I had become quite friendly and we'd made it our business to meet once a month to review the progress of the business. This was a great benefit in two ways. It gave me a deadline which had to be met for producing the fairly crude management reports and gave me someone to whom I'd have to justify my decisions. From Ron's point of view, our regular meetings gave him a thorough understanding of what was a unique business. I always tried not to give him any nasty surprises and he invariably provided extra support during the regular times of need. Over the next ten years or so Ron and his wife Ayleen became very good friends of ours.

The bigger premises meant that I could engage more staff and the next newcomer was a school leaver, John Clarke. Bearing in mind the excellent training which I'd had as an apprentice, I was reluctant to call John an apprentice because we couldn't give him the training that would be entailed. Instead, we called him a trainee and gave him as wide a variety of work as we could. The big old mill was very poorly insulated and our large workshop/warehouse became very cold and draughty in winter. I hadn't realised how cold until one day I came into the workshop in a donkey jacket to find John smelling of rubbing liniment. He'd been using Fiery Jack to rub on his hands to keep warm but hadn't complained at all! I immediately arranged to have large paraffin heaters strategically placed around the shop floor. Muriel's next door neighbour was a fitter called Bob Hamilton, who knew from Muriel that we were expanding and taking on new staff. He joined us too at that time and would later play a key role in a very special diversification.

Muriel and Carol had made it clear from the outset that they only wanted part-time work, but the pace of growth was putting a big strain on our administration systems. I kept putting pressure on them to increase their hours which, thankfully, they were able to do to a certain extent. However, it was obvious that we'd need another accounts clerk. We were in our fourth year of trading and if we doubled revenue again, as was very likely, then revenue would hit £100,000 p. a.

We were under strain in other areas too. We had more 'phone lines installed but I always wanted the 'phone to be answered promptly by competent, knowledgeable staff. I regularly took Muriel and Carol into the workshop to show them what each piece of equipment could do and coach them in the technical jargon used when discussing lifting equipment. They were excellent when dealing with customers on the 'phone but a lot of chauvinistic male engineers are only comfortable dealing with other men. My regular contact on a daily basis with William Allen was a young man called Alan Mann. He'd always dealt with my many orders, some very demanding, very smoothly, politely and efficiently. He dealt with me as I wanted my staff to deal with LGH's customers. I offered Alan a job as the first point of contact for customers and he accepted, but I was uncomfortable about taking him from the company which had helped me so much during my first few years. However, my need was greater than theirs and I felt, as did Alan, that his career prospects would be better with LGH in the long term.

This was before the advent of mobile telephones, of course, and I spent a lot of time out of the office calling on potential customers or acting as a delivery driver. I felt it was important that I could be contacted at all times and invested in a paging device. If my staff needed to speak to me or get a decision on some question they could call a message centre, who would then alert my pager to let me know that a message was waiting for me. I'd find a public telephone and call the message centre, who'd relay the message to me. By the standards of sophisticated mobile telecommunications which exist forty years later it was crude and time consuming, but at the time it was a brilliant way of keeping in touch with my office.

It wasn't all work and no play, though. In July 1973 the local Round Table were to hold an 'It's a Knock-out' competition for teams from local businesses. Each team would consist of six men and six women, which would be tough for my little company to field but, on a whim, I entered LGH into the contest. We were one of about ten local companies to enter, including huge companies such as GKN and

BICC. We were given a list of the different contests in which we'd have to take part and we started training in earnest by going to a local football pitch twice a week. Virtually every employee of LGH was in the team, plus the odd husband, wife or neighbour to make up the numbers. Training was going well and proved to be a good team building exercise and we had a lot of fun together. Then Carol, who was a keen team member, developed appendicitis and Irene stepped in as a last minute reserve.

The competition was held on the playing field of a local school. On the day, which was beautifully warm and sunny we acquitted ourselves very creditably and came third overall, having beaten companies with hundreds of employees. But the occasion was notable for a very different reason. The event involved 120 competitors from ten different companies, with eight different quirky team games using lots of different apparatus and occupying about five acres of land in front of hundreds of spectators. This was potentially a logistical nightmare to organise. In the event, the competition ran very smoothly and the whole Round Table team worked brilliantly together to ensure that everything happened as it should. This team was held together by one young man, who acted as compere and orchestrated everything in a timely, smooth and humorous manner. I was very impressed, not only by his organisational skills but also by his affable personality. At the end of the day I sought him out to thank him and congratulate him on a job well done. As we chatted, I discovered that he was a currently unemployed sales representative. I'd been thinking for some time that I'd soon have to be employing a sales person if LGH's growth was to be sustained. I offered Gordon Worswick a job right there and then and he would go on to have a stellar career and ultimately make a massive impact on the future development of my company.

This financial year from May 1973 to April 1974 was to prove to be a momentous year in three very different ways and it could be said that the whole future of the company was defined by what happened that year, although that wasn't obvious until many years later.

I used the local newspaper again to advertise our vacancy for an accounts clerk. I received letters from a few promising applicants and also a 'phone call from a sales representative from Burroughs Office Equipment. I rarely turned reps away if I thought they might have an interesting proposition, so I agreed to see him. He was a bright and friendly young man called Mike to whom I immediately took a liking. He'd seen our advert for an accounts clerk and said that he could sell me a machine which would eliminate the need for another member of staff and save me the cost of an extra salary. He went on to explain that his company made very sophisticated office machinery which could be programmed to carry out virtually any accounting task. I was naturally very sceptical and pointed out that a hire business was different from most others because our equipment didn't get sold in a one way transaction. It also came back to us and invoice values to customers varied with the length of hire. I didn't think any machine could cope with this and the many other intricacies of our business. Mike said he'd like to have the opportunity to prove me wrong and set up an appointment for a demonstration at his Bolton Office/showroom. This proved to be an eye opener for me and it was clear that office machinery was making massive progress at that time and I'd ignore it at my peril.

One of my badminton-playing Monday night group was Richard Foster, Ray and Kath's brother-in-law. Richard worked in a sales capacity for Instron, a high tech Swiss company, and he regularly visited large, sophisticated companies and universities who had the latest and best office equipment available. I told Richard of my visit to Burroughs, which had sparked my interest in electronic solutions to our administrative procedures, and asked him which companies he'd recommend I should speak to in addition to Burroughs. After some thought he said, "I'd go for Olivetti, Philips and Wang". I'd never heard of Wang but Richard said that they were an American company making what they called 'advanced programmable calculators' and were represented in Europe by a small company based in Harrogate called CS Computer Services.

I contacted all three companies and invited them to come to see me to present their solutions to my requirements. That was a revelation. Philips and Olivetti were giant corporations and they were clearly unimpressed by our rambling old mill building and wooden partitioned offices. They didn't take my enquiry seriously and responded in a cursory manner which gave me no encouragement at all. CS Computer Services (CSCS), however, had a totally different attitude. The two partners of the newly formed business, Ken Atkinson and Brian Fox, came to see me. They were destined to have exceptional careers in the computer world but at this time were just two young men trying to establish their start-up computer business. A few months earlier they had been employed by ICL, the largest British computer manufacturer, and had been approached privately by Ron Easter, a printer friend of theirs from Blackpool, who had a technical problem. Ron printed Bingo cards and his problem stemmed from the fact that Bingo games were getting bigger. Bingo halls all over the country were linking up to form games with thousands of participants simultaneously instead of just a couple of hundred. The big Bingo hall operators were demanding that their suppliers could guarantee that very large batches of cards could be produced without any two being alike. At the time no printer in the world could meet their requirements so Ken and Brian attacked the problem in their spare time with great energy. Brian was a maths graduate and eventually cracked the problem using one of Wang's advanced programmable calculators to write the software which controlled Ron's printing machines and enabled him to make a killing in the Bingo card market. Ken and Brian saw the commercial possibilities of Wang's equipment and negotiated the exclusive selling rights for Europe. They set up CSCS and Ron was their first customer.

The two brilliant young computer wizards convinced me that they could design a computer program which would cope with all of the idiosyncrasies of my unique administrative system and would massively reduce my need for more and more accounts staff to calculate and type more and more invoices as my business grew. It would print invoices and statements faster than I could possibly imagine and all of the statistical and business data that I could ever need would be available at my fingertips. It was magical and fantastic and wonderfully exciting. They quoted a total price of £13,000 to cover both the hardware and the bespoke programming and it would take 6 months to complete the necessary work, which would have to be ready for the start of the next financial year on 1st May 1974. This represented about 20% of our previous year's turnover and considerably more than the profit we'd earned. It would be the first computerised plant hire system in the world and the first one in the lifting equipment industry. It was audacious to even contemplate such an idea but having seen the future there was no turning back. I took a deep breath and placed the order and became Wang's second European customer.

CSCS sent their brilliant systems analyst, Harrald Hunter, to prepare the specification for the software. Harrald and I spent dozens of hours discussing how our systems worked in the most minute detail. He asked probing questions which got to the heart of every conceivable situation. He also had extensive input from Muriel and Carol, together with Alan Mann. At times I despaired that a machine could cope with so many complex variables but Harrald kept reassuring me that "if you can describe it, I can program it".

The hire system required that we set up a Plant Register showing for every one of our hundreds of items of plant - serial number, cost, depreciation rate, book value, current test certificate number, due examination date, due test date, number of days hired this period/this year/life, hire revenue earned this period/this year/life - and express these figures in percentage utilisation terms. The system would have to cope with customers having different discount structures and would have to deal with revenues from sales and maintenance activities in addition to our core hire business. I wanted analyses of customers' accounts to show what they were spending on each activity and how quickly they paid our bills. I wanted also to be able to analyse utilisation data to determine whether chainblocks were better earners than jacks, for instance, or Tirfors were better than Pul-lifts. Whatever I wanted, I could have! For a young businessman obsessed with measuring performance it was a dream come true.

Harrald went back to the CSCS offices in Harrogate to work on developing the programs for our new computer and business at LGH continued apace. Irene and I hadn't had a holiday since 1969, partly because we couldn't afford one and partly because I didn't want to take time off. However, she persuaded me that we were all due for a break and we had what seemed to be a very expensive two weeks in Gran Canaria. On returning to work I found that trading had been at record levels whilst I'd been away and my colleagues, who had coped admirably, were keen to rub this in. Alan had settled in well and his calm, unflustered telephone manner was a lesson to us all. Almost all of our orders were received by telephone and the customers always wanted their deliveries 'yesterday'. The questions from customers were usually concerned with technical specifications and availability. Only as an afterthought was price questioned, and only then as a formality, so that the purchase order could be raised correctly. Most hires were initiated in the belief by the customer that the equipment would only be required temporarily to cope with a specific contract or to supplement a shortcoming in their own plant stock. Very often, however, either because of contract over-runs or poor managerial control or sheer forgetfulness, the hire period would extend for many weeks and sometimes, many months. We would submit our invoices every four weeks but, because our values were relatively small, there were no alarm bells ringing in our customers' offices.

One day Alan told me that he had a pal called Terry Friend who ran a Post Office in London. Terry had previously worked for Felco, the chainblock manufacturers, and was familiar with lifting equipment. The Post Office kept him busy in the mornings paying out pensions and so on but he was free during the afternoon. He had an empty garage and wondered if I'd be interested in storing some of our plant in his garage whilst he tried to build up a customer base for our hire concept in the London area. This seemed like a no-lose proposition but I realised that there were quite a few principles to establish at the outset which might have far reaching consequences in the future.

I needed to decide how we'd remunerate Terry and who'd be responsible for invoicing customers, Terry or the Atherton office. Would we supply him with a van? How would the equipment be maintained after it had been hired? How would we cope if Terry was on holiday or became sick? Would we have a whole new set of stationery printed with the London address? Would we pay Terry's 'phone bill? And many other questions which needed answers before we could proceed with confidence. It's obvious now, though it wasn't quite so clear at the time, that we were establishing a London Branch of LGH. Eventually we'd go on to open thirty-four branches, all operating within the framework established almost casually at that time in 1973.

By November 1973 the hectic summer months were behind us and everything was settling into a smooth routine. We had a very talented group of staff who were extremely competent at their various tasks. Princess Anne married Capt. Mark Phillips on 14th November but that date became significant to me for an entirely different reason.

My parents had sold the Fish and Chip shop and moved to a 6 acre smallholding in the village of Hapton, near Padiham. Dad raised chickens and had a couple of pigs and a few lambs. My mother had a large vegetable garden. It was my habit to visit them about once a month and I'd go with my dad to his local club for a game of snooker and a couple of pints. We did this on that fateful day, with dad handing me my usual snooker lesson, and as I started the 25 mile journey home at about 11 pm the weather was murky and drizzly. I was driving my pride and joy 1600cc Capri GT and, as I came to Haslingden, I could choose one of two alternative routes. The easy but slow road through the Rossendale Valley or the deristricted high road which clung to the side of Holcombe Hill with stunning views (when it was light and clear) of Ramsbottom way below in the valley. I chose the high road and looked forward to an exhilarating drive on this quiet winding country lane.

As I climbed, the weather became worse. The rain turned to sleet and then to hailstones. It started sticking to the road and I was driving too fast for the conditions. The car skidded right on a corner. I corrected the skid but over-corrected and went the other way, totally out of control, to the left where the hill fell away steeply. I crashed through the hedge and some small trees that were growing up from the field and the car plunged down the hill, rolling over as it did so. The car was badly smashed and every window, including the windscreen, was broken. This was before seat belts were mandatory but I was wearing a thick overcoat, which I think may have cushioned me slightly. The car had come to rest the right way up in a muddy field about 100 yards from the road and I was hurting all over but, as far as I could tell in the pitch dark, I wasn't bleeding. I was fully conscious and my head hadn't been impacted. It was obvious I'd cracked some ribs on the steering wheel and my back was hurting. Every film I'd ever seen showing crashes similar to this ended with the car exploding in a fireball and I was terrified that this was about to happen. I imagined petrol leaking from the carburettor onto the hot exhaust pipe and was sure it would blow up any second.

I couldn't get out! The doors were smashed and seized up so, in desperation, I managed to crawl through the broken windscreen and slid over the bonnet to the ground. I lay there in the wet freezing mud and contemplated my position. I was clearly hurt badly and needed to get to a hospital, but at least I could move. I reckoned that if I stayed where I was in this dark lonely field I wouldn't be found until morning and there was no way I'd survive in the freezing cold. There was no option, I had to get back to the road. I half crawled, half walked back up the steep field towards the road. When I got there I had to somehow get through the thick hawthorn hedge but finally I made it.

The lane was unlit and by now it must have been nearly midnight. Would there be any more traffic that night? I was getting increasingly doubtful but, after what seemed an eternity, I saw a car's headlights approaching. A wave of relief swept over me and I stumbled to my feet and pulled my coat and jacket open so that the driver would see my white shirt as I waved him down. He saw me and stopped about 30 yards past me. I crawled and staggered to reach him as his wife opened the passenger door and looked at me. I must have looked awful because as I got close she said to her husband "he's drunk George, drive on". I shouted to tell them that I'd had an accident and was hurt and thankfully George believed me. They took me to Bury General Hospital in double quick time and I'll be eternally grateful to these wonderful Good Samaritans whose names I omitted to take.

The X-rays taken that night revealed that, in addition to the several cracked ribs, three of my lumbar vertebrae were fractured. They strapped up my chest tightly and found me a bed. The following day I was told that, once my ribs had started to heal in a few days' time, I would have to be encased in a plaster cast from my neck to the top of my thighs. I'd have to keep this on for three months. I wouldn't be able to work, my business would fail. Get me a private room with a telephone so I can run my business from my hospital bed! These were the thoughts that flooded my head. Then I thought how well the LGH team had managed whilst I was on holiday. They were all good, honest, hard-working, skilled people who I had hand picked and trained. This was a chance to show them how much I trusted them and would give them the opportunity to show how good they could be. I decided that I couldn't half run the business - it was all or nothing.

I asked Alan to come to see me in hospital and told him that for the next three months the business was effectively his. He would have to make all of the decisions as he went along. He wasn't to consult me on a single issue until I was fit to resume work. Muriel and Carol visited me in hospital also and I told them of my decision and they reassured me that all would be well. I stayed in hospital for another few days after my full torso plaster cast had been applied.

One day, I had the headphones on and was listening to the radio when they played a Shirley Bassey song, Make the World a Little Younger. This seemed to hit a nerve with me as it seemed to suggest that I could go back in time and have another go at that corner and this time not crash. I started sobbing, gently at first then uncontrollably, with my head under the sheets. The nursing Sister came to me and asked if I was ok then amazingly said, "This is good news Bill. We've been waiting for something like this. It's delayed shock and you needed to get it out of your system. You can go home tomorrow". For me, the three months dragged interminably and I lost a lot of fitness through not being able to play badminton and squash, but eventually I was able to pick up again at work where I had left off so abruptly three months earlier. The staff had risen to the challenge magnificently and the business was in a healthy position. Incredibly, the cash-flow had been strongly positive and for the first time ever we had a credit balance at the bank!

There was a positive side to this incident as, for the rest of my life, I found it easy to delegate and was always ready to give promising young staff the chance to take more responsibility. There were two lasting downsides. Although I resumed playing active sports I was for ever left with a susceptibility to suffer from sciatica. The other indirect result was that I failed to achieve Chartered Engineer (CEng) status, which was the highest professional qualification to which I could aspire. I had my HNC (Mech Eng) and all of the required endorsement subjects. I'd been admitted as a Graduate Member of the Institution of Mechanical Engineers (GradMIMechE). The next step was to gain Associate Member status, which would automatically grant me the coveted CEng qualification. In order to become an Associate it was necessary to demonstrate a level of seniority in the engineering profession, either through academia or management in industry. I was getting ready to apply when I lost my job at Coubro and then the Institution announced a change of rules. They were tightening up standards and the night school study route would be closed for Associate Member applications after the end of 1973. I thought I might struggle to convince the Institution of my managerial seniority as LGH was such a small business and delayed my application as long as possible. With all the trauma at the end of the year I failed to submit my application in time and was denied the chance of proudly displaying CEng after my name. It still rankles to this day that, partly through my own lethargy, I failed to do full justice to the thousands of hours of study I'd put in at Burnley, Accrington and St Helens Technical Colleges.

During my enforced absence from work my colleagues had to deal with an unprecedented situation. In early 1974 the Government introduced a three day working week. This was an attempt to conserve electricity, the production of which was limited due to dwindling coal reserves as a result of a miners' strike. We were allowed to use electricity on three consecutive working days but not on the other two. On any given day some of our customers would be working so, as a service company, we had to be open for five days even though we had no electricity for part of the time. Paraffin heaters and battery powered lights came to the rescue and we got through this national crisis relatively unscathed. It turned out that the Heath Government had been ill-prepared for the conflict, with low coal reserves and considerable public sympathy for the miners, who were seen to have won the battle. Prime Minister Edward Heath fell on his sword and resigned. Ten years later the miners' union would take on Margaret Thatcher with a completely different outcome.

One of the side effects of the miners' strike was that prices started to rise and inflation, which was already over 10%, became rampant. It continued to rise until it peaked at almost 27% in August 1975. I figured that our hire rates would have to reflect today's cost of buying plant rather than the historic cost. With such rampant inflation, the like of which none of us had previously experienced, it would be easy for a plant hire company to convince themselves that they were making good profits on old plant. The reality was that insufficient reserves would be built up to replace the plant at the end of its useful life. I was dismayed to find that all of my main competitors were failing to raise their hire rates anywhere like in line with inflation. This in turn put downward pressure on our hire rates at just the time when I felt compelled to raise them.

The only solution, I felt, was to call a 'summit conference' of all of the major players in our little sector of commerce. I was very much the new kid on the block but I felt very strongly about this and was determined to give it a shot. I booked a room in a Birmingham hotel and invited every company with a significant hire offering in the lifting equipment field to send a senior manager to attend. They all did. Cheadle, LBT, Coubro, Sowerby Welch, Ray Bills, East Ham -

they were all there. I'd prepared lots of statistical data to back up my arguments and stressed that I wasn't trying to establish a cartel. I'd taken the liberty of obtaining the latest accounts of some of the companies and knew that some were far from healthy. The reception my suggestions got was lukewarm at best and most seemed to think that my business must be in trouble or I had some other ulterior motive. The meeting was drawing to a close with no agreement to implement hire rate rises in line with inflation when father figure Mr Welch spoke to thank me for arranging the meeting and said "I can't speak for anyone else. I found your presentation very interesting young man, but I'm very happy with the profits we're making and won't be raising our rates". I happened to have a copy of his latest accounts in my briefcase showing that his company had just made a loss. I didn't embarrass him by revealing this but I felt I'd wasted my time and maybe shown too much of my hand to my competitors. I came back to Atherton thinking that if they couldn't see the sense of what I was saying then that was their problem. The following day I raised our rates by 20% and in the next six months saw unprecedented growth in hire revenue and profits.

My good friend and neighbour, Ray Garside, had also started his own business with a partner called Walter. As a printing ink salesman, Ray had met many people in the printing industry and had spotted what he believed was a promising commercial opportunity. Plastic bottles, particularly in the cosmetics and shampoo fields, were presented with labels or, more rarely, with printed images directly onto the bottle. The bottle manufacturers had little capacity and even less appetite for printing the bottles and Ray and Walter set up Cannon Plastics to act as sub contract printers to the plastic bottle industry. They bought specialist machinery and employed local girls as machine operators. Ray kept working for Coates, selling ink, whilst Walter ran the business. I thought that the idea was sound and could see a bright future for the business as plastic packaging proliferated. However, things didn't go as well as planned.

One day, as I was walking back to work from lunch at home, I came across Ray on the avenue, looking glum. He told me he was off to see Ron Gleave, his bank manager (yes, same one) to wind up the business before the losses became too great. I was really sorry to hear this and felt that the business just needed more time to become established and it could prosper. I persuaded Ray to cancel his appointment at the bank as I thought we might be able to work something out. Walter wasn't prepared to risk any more and his share of the losses to date was as much as he was prepared to lose. With Ray's agreement I offered to shoulder Walter's share of the losses in exchange for his 50% partnership in Cannon Plastics. Walter agreed and that's how Ray and I became partners.

The wheel had turned full circle and I was a printer again, about 15 years after closing down Mailsales. Ray and I subsequently went to see Ron, who was delighted at the new arrangement. I didn't have to put any capital into the business but stood as personal guarantor for the bank overdraft, which meant serious problems if we went bust. We engaged an experienced screen printing professional, Colin Evans, to run the day-to-day activities and Ray resumed his day job with Coates. Colin massively improved the quality of the output from the fickle screen printing machines and reject levels were reduced. There was a happier atmosphere on the shop floor and slowly but surely over the next few years the business became profitable and the earlier losses were wiped off the balance sheet.

We had to move two or three times to accommodate the growing business and Ray went into the business full time. It was very satisfying for us all and I was especially gratified because, but for me, the business would have folded, though I'd actually contributed virtually nothing to the recovery process except to give Ray a little more time. This caused me a problem as I could see that, with continued success, my share of the value of the partnership would grow even though I wasn't contributing anything. To me it was an interesting diversion. To my friend Ray, it was his whole career. I offered Ray the chance to buy me out which the bank facilitated and he went on to run a successful business until he sold out and retired.

During this time, two relatively small incidents conspired to have massive repercussions, not only for LGH but for one of Britain's iconic lifting equipment brands. It made perfect sense for us to stick to certain brands and specifications of equipment for our hire stock. To mix brands would make stocking spares chaotic and would inevitably lead to confusion among our customers and staff. The only brand of chainblock which we used was Felco and our only source was William Allen. Felco were the undisputed brand leader in the UK and were considered to be the highest quality chainblock available. We'd never had an accident involving any of our equipment and we were intent on jealously guarding that record when we received a 'phone call from Cappers, one of our best customers, to tell us that one of our 10 ton Felco chainblocks had failed and dropped an extremely valuable load.

It turned out that no one was injured and miraculously the load was not damaged, but our investigation showed that the teeth on the main load bearing gear axis had stripped off and had allowed the load to fall. This was obviously very worrying and the Health & Safety Executive inspectors wouldn't at that time release the failed gear wheel to us for further testing. We contacted William Allen to solicit their support but they had no technical resources. They contacted Felco on our behalf but they weren't prepared to send a technician/inspector from London to the North West and in any case denied responsibility, claiming our maintenance standards must be suspect. We felt vulnerable and isolated and it was inevitable that the finger of blame would be pointing at us. Then, catastrophe, another accident, this time involving a 2 ton Felco chainblock. This was a long height of lift and the load, which wasn't particularly valuable, had been totally destroyed after falling thirty feet through the air. Again, thankfully, no one was injured. The failure was identical. The main gear wheel, which was identical in the two ton and the ten ton blocks had failed in exactly the same way by the teeth stripping off. Both blocks were relatively new and neither had been overloaded or mis-used. Lifting equipment is designed with very conservatively high factors of safety in order to minimise the occurrence of accidents such as these. What could have happened?

Our investigations showed that the two blocks had very similar serial numbers, suggesting that they'd been assembled at the same time from components in the same batch. We sent the failed gear wheels and teeth to a University Metallurgical lab for testing and the report confirmed our suspicions. The gears had been incorrectly case hardened, resulting in chronic brittleness of the steel, which directly caused both accidents. I was livid. Not just because of the accidents which could easily have put my young company at risk if serious injuries had occurred but mainly because of the almost total apathy with which the manufacturer dealt with two catastrophic failures of their products. I was not prepared to risk being in that position again.

Coincidentally, only a few days earlier, I'd received a letter from a Dutch company from Amsterdam called Louis Reyners. They were European distributors for a Japanese chainblock manufacturer called Nitchi and were looking to appoint an exclusive UK distributor for the full range of Nitchi products, including Pul-lifts and Electric Chain Hoists in addition to their range of chainblocks. At that time, I wouldn't normally have even looked at a Japanese chainblock, but this situation wasn't normal. I had to evaluate all options, including this one. I responded positively to the letter and set up a meeting at my Atherton office with their sales manager, Rob Dorpmans.

The Dutch are great linguists and Rob was no exception, being fluent in five European languages. He explained that Nitchi manufactured a very high quality range of hoists and his company had secured the rights to market them throughout Europe. Their strategy was to appoint an exclusive stockist/distributor in each country, who would be expected to carry extensive stocks and actively promote the brand. The stockist would be free to determine prices and profit margins and could appoint sub-distributors in their territory.

This was a whole world away from the complete reliance on William Allen's and the prospect of being a main distributor, with all the potential that was entailed, excited me tremendously. But all the commercial opportunity was useless if the products were of inferior quality. I asked for samples from the range of products for evaluation purposes which John, Trevor and Bob took apart and re-built, examining every component and measuring the performance against the equivalent Felco products. The report which they submitted to me was unequivocal in its praise for the excellence of the Nitchi range. The designs were sound, the engineering was perfect, the built quality was faultless, the finish was excellent. And the prices were much better than any British built equivalent. My only problem was that we had a fleet of hundreds of Felco blocks which would become surplus to requirements and would prove expensive to replace. Chainblocks represented our biggest single source of revenue and were very important to us. We did the deal with Rob and became Nitchi's UK Distributor. In the end we were able to phase in the Nitchi range almost seamlessly and our continued rapid growth rate meant that quite soon the Nitchi blocks dominated our stocks.

Although this didn't seem to be an earth shattering decision at the time it is probably true to say that it influenced the future of the British chainblock manufacturing industry. Felco barely knew of our existence at the time and their failure to give us technical support in our moment of need when their products proved defective precipitated our subsequent actions. Over the next forty years, we were the biggest buyers of chainblocks in the world. Every block we bought was made by Nitchi. It could have been Felco.

Chapter 10 - The Branch Route

April 1974 saw the end of our fourth trading year and, as predicted, we'd doubled revenue again to reach what seemed a significant milestone of £100,000 turnover. The audited accounts showed a disproportionate increase in profits to over £20,000, even though staff costs had risen steeply. But there was no time for back-slapping, as the new computer system was ready to initiate. I'd told Harrald that we'd opened a branch office in London and asked him to ensure that the system could handle multiple locations and give separate reports for each branch if and when they happened. We'd taken on a young woman school-leaver, Linda Wood, who joined Muriel and Carol on a short training course at the Harrogate offices of CSCS and it was clear that she had a natural aptitude for this new technology. She became our main computer operator for many years to come.

Apart from a few teething problems, the new system was introduced quite painlessly and it soon became obvious that the efficiency of recording transactions and the speed and accuracy of the invoicing and accounting procedures alone made the investment worthwhile, not to mention the brilliant management reporting that was available. No more counting red golf tees on a peg board. The computer would list every item of plant on hire at any given time at the touch of a button and give me the revenue earnings instantly. No more laborious entering data for plant on a card index system. The whole system worked even better than I'd hoped and put my little business way ahead of the game as far as our industry was concerned. Were we good enough to make that advantage pay off in a commercial way?

One of the conditions of my agreement with CSCS was that they could sell the Plant Hire system which they'd developed for LGH to other companies. The system was the first of its kind in the world and Brian and Ken had seen great potential for multiple sales. It was agreed that LGH would earn a generous commission from such sales.

We would act as a reference site and allow potential customers to see our computerised system. However, it didn't prove to be that easy. When I started hiring lifting equipment at Coubro I'd never worked for a Plant Hire company and had no previous experience of designing or operating a hire admin system. I made it up as we went along in as logical a way as I could conceive. The LGH system was naturally a clone of that system. It turned out that it was different from standard hire company procedures in several subtle but significant areas. For instance, all of our plant was 'non-operated', whereas most hire companies supplied an operator with their plant. Also, I'd decided that as there were seven days in a week, one day's hire above the minimum week's hire would count as one seventh of the weekly rate. The industry norm was to use a five day week and a day would be charged as one fifth of the weekly rate. Ultimately, CSCS failed to sell a single system based on our template despite our hosting several visits from potential customers.

My motor mechanic brother-in-law, Roy, was self-employed with his own garage. At week-ends a young skilled engineering fitter would work part-time for Roy to boost his earnings. Roy 'phoned me one day to tell me that this young man, Peter Ashworth, who was very conscientious, was seeking a new job and he thought I might be interested. If LGH was to double in size again then we'd need every help we could get and ambitious skilled young engineers didn't grow on trees. I arranged for Peter to come to see me and it was obvious from the outset that he had special qualities. He wanted to get into sales and felt he had more to offer than being at a bench in the workshop. At the time, we were getting quite a bit of work from across the Pennines in Yorkshire but our customers there were proving difficult to serve. It was hard to justify sending a van or truck all the way to Leeds or Bradford with a piece of lifting equipment being hired at £5 per week. I told Peter that I'd provide him with a van and he could cover the Yorkshire area both as a sales rep and as a delivery driver. He would spend his days in his territory and telephone the office at Atherton regularly to check if any of his customers had placed an order in which case he'd come to pick up the equipment and make the delivery. I set Peter a target for hire revenue in his area and promised him that when he hit the target then we'd establish a branch in Yorkshire and he would be the manager. Peter grabbed the opportunity with both hands.

I thought the target I'd set for Peter would take several months, perhaps a year to achieve. He made it in just a few weeks and proudly reminded me of my promise. I was thrilled. This proved that the concept of hiring lifting tackle could be applied anywhere. I gave Peter the job of finding the location and, in the meantime, he was to continue building our customer base in his area. In that first year he worked tremendously hard and covered 85,000 miles in his van. Peter eventually found the premises which he felt were perfect for LGH's first 'proper' branch. Much to my surprise, the location was the village of Bircotes, near Doncaster in South Yorkshire, rather than the Leeds area, as I'd expected. Also, this was a freehold ex transport garage much bigger than I thought we'd need with an adjoining detached house which had been transformed into offices. Peter was working very hard and I was impressed by how quickly he'd developed the territory. Despite my misgivings I agreed that we'd go ahead. The location proved to be an inspired choice. It was in the middle of the vast Yorkshire coalfield and British Coal would become an important customer. It was surrounded by many huge power stations which were constantly being maintained and in turn utilised massive quantities of lifting equipment. It was easy to reach the large industrial conurbations of Sheffield and Rotherham.

In the meantime our infant London Branch had been making slow but steady progress when we were hit by a bombshell. Terry had a heart attack and of course couldn't continue working either in the Post Office or for LGH. We had to make some quick decisions. It seemed that we had three options: (a) close down the London operation and recover all of our plant (b) find someone else in the London area to take it over or (c) send someone from Atherton to London to keep it going. London, our capital city, was a hive of construction activity. If we had ambitions to be a serious player in this industry, then we had to have a presence there. I decided on the third option and offered Alan Mann the chance to be our London Branch Manager. He was newly married without children and he saw it as a life changing opportunity. He headed South and found us premises in Upper Norwood, SE19, to keep the ship afloat.

Soon after this I was with a fabrication engineering customer in Turton, Bolton. During a general conversation I told their MD, John of my recent branch developments. He told me of the large amount of work his company was securing from Aberdeen and urged me to consider this for the next branch of LGH. Oil had recently been discovered in the North Sea and all the major oil companies in the world were jockeying for position to exploit this discovery. Aberdeen was the epicentre of the UK offshore activity and it was booming as all and sundry staked their claims for a chunk of the spoils. When I told John that I might be interested he gave me the name and number of a chap called Mike who used to work for them in a sales capacity in Aberdeen and was still living there but currently out of work. I contacted Mike the following day and arranged to meet him in Aberdeen a few days later.

I'd never been to The Granite City before so, when Mike picked me up from the Airport in a taxi which he was driving, I asked him to drive me round the town to give me a feel for the layout. I interviewed him as we drove and was unimpressed by his quiet, somewhat nervous, attitude. He didn't seem to know much about the oil industry either but, then again, neither did I. There were no other candidates and I knew no-one else in Aberdeen so I gave him the benefit of the doubt and offered him the job of opening up an Aberdeen branch for LGH. We had some lunch together then, as there were a few hours left before my return flight to Manchester, I asked Mike to take me round the streets to look for potential customers for our new venture. This proved to be relatively easy and we found the offices of a few contractors who were providing various services to the big oil companies. I thought it would be good training for Mike to see how to go about introducing LGH to new clients. I've already said that I didn't consider myself to be much of a salesman but I couldn't believe how easy this was. I got substantial enquiries for purchasing lifting equipment from the first four calls we made together with promises of hire business when we were up and running. This was going to be a gold mine! When Mike dropped me back at the Airport I asked him to start looking for premises to rent as soon as possible and in the meantime continue building up a portfolio of potential customers. The following day from my office in Atherton I submitted quotations for the four enquiries I'd received and subsequently gained orders from three of them. These were the only enquiries and orders received from Aberdeen during the next three months! What was Mike doing? Nothing, was the answer.

I'd been given the name of a reputedly excellent sales representative working for a competing lifting equipment company in Aberdeen. He was called Bill Davidson and I arranged to meet him. He was tall, smart, knowledgeable and ambitious. I offered him the job of developing LGH in Aberdeen and when he accepted I sought out Mike to tell him his services were no longer required. Bill soon found premises on Riverside Drive and quickly established what was to become a thriving branch.

These were thrilling times for a young businessman and when April came round again at the end of our fifth year of trading our Wang computer churned out the figures showing a turnover of £202,000 with a healthy profit. Amazingly, we'd doubled again! I worked out that if we kept up this rate of growth for another fifteen years or so we'd be the biggest company in the UK. The meetings with our bank manager, Ron Gleave, continued every month and despite, or rather because, of our spectacular growth, cash flow remained a constant problem. Ron was still very supportive and he considered LGH to be his star account, but he had to work within tightly defined lending parameters and certain security ratios had to be maintained. It always seemed that we were walking a tightrope between growing the business and having the cash to invest in the plant which was necessary to produce the growth.

We had a local competitor called Leigh Lifting Services, owned by a slippery rascal called Mike Potts. A few years earlier Mike had been a rep for Yale who made a range of quality lifting products. It was Mike's task to set up stockists and distributors for Yale's products. One day, when I was Coubro's manager, he came to see me and waved a piece of paper under my nose. It was an order worth a few hundred pounds from an end user to purchase two 1 ton Electric Hoists. He offered to let me have the order if I'd place an order with him for four hoists which would make us a stockist and thus qualify us for 20% discount. He promised to let me have leads to help me sell the other two.

I gave him the order which he then took to another lifting equipment company. He offered them 30% discount if they'd order eight and become a distributor. He'd turned an order for two into an order for eight. I said he was slippery! Mike and I tolerated each other and occasionally did some reciprocal trading and one day in 1975 he 'phoned me to ask if I'd be interested in buying from him two second hand Morris worm gear hand chainblocks of 30 ton capacity each. I was staggered. I'd never heard of such large capacity blocks. They were massive and weighed one and a half tons each. They must be the biggest chainblocks ever made. The worm gear design was old-fashioned but Mike assured me they were in excellent condition and he'd include delivery and throw in wooden packing cases for a total price of £50 each. They were clearly going to be white elephants and money was tight but the temptation to be able to claim that we stocked the 'biggest chainblocks in the world' was too great to resist. I bought them.

We stored them in a corner of our workshop near the base of the chimney and promptly forgot about them. Then, a couple of months later, Mike called me again. "Hey Bill, you know those 30 ton chainblocks that are unique and the only ones in the world? How'd you like another five at the same price?" I was stunned and certainly didn't want or need another five and nor was I ready to fork out £250 for something I didn't want. Mike said it was OK as he'd now just hawk them around the trade and someone was bound to take them. Heck, they were practically worth that as scrap! In fact, that was how Mike had acquired them, as surplus to the requirements of a local aerospace company who probably only ever used them once. I was trapped. I'd no longer be able to claim the unique offering of the biggest in the world. I had to have them. When they were delivered John Williams looked at the huge boxes in dismay and said "What the hell are you trying to do Bill, get a monopoly of 30 ton chainblocks?" "Yes John", I replied "that's precisely what I'm trying to do".

The chainblocks sat in a corner for a year or so without a single enquiry for them. Then, out of the blue, I got a call from the sales manager of Felco, the UK's largest chainblock manufacturer. They had an enquiry from an oil company in Turkey for the sale of two 25 ton chainblocks. Felco didn't make anything over 20 tons but they'd heard I might be able to help. I agreed that their Turkish customer's English engineer should call me to discuss a deal. When he called I explained that the blocks were available but were part of my hire fleet. They were rare and irreplaceable and I couldn't possibly sell them. After considerable wrangling I let him persuade me to sell them to him for £800 each plus VAT, buyer to collect and bring the cheque with him. He snatched my hand off and I was able to ease a dangerously tight cash-flow crisis at a stroke. It was good to show

John the cheque and imply "I told you so". He rarely questioned my judgement after that.

A few years later, two more of these antiquated mammoths did even better for us. One of the giant international oil companies had an exploration rig out in the North Sea and placed an order with our Aberdeen Branch to hire two 30 ton chainblocks at £100 each per week. A year later they still had them and 'phoned us to say that they were very sorry but they'd 'accidentally' dropped our blocks into the sea over the side of the exploration platform. Would we please consider the hire to be terminated and charge them the replacement value of the equipment. We explained that the items were irreplaceable but in recognition of the fact that they were good customers and the items had already earned £5000 each in hire revenue, we'd only charge a further £2,500 each for the written off items. Everyone was happy. Our original investment of £350 for seven of these blocks had resulted in revenues of over £16,000 and we still had three left! Mike Potts, eat your heart out!

Our elder son, Ian, had been doing particularly well at what was now Park Lee Junior School. His reports were consistently good and parents' evenings were always a pleasure. He clearly had an academic talent which would be best fulfilled at a Grammar School. Unfortunately Grammar Schools no longer existed in our area having been replaced by Comprehensive Schools. Remembering the benefits which I felt I'd gained from having attended Clitheroe Grammar I was keen that Ian should have the same opportunity. He was entered for the entrance exam for the Junior Division of Bolton School the pre-eminent private school just a few miles from Atherton. He passed and subsequently attended the school for the next nine years. Lorraine was also bright but when offered the chance to sit the Bolton School exam told us that she'd prefer the local Comprehensive School, Hesketh Fletcher.

With the business going well I felt confident that we could afford to improve the standard of living of our family. Whilst the semi dormer bungalow with its basement on Lancaster Avenue had been great for us we'd been there for approaching eight years and it was time to trade up. Our friends Ray and Kath had announced that they were moving to Lostock in Bolton and David and Carol were likely to move too. We also searched in the Lostock area which was the prime residential area for the district and was close to Bolton School. Coming from a house with a large basement made it difficult to find a house of comparable size which was affordable. Eventually we found just the right house in Atherton set in 3/4 acre of gardens and with terrific potential for renovation and extending. We bought it with the help of what we were told was the biggest mortgage ever arranged at that time by the Wigan Branch of the Halifax Building Society. The house, called Ladyhill, had been built in 1937 for Sir Humphrey Brown who at the time was chairman of Lancashire Collieries. After the nationalisation of the mines he became deputy chairman of the National Coal Board. It was a perfect choice for us with three young children and we still live there almost forty years later.

As I noted earlier, young women can be notoriously difficult to employ. They have this annoying tendency to get pregnant just as they've become indispensable to the business and Muriel was no exception. She took maternity leave towards the end of 1975, which meant that we had to juggle around with her various duties. Carol took on more responsibility and taught Irene how to do the wages which, with four Branches, was now becoming a serious job.

The inexorable growth of the business continued. More customers, more orders, more plant, more revenue, more staff .... it seemed that the business had acquired a will of its own. It felt to me that LGH was driving me now instead of the other way round. By April

1976 we'd almost doubled in size again with a turnover of £395,000. Profits were good and virtually every location was performing well.

The exception was London. The initial spurt of growth after Alan had taken over had dried up. How could this be? Alan was highly competent, he had some decent, if not brilliant, staff. The city was alive with potential business but it wasn't happening for us. I travelled to London by train in an attempt to get to the bottom of this vexing question. Alan picked me up at Euston Station and, as we drove eastward to his branch, I outlined my concerns. I explained that his big city branch, despite being our first location outside Atherton, was being outgrown by the other three locations. What was going wrong? I told him I'd give him three months to sort it out and show me that he was capable of running a branch of which we could all be proud. He was hurt and deeply shocked at my criticism and protested that he and his staff were working hard to achieve success. When I left that evening to catch the train back home our relationship was very strained. One week later he 'phoned me to resign his position. He had holidays due and wished to leave immediately. It turned out that he'd had his own lifting equipment company up and running for several months and he'd been passing all the most lucrative orders from my company to his own. He also poached the best staff, who went with him and had been in on the swindle too. It was a dark time for LGH and our branch concept. We were clearly susceptible to this kind of subterfuge and would have to be especially vigilant in the future. I reluctantly decided to shut down the London operation for the time being and found another, more lucrative home for the plant which Alan had left behind.

Chapter 11 - Keep It Going

The demise of our London Branch coincided with an unexpected approach. Although LGH was still small, we had caused quite a few ripples in the very fragmented lifting industry. In turnover terms, we had grown in only five years to be larger than many companies who had been established for decades. There were only two other multi-location lifting equipment businesses who were dominating the market at that time - my old employer Coubro and their arch rivals Lloyds British Testing (LBT). Neither was particularly interested in hire so our main competitors were Cheadle Plant Hire in the North West, Raymond Bills in the Midlands and Sowerby Welch, together with East Ham Plant Hire in the South.

The surprising approach I received was from a young extrovert sales rep from LBT called Maurice Roberts, who was based in Dudley in the heart of the Black Country, the centre of the UK's forging industry and a significant potential market for the hire of lifting gear. Bill Davidson in Aberdeen had also come from LBT and it was possible that Maurice had spoken to him. I invited Maurice to Atherton, where he told me that he was ideally suited by inclination and experience to open a Branch for LGH in the Midlands. His eyes nearly popped out of his head when he saw the vast amount of beautifully maintained equipment which we had in stock available for hire. His keenness and ambition were palpable and I had to give him a chance. Besides, what else could I do with all the plant lying idle in London? So our Dudley Branch was born and the UK had four strategically located LGH Branches, with a gaping hole in London.

Then yet another LBT man approached me. This was Bert Soper, an LBT Branch Manager from Teesside in the industrial North East. LBT had hired some equipment from us and Bert had driven from Middlesborough to collect it from Atherton. Before he set off on the return journey, he asked to see me and he was stunned by the sheer quantity and quality of our stock. He told me his own company's meagre investment in hire stock was making life difficult for him and it was impossible to compete with professionals such as LGH. "I want to be part of this and could open a Teesside Branch", he almost pleaded. Bert had a soft Welsh lilt mixed with a slight Geordie twang, which I found endearing. He was older than most of my colleagues but I took a liking to him and trusted him. I'd never visited the North East so I arranged to meet him in Stockton the following week. On the day of our meeting I drove up the A19 towards Stockton. I clearly remember coming over the crest of a hill in lovely open countryside to be hit suddenly by a panorama of chemical plants which seemed to stretch as far as the eye could see. Nirvana! Paradise! How had I not known this existed before? Thank you Bert, let's do it.

Engaging Bert so soon after Maurice and Bill gave me guilty pangs. LBT would think I was attacking them by stealth and poaching all of their best people, even though it was the staff who were approaching me. It turned out that Maurice and Bert had been friendly rivals in their LBT days and I encouraged this to continue. Both branches were very successful and followed remarkably similar growth patterns, first one gaining the upper hand then the other. It was all good fun.

Gordon was doing a great job as a sales rep for Atherton and the other four Branch Managers acted as salesmen for their own locations. I encouraged them to think of their branches as their own businesses and fostered a spirit of competitiveness by letting them have monthly figures showing all the key parameters for each branch in league table format. No one wanted the wooden spoon so this was a form of motivation. Managers earned bonuses proportional to the contribution made by their branch without any reference to the overheads being incurred at Atherton, which was increasingly being seen as Head Office.

Some Managers had a particular area of expertise or a special interest which I was keen to encourage and exploit for the benefit of the company. For instance, Peter Ashworth at Doncaster exhibited a passion for winches and he developed by far the largest winch hire fleet in the company. He stocked winches large and small, diesel, electric, hydraulic, pneumatic, hand operated - you name it, Peter could supply it. One advantage of winch hire compared to our more usual lines was that, because they were relatively large and expensive, we could finance their purchase through HP and the hire revenue potential was proportionately higher with longer hire periods expected. With this advantage, Doncaster gradually overtook Atherton as the location with the greatest revenue. Peter was fond of reminding me that he'd been a Lucas apprentice and I hadn't been good enough to get a job there. I was equally fond of reminding him that he worked for me, not the other way round!

Chapter 12 - Driving On

The next few years were so hectic that, looking back, it's difficult to know how we managed to carry it off and my memory of that time is something of a blur. The transformation of LGH from a loosely connected collection of branches, operating at the periphery of the lifting gear industry, into a highly organised, well managed and very profitable group of businesses was about to commence.

I'd never really understood, or even thought about, the distinction between sales and marketing and was becoming a bit uncomfortable with the inconsistent presentation of our business to the world at large. I knew that, if a company had a lifting problem, they'd be well advised to consult LGH as professionals in that field, so I decided that it was high time that we consulted Sales & Marketing professionals. Using a trade directory, I found three Manchester based firms and invited them to meet me at Atherton. Following the meetings, the three firms submitted detailed proposals and budgets for a professional marketing campaign. All three were very impressive, but one was exceptionally exciting. This proposal from Geoff Ashworth, partner of ICA Publicity, convinced me that a substantial investment in marketing was essential to underpin LGH's continued meteoric growth. However, he stunned me by saying that our original logo would have to go! I'd designed that logo at the outset and it appeared on all our stationery, signs and vehicle livery. It would cost a fortune to change that.

Geoff's firm designed a new proposed logo incorporating three hooks, symbolic not only of the lifting gear industry but also of the three facets of our business, hire, sales and service. It also displayed our three letter abbreviation, LGH, and the motto 'puts safety first'. The logo would be displayed in three colours, black, white and green but the green wouldn't be our existing dark green 'house' colour, it would be (shock, horror) a unique shade of a kind of lime green. It was a work of genius and I firmly believe that its adoption played a significant part in the extraordinary continued growth of LGH.

The company's administration was firmly centred in Atherton, where functions such as payroll, sales invoice processing, purchase ledger, plant register records, personnel records, monthly profit and loss accounts, banking, insurance, legal etc. were all conducted. It was clear that there would be increasing pressure on office space as we grew the business. The present wooden partitioned offices were hopelessly inadequate and we would soon either have to move or build an extension to our Hamilton Street premises. I obtained quotations for building a new custom designed workshop and offices building on the new Chanters Industrial Estate, which was being developed only about half a mile from Hamilton Street. This, however, proved to be too expensive for us to afford at the time, so we invited two builders to look at extending the old mill building.. Allen Brothers of Wigan won the contract on a design and build basis and proceeded to apply for planning permission. The value of the contract was £45,000 and NatWest Bank facilitated a commercial mortgage over 10 years, which I felt we could handle comfortably. What I wasn't prepared to do was invest this kind of capital on someone else's land without security of tenure. We still only had a one year rolling lease with Leslie Fink, so I contacted them to let them know of our plans and to request that we have a new 99 year lease. They explained that it wasn't their practice to grant long term leases and the best they could offer was a 10 year lease. I protested that this wasn't enough to give me the confidence to invest £45,000 and, after much discussion and haggling, we compromised at a 77 year lease. The value to LGH of this longer term would become of great significance a few years later.

We now had efficient and comfortable new offices, a computer based admin system which was the envy of the industry, an impressive new image based on ICA's proposals and evidenced on signs, vehicle livery, stationery and a beautiful new catalogue. Press releases were going out regularly and we were advertising quite heavily in a number of trade magazines. The branch network was performing well and the business model appeared to be robust. By April 1976 turnover had reached £395,000, not quite double the 1975 figure, and the following year it hit £650,000.

Atherton was proving to be a very fortuitous location for LGH. It was close to the developing motorway network, it was situated conveniently between Manchester and Liverpool, the two biggest North West cities, and there was a ready supply of skilled engineering and commercial staff from a background of cotton mills, mining and nut and bolt manufacturing. However, the North West was a huge area for a sales representative to cover and Gordon Worswick was still on his own in sales. This was a good opportunity to offer an internal promotion by appointing a new sales rep from within the business.

The position was advertised and three candidates were selected to be interviewed by Gordon, John Williams and myself. Two of the candidates were fitters from the workshop who were both highly skilled and very experienced in the use of lifting equipment. The third was Carol Slane, a woman!! At that time, the lifting equipment industry was totally male dominated. There was not another woman in a sales or technical role in the whole country but she interviewed so much better than the two men that we all agreed that it would have been unfair not to give her the chance. Carol went on to have a long and successful career in sales with LGH and will continue to feature in the story. One of the male candidates immediately resigned on being told that he had been unsuccessful. He went on to have a moderately successful sales career with a competitor.

By 1978 I was playing squash for Horwich Leisure Centre's 2nd team in the North West Counties league Division 6. This was reputed to be the largest squash league in the world with hundreds of teams and thousands of players. One of the teams we played against regularly was JJB sports and twice I was drawn to play against their company chairman, Dave Whelan, who played for one of the JJB teams. He was extremely tenacious and beat me 3-2 on each occasion. In those days he wasn't the famous high profile billionaire he would later become - he was just one of the lads having a night out playing squash.

I also played regularly at a private squash club in Leigh called The Lancastrian. The club manager was a professional called Paul Hendry, who one day suggested to me that I might like to consider sponsoring a professional squash tournament. He assured me that he could guarantee entries from eight of the world's top fifty players and a further eight lower ranked pros. The tournament would be known as The Lifting Gear Hire Lancastrian and would have a total entry of eighty players, comprising sixty-four top amateurs and sixteen pros. LGH would pay £700 and this would be augmented by entry fees from the amateurs and ticket sales from spectators, so a prize fund of £2,500 could be offered. We agreed to this proposal and the event was a tremendous success, giving us exposure in local and national press and a wonderful way of entertaining our customers in a relaxed and enjoyable environment. The tournament became a regular fixture on the professional squash circuit and went on to count towards world ranking points. To reduce the pro players' expenses, the club members and our colleagues would accommodate them in our houses for the duration of the tournament. One year Ross Norman, a young up and coming New Zealander, stayed at our house and won our tournament. Some years later, in 1986, he became the first player in over five years to beat the legendary Jahangir Khan on his way to winning the world championship.

Not only was the growth pressure impinging on office space, but our brilliant computer system was beginning to creak at the seams. The problem stemmed from the fact that the Wang system would only permit data input from a single terminal and, as the volumes of data increased in proportion to revenue growth, it became increasingly difficult for Linda to keep up with the company's needs. Wang had a new development ready to launch but it was not yet available in the UK. It was called the Wang VS, which would support multi terminals, and they were so keen that we should upgrade to this computer that they invited me to the USA to see the prototypes which would soon be available. I'd never previously been to America and Wang's offer to pay for my trip was too good to pass up. I agreed with Wang that after my visit to their offices at Lowell, Massachusetts I'd stay on in the US for a few extra days at my own expense to conduct some business of my own. That proved to be a hugely significant decision in the whole scheme of things.

I flew from Manchester to Boston via JFK and La Guardia. Someone had advised me to book the flight right through to Boston, which would oblige the airline to transfer me to La Guardia from JFK by helicopter straight over Manhattan Island. What a thrill that was, my first helicopter flight. I had a video camera with me and filmed the views of New York from the air. During the flight I asked the pilot if we'd be flying near to the Statue of Liberty and he said "Would you like to?" He promptly changed direction and flew to the iconic statue, circled it twice and shouted back from the cockpit, "Did you get that?" Welcome to America!

Wang Laboratories' car collected me from Boston Airport and took me to their impressive offices at Lowell. On arrival, I checked in at reception and was asked to wait in an ante room for my host, Clifford D Castle III. The third! I'd never before met anyone who was even a second never mind a third. I was given coffee and a biscuit, which the receptionist called a cookie, and used the rest room while I waited. After a few minutes, Mr. Castle's secretary came to collect me and showed me to his palatial office. I was tired and jet-lagged but in awe of everything and keen not to miss a thing. He invited me to be seated and then said, "I understand that this is your first trip to America, Bill. You'll have to be prepared to find we Americans a bit brash and blunt. We call a spade a spade; your flies are undone." What? Oh no! I'd left the rest room a bit too hurriedly but the resultant humour softened the introduction and the trip to Wang went well. They were very keen to sell me the new VS model, which would have been the first one in Europe, but they failed to convince me that the necessary technical support would be in place in time to meet our needs so I didn't place an order with them.

I'd taken my squash kit to the US in the hope that I might get a game there with their different size of court and harder ball. I asked Clifford if any of his colleagues played the game and he promised to fix me up with an opponent. This proved to be harder than he'd expected and it was only on my last day there that a British ex-pat called Jack Taylor contacted me to say that he'd fixed it for me to play at his club, The Harvard Club, at 6.00 that evening. He told me to check in with the receptionist and to use his membership number to charge anything I wanted to his account. I took a taxi from my hotel to the club in good time and the receptionist greeted me warmly then turned away and called out "Mohibullah. Mohibullah, Mr Parkinson's here for you." What? Don't tell me I'm playing Mohibullah Khan, who only a few years earlier had won the British Open. I was walking on air. It was like turning up for a casual game of golf to find Jack Nicklaus waiting for you on the tee. He was wonderful to me, first by completely fooling me with every shot he played then, once he'd shown who was the boss, by allowing me to play long rallies with him. A truly special episode in my life.

After leaving Boston I flew to Buffalo and visited Columbus McKinnon, a prominent US lifting equipment manufacturer. In the UK, I'd set my technical colleagues a challenge to develop a way of making the installation of a chainblock onto a runway beam at height more simple and safe. Trevor Lamprell produced a design of a gadget which we patented and started making, selling and hiring. I had an appointment to meet CM's Vice President (Marketing) to see if they'd like to be our exclusive US dealer for our product which we called 'Easirig'. He was impressed with our design, understood the need for such a product and told me that it was on their 5 year plan to develop such a device. I suggested to him that we'd saved them a job as it was available here and now. They thought about the proposal for several months before declining to take the distributorship and we never successfully introduced the 'Easirig' into the US.

Whilst in this area, I decided to take a look at one of the world's most famous sights, Niagara Falls. This was February 1979, one of the most severe winters on record, and the Falls were completely frozen. There was barely a trickle of water making the drop to the river below but it was stunningly beautiful, with massive patterns of ice formations. This iconic tourist trap was deserted. I was virtually the only person there. It was uncanny. I decided to ride up and down in the lift and fantasise that this was the one used by Marilyn Monroe in *Niagara*, but found out later that the lift she used was on the Canadian side of the Falls. I left Buffalo Airport with snow several feet deep heading south for Miami in Florida to visit my cousin Lois.

My mother's sister, Harriet, had left England in the 1930's with her husband, Harry Dring, to become missionaries in Formosa, Argentina. They had two daughters, May and Lois, who went on to marry two brothers, John and Rolf, the sons of a Norwegian couple who were also missionaries in Argentina. The two young couples ended up living in America and it was to see Lois that I was heading for Miami. When I disembarked, after a flight lasting about three hours, it was to see palm trees waving around in a lovely warm breeze. I'd just left five feet of snow and was still in the same country! "This is a big country," was my over-riding thought. I stayed for a few days with Lois but didn't see her husband Rolf who was on a business trip to Europe. He was Financial Vice President of Eastern Airlines, who were about to place a massive order for many European Airbus planes if they could secure the biggest corporate loan ever from a consortium of European banks.

This trip to America fired me up and gave me an appetite for more. I hadn't bought anything and I hadn't sold anything but what I'd seen was opportunity. I determined that one day I'd be back and next time I wouldn't be leaving empty handed.

Chapter 13 - Crisis Time

Once I returned to the UK, having decided not to buy another Wang machine, my first priority was to find a replacement for the 5 year old computer which had served us so well. Computer technology had moved on apace, in accordance with Moore's Law since 1974, with great advances made in speed of operation, data storage capacity, ease of programming and a reduction in cost. One of the best and fastest growing British computer manufacturers at that time was Systime, who were based in Leeds. The largest engineering company in Atherton was Staveley's, who had recently set up a subsidiary based on selling and setting up Systime computers. It made sense, it seemed, to use a local company to support our computing requirements, and I invited them to make proposals to us for replacing the Wang 2200 machine. I wasn't to know it at the time but that relatively simple decision resulted in a crisis which almost wrecked my business.

Compared to the original Wang system five years earlier, the creation of the Systime suite of programmes should have been quite straightforward. After all, the basic fundamentals of the LGH Administrative system remained the same as before, so there was no clever, original work to complicate matters in that respect. We were basically asking for a copy of the Wang system but with multi-terminal input capability and considerably more storage capacity and processing speed. On reflection, the team who worked on our programming were inexperienced in creating bespoke software on this scale and with this level of complexity and the progress towards the contractually agreed completion date kept slipping.

We were not aware of the extent of the slippage and we made a full commitment to close down the Wang computer on 30th April and go live with the Systime computer on 1st May 1979, following two months of parallel running. It gradually became clear that there'd be no time for parallel running, but we were still hopeful of going live on 1st May. Further delays, teething problems, crashes and other assorted failures meant that we weren't able to produce a single invoice in May, after switching off the Wang.

June came and went and still we were unable to produce invoices. As ever, cash flow was tight, and it was clear that this would be seriously exacerbated by this lengthy delay in producing our sales invoices. Documentation for input to the computer was piling up alarmingly and equipment was being 'off-hired' before we'd even recorded the 'on-hire'. It was chaos.

I called a meeting between our management and the Staveley's top brass and gave them specific threats of legal action to recover the losses which we were incurring, with punitive damages for breach of contract. I expected this threat to shake them into action to mitigate our losses by finishing the outstanding work quickly. The Staveley's CEO, who had only recently joined them, quietly and calmly sat through my angry tirade then shocked us all by announcing, "Bill, when you're bleeding to death and have only minutes to live, one more cut isn't going to make any difference". He explained that the parent company was going bust but he was determined to ensure that the computer subsidiary finished our contract. Any talk of claims for damages was worthless. As Staveley's were also NatWest customers, my bank manager, Ron Gleave, was well aware of the problem and was supportive of a temporary loan facility for LGH to help us to cope with the drying up of cash receipts over the next few months. The new system was eventually completed and, after some initial teething problems, gave excellent service for several years.

It was a close call. Without such an understanding bank manager providing emergency funding we too would have gone under. We'd been let down, but it was my fault and I had to take responsibility and learn from these mistakes. I'd been too complacent and trusting of very nice people whose credentials I took for granted. It nearly cost me my business and I realised it must never happen again that the incompetence of one supplier should jeopardise everything I'd worked for.

The old Wang system was now redundant and I tried to sell it, but no-one was interested in a second-hand computer. I asked our children if they'd be interested in having it at home and the elder two, Ian and Lorraine, weren't keen, but Steven, at seven years old, couldn't wait to get his hands on it. We installed it in his bedroom and I gave him the operating manual, which he studied avidly. In no time at all he was writing simple programs in Basic language and progressed quickly to more complex tasks, at an age when a lot of children can barely read. We didn't know it then, but this was the start of Steven's professional career in the computer industry. Having graduated with a degree in Computer Science and Engineering at the University of Southern California, he still lives and works in San Jose in the heart of the Silicon Valley.

Chapter 14 - Acquisition Time

We continued to expand on all fronts, with the head office/branch model working very well. Cash flow continued to be my biggest headache, as we spent ever bigger sums on the plant fleet that underpinned our growth. My bank manager, Ron, and his wife were keen and highly competent Bridge players and encouraged Irene and I to play with them at occasional evenings at their home. I became quite keen and soon joined them at weekly evenings of competitive Duplicate Bridge at the Pilkington Sports and Social Club. There I got to know a Cambridge graduate called John Ashworth, who had recently left the teaching profession and had taken a crash course in accountancy. Ron thought that it was about time that we had an accountant at LGH to help with the management accounts which he and I looked over each month. I offered John a job and. though he wasn't a fully qualified accountant, his intelligence and facility with numbers ensured that he was able to greatly improve the production of our monthly accounts. Our turnover reached £850,000 in 1978 and the magic figure of one million was passed the following year, when we hit £1.2m.

One of our main competitors during my Coubro time was Wilcox Chains Ltd. who were an old established Manchester firm of traditional lifting gear engineers. They'd been founded in about 1870 and operated from very old dingy premises off Bridgewater St., near the Rochdale Canal. They were owned by two elderly gentlemen who were brothers-in-law, called Fred Vaughan and Albert Oakden, neither of whom had any children to follow them in the business. I surmised, correctly as it later turned out, that they might be looking for an exit from the business in order to retire. I approached them with a view to making an offer but they wouldn't even talk to me about it. They obviously thought that a young man who'd only been in business for a few years couldn't possibly afford to buy the well-established 100 year old pillar of the lifting gear industry.

They were right in one respect. I didn't have the capital to make an outright bid for their company, but I would have made them a generous offer and spread the payment over a number of years. It would have been on similar lines to my first business acquisition, Mailsales, in my youthful printing days 20 years earlier, but on a completely different scale. The logic behind my approach was two-fold. First, I felt that the engineering capability at Wilcox would be useful to LGH, who were frequently being asked to design and make spreader beams, overhead runways, jib cranes, special lifting attachments and a multitude of other engineered products. LGH didn't have the capability to make such products but Wilcox did. Secondly, I felt that Wilcox was appearing somewhat dated and old-fashioned. There'd been little investment in the business for years and I was convinced that we could run the company more professionally and probably more profitably.

Shortly after my overtures had been rejected by Messrs. Oakden and Vaughan, I was annoyed to learn that they'd sold out to Manchester Liners. I gave up on the idea until a couple of years later, in late 1979, I heard that Manchester Liners were prepared to get out of the lifting business and would listen to offers for Wilcox. This was my chance. I met with their management and offered them £75,000, which was accepted. However, as always, I didn't have the ready funds, so negotiated to pay them £25,000 deposit and two further payment of £25,000 for the next two years, plus interest, making a total consideration of £87,000. The deal was done and the contract was signed. At that time Wilcox's trading performance was poor. Manchester Liners had used the business to provide sinecure employment opportunities for retiring ships' captains so that they could wind down their careers in an undemanding managerial role. Not surprisingly, with no commercial drive to spur them on, the staff had become complacent and lethargic. I had just the man in mind to run the business and shake everyone up.

Malcolm Jones was currently managing a small satellite branch for Lloyds in Skelmersdale. I'd met him a few times and we'd done some reciprocal business together. He impressed me as a tough, no-nonsense Scouser who might be ready for a challenging career move. I arranged to meet him and offered him the Wilcox manager's job, with a generous salary and attractive commission based on profits. I thought that he'd jump at the chance but he made me work hard at convincing him during two or three subsequent meetings and squeezed an improved remuneration package out of me. He finally accepted the job and handed in his notice to Lloyds.

In the meantime, Irene and I had decided to take our first ever skiing holiday, in Kitzbuhel, Austria. This was an expensive holiday with three children and I'd needed to raise some cash to fund it. I'd bought some Krugerands a couple of years earlier at about £117 each and gold had been going up in price recently. It was now standing at over £200 an ounce. I consulted Ron on the question of whether or not to sell and he said, "Bill, it's never wrong to take a profit". This sounded like wise advice so I sold my eight Krugerands, which just about paid for our holiday. Whilst we were in Austria I kept seeing English newspapers which were screaming headlines on a daily basis 'Gold hits new high!' It peaked at over $800 an ounce in January, giving me much food for thought.

My thoughts about gold and poor timing of disposals were soon interrupted by further bad timing. We were all enjoying our first experience of skiing and were making good progress on the slopes. The children, as usual, were improving rapidly and were taking their own classes. After a week, I was in a class near the base of the legendary Hahnenkamm mountain, which was being prepared for the famous downhill ski race in a few days time, featuring ski ace Franz Klammer. The instructor was teaching us 'side slipping' across the face of the slope at very slow speeds when a German girl ahead of me fell and, in my clumsy effort to avoid her, I also fell. Because I was going so slowly, the bindings of my skis didn't release as they would if I'd fallen at speed and my tangled skis caused my ankle to break. After I'd convinced my instructor that I really had broken my ankle in such an innocuous looking fall, he put his head between my legs and lifted me onto his shoulders and promptly skied as fast as he could down the half mile to the medical centre at the foot of the mountain. I've never been so terrified in my life as I was during that hair-raising descent.

We returned to England and I arranged to meet my new colleagues at Wilcox Chains. I hobbled in on crutches with my ankle in plaster and went round all the various workstations, introducing myself and finding out what each member of staff was responsible for. As I came to the blacksmiths' department, I stopped to talk to a welder who was working on a chain sling. This was high tensile strength steel and he was using a very high quality intense welding process called atomic hydrogen. I donned a welder's mask and watched him work for a few minutes. When he paused in his work, I took the mask off to thank him for the demonstration but then he struck up the arc again. I was wearing contact lenses at the time and the glare of light was incredibly intense. After a minute or so my vision returned to normal and I thought no more about it at that time.

At lunch time I had all of the staff gathered together so that I could address them collectively. I told them that the business was losing money and that they were in a self-perpetuating downward spiral which would inevitably lead to the failure of the company. Trading losses meant that there was no cash available for investing in better equipment, good stock levels, decent vehicles etc. It also meant low wages and a failure to attract talented staff. I explained that I couldn't work miracles to change this situation but I could give them a short period of breathing space, which would give them the opportunity to reverse the direction of the spiral. I announced an immediate 10% increase in all of their salaries and told them that a dynamic new manager would be starting the following week. I expected nothing but total commitment and hard work. Those who were not prepared for this could leave right now.

I went home thinking that we had a chance to make it work, but my eyes had started to itch. I took my lenses out and the itching became painful. By the time I went to bed the pain was intense and it was clear that there was something seriously wrong. I remembered seeing the atomic hydrogen welding arc and guessed that I was suffering from what welders called 'flash'. Irene called our doctor, who was also a neighbour, and he kindly came to see me and administered some anaesthetic drops to my eyes. It turned out that the 'flash' had, in effect, welded my soft contact lenses to the surface of my eyes and scarred them. It was several weeks before the healing process was complete.

Malcolm took up his duties as manager and immediately asked ICA Publicity to re-design the Wilcox stationery, catalogues, vehicle livery and signs. He then bought a new truck and van and had them painted in the new livery. The whole place was tidied and obsolete stock was sold for scrap. The sales ledger was scrutinised and it was clear that debtor control had been a very low priority for years. It now became the number one priority and the average debtor days were dramatically reduced over the next few weeks. Malcolm had many contacts in industry and he persuaded many of them to give Wilcox a chance for their lifting equipment needs. Business started to improve. I'd opened a bank account for Wilcox with a £10,000 'seed' deposit. After six months they had a credit balance of £120,000! It would have been possible to immediately pay off the amount owing to Manchester Liners using Wilcox's own money. I couldn't believe how easy this had been and the experience would give me the confidence to repeat this exercise several times during the years to come, although not always with the same degree of success.

Chapter 15 - Consolidation

My business was ten years old and I was forty years old. I felt that there was no limit to what we could achieve. We had continued to open new branches steadily, but there were still many industrial regions of the UK where we weren't represented. It still niggled me that we were still not operational in London. The cash flow constraints imposed a tight discipline on us, which limited capital expenditure, and that in turn controlled the rate at which we were able to expand. I think that this was beneficial to the company as purchases of new plant had to be carefully considered and fully justified. Every time we bought a piece of plant, in effect we were making a bet that we could hire it out often enough to get our money back, at least. This was especially true of the larger, more expensive items such as winches.

Under Peter Ashworth's management, our Doncaster branch was building a formidable fleet of powered winches - electric, diesel and hydraulic from 1 ton to 20 ton capacity. The staff at Doncaster developed an expertise in the use and maintenance of winches which could be called upon by the rest of the branch network. Right from the outset we encouraged inter-branch trading. Each branch was a separate profit centre and was deemed to own its own plant. If a branch obtained an order for the hire of, say, ten 5 ton chainblocks, but only had four in stock, then they could rehire the others from one or more of the other branches and an inter-branch discount of 50% would apply. In other words, the revenue earned was split equally between the branch achieving the order and the branch owning the plant. This principle remained constant and I'm sure prevented unnecessary expenditure on plant which we already owned. It helped that most of our branches were located within 60 or so miles of their nearest sister branch and would arrange to meet in the middle to transfer equipment.

On one occasion, I visited our Dudley branch on a routine visit. Maurice, the manager, and Bert, his Teesside counterpart, were still locked in fierce but friendly rivalry, which was healthy for the company. I knew that Maurice had a potential sizeable bad debt problem resulting from a dispute with a good customer. This had been dragging on for some months and I was anxious to see a resolution. I asked Maurice to explain the technicalities of the dispute, which he did quite logically. It seemed we had a good case to be paid in full and I suggested that he write to the customer to put our case. "Oh, I already sent three letters" Maurice explained, "but they're not responding". I asked to see the correspondence file and when I read the letters was horrified to see that they were full of grammatical and spelling mistakes. I asked for Janet, Maurice's secretary to join us and told them both, "It's ultimately the guy who signs the letter who is responsible for the quality and accuracy of the content, but the typist shouldn't knowingly type mistakes and if she suspects a spelling error she should use a dictionary. Janet, I'll buy you a dictionary". Janet was quick to point out that she already had a dictionary but the word in question - Sykological - wasn't in her version.

On my return to Atherton I gave this salutary experience some thought. I had branches around the country which I thought were operating to consistent standards, but what if they weren't? I was busy at Atherton and wasn't getting around the country as often as I should. Most of my managers had been invited to join us - they'd never had to write an application letter. They might be illiterate as far as I knew. Even more importantly, what about maintenance standards of our own plant, with all the safety implications that were entailed? It was vital that we introduced defined policies which would become standard practice for all branches both now and in the future.

I tackled the letter issue first. Business letters at that time were written using electric typewriters. Each branch had purchased their own machines and the typefaces varied in accordance with the manager's preference. Also, each typist had been taught how to lay out a letter in a different style. Indented paragraphs or not, signature on the left or right etc.? I decided on a standard typeface and layout which would be adopted henceforth by everyone in the company. I wrote model letters to fit every occasion - quotations, payment chasing, apologies, complaints etc., and prepared a file of correspondence standards for each manager and typist in each branch. Not only did this improve our standards of correspondence, but it sent a strong signal to everyone working for LGH that as far as our presentation to the world at large was concerned, anything less than perfect was unacceptable.

To achieve conformity in maintenance procedures would be a much more demanding task. Over the years, it would consistently be the concern of senior management and would result in significant investment of time and money. At this time, though, I just wanted to be sure that we weren't cutting corners that could result in unsafe equipment. I asked John Williams, who by now was running Atherton branch, to help define best practices. We invested in the latest testing equipment, which made it much simpler to apply proof load tests to our equipment, which in turn ensured that tests were not missed. John regularly visited the branches specifically to audit their maintenance procedures and there was a visible improvement throughout the company. The company applied to join the Chain Testers' Association of Great Britain (CTA) and our procedures and standards were subjected to their technical audit. The CTA was the national trade body to which all reputable lifting gear companies belonged.

Our relationship with our Nitchi chainblock suppliers, Louis Reyners from Amsterdam, had developed well and their Sales Manager, Rob

Dorpmans, visited us every few months. We were supposed to set up stockists throughout the UK but all of the potential stockists saw us as competitors and wouldn't enter into a business relationship with LGH that they perceived would be of benefit to us. However, our own consumption of Nitchi products was more than enough to satisfy Louis Reyners that we justified the exclusive National Distributor contract.

I told Rob that I'd be keen to visit the Nitchi factory in Osaka, Japan and he said that his company would stand the cost of such a trip if we hit ambitious sales targets the following year. Rob had told one of his Dutch customers about LGH and described how we were rapidly growing a hire operation in the UK. This customer was called A. Kwint and, in a way, was similar to Coubro, having started life many years earlier as ships' riggers in the northern port of Gröningen. Their Managing Director, Mr. Smit, contacted me and said he'd like to visit us, to which I agreed, curious and suspicious at the same time.

Mr Smit visited Atherton, together with Kwint's Technical Director, and,during the visit we discussed the possibility of a joint venture in Holland, based in Gröningen but with representation also in Kwint's branch offices in Rotterdam and Leeuwarden. This would be our first tentative step overseas and it was important that we made all the right decisions as this might prove to be the blue-print for similar partnerships elsewhere. We agreed to meet again in a few weeks' time in Gröningen to finalise the details. Gordon Worswick, John Williams and myself flew from Manchester to Schipol Airport in Amsterdam, from where we were collected by Mr Smit.

On the drive North to Gröningen we stopped at a restaurant for lunch and, just as we were about to tuck in, Mr. Smit stopped us in order to say grace. How could we not trust such a devout Christian? We were impressed by the facilities at Gröningen and gained confidence in the ability of Kwint to run a hire operation. Our subsequent agreement was based on an equal partnership, with each partner contributing an equal amount of capital to fund the start-up. Kwint would supply the office and workshop storage accommodation at a nominal rent and would transfer a competent manager to run the new company, which would be called Kwint LGH BV. We would supply the knowhow for the administrative systems. The big advantage for us was that we were getting an entrée into Europe at little cost in a low risk venture with a partner who had an established branch infrastructure and a pre-existing customer base. The downside was that we had little day-to-day managerial control and we were teaching someone else in our industry how to do what we did best.

The sales targets which Rob had set in order for me to qualify for a free trip to Japan were narrowly missed and new targets were set for the following year. These were also missed and Rob kept raising the bar in such a way that we always narrowly failed to achieve the target until, eventually, we made it. The prize was to be invited, at Louis Reyner's expense, to visit the Nitchi factory in Osaka and, as a bonus, on the return journey we'd spend a few nights in Hong Kong and Bangkok. We flew into Tokyo and transferred to Osaka on the famous 'Bullet' train to be met at the station by Nitchi's owner, Mr Kimura, in his chauffeur driven Jaguar car. We checked into our hotel and the following day were treated to a comprehensive tour of the Nitchi facilities, which were most impressive and reinforced my confidence in their products, which were the most important cornerstone of LGH's hire offering. The following day Mr. Kimura took us to Kyoto, which had been the old capital of Japan, and contained a fascinating mix of ancient temples and lovely gardens.

Chapter 16 - Family Holidays

In 1976 I'd bought quite a large double axle second-hand Tabbert caravan and we embarked on our first overseas caravan holiday as a family. We chose Brittany, on the North-West coast of France, and had a wonderful time in the continuous sun of that legendary summer. The following year we were tempted back to the West coast of France, crossing by ferry and towing the caravan behind my 3 litre Granada to Royan, in the Bordeaux region. The summer of '77 was almost as good as '76 and again we had a wonderful two week long family holiday. We were now seasoned caravanners and decided the following year to be more adventurous. We ventured on a four week holiday, which would take us to the French Riviera, Monaco, Italy, Switzerland and the Black Forest region of Germany.

I had the caravan serviced before departure to ensure that there'd be no mechanical failures and we set off full of excitement and anticipation. In the event, and for several different reasons, the trip turned into a nightmare. Firstly, as we travelled South on the French Autoroute, a motorist passed us and waved frantically for us to stop. When I did so I was horrified to see that one of the caravan tyres had burst and was on fire! I was able to put out the fire, remove the wheel and replace it with the spare. Because we had four wheels on two axles I'd been unaware of a puncture and the friction had caused it to ignite. It took several days to obtain a replacement tyre for the damaged one and in the meantime we suffered another puncture of a caravan tyre. A week later we suffered yet another puncture: three in the space of about ten days.

We made it to the Riviera for our first ever experience of the Mediterranean at Nice, and met up, as previously arranged, with Irene's sister Doreen and brother-in-law Roy and their children, Neil and Janet. Everything was going fine when I decided it was time to see if everything was well back at LGH in Atherton. Our receptionist,

Judith, seemed relieved when she answered my call and said, "Did you get our message asking you to call which was broadcast on Radio Luxembourg?" I was incredulous! Why would they want me to call so urgently? Judith explained, "Irene's mother's died suddenly and we wanted to let her know. The funeral's in three days time." I had to go back to the camp site to tell the two sisters that their mother had died. We then had to make arrangements to get them back to England for the funeral.

In those days it was normal for each family to have one passport, usually in the husband's name. His wife and children would be named on his passport. The wife could only travel abroad in the company of her husband, so Irene and Doreen had a serious problem which was compounded by the fact that it was Bastille Day, a French national holiday. We managed to contact the British Consulate and explained the situation and they very efficiently arranged with the French and British Immigration officials for the sisters to fly home without passports. For the return journey, after the funeral, a few days later, they obtained temporary visitors' passports from the Post Office in the UK. In the meantime Roy and I remained on the Riviera coast and took care of the five children by taking them to the beach at St Tropez and letting them play in the sand and rock pools, whilst we watched a group of topless young women playing volley ball. It was tough and we couldn't wait for our wives to return.

A few days later, Roy and Doreen returned home and we continued our holiday by heading East along the coast towards Italy, calling at Monaco on the way. We were turned away from Monaco as caravans weren't allowed into Monte Carlo, so we found a nearby camp site, unhitched the caravan and made the visit by car. The following day we crossed into Italy then, unknown to us, slightly doubled back into France and found an idyllic camp site in a rugged area with the beautiful white water torrent of a stream rushing by. We were awoken at dawn the following morning by a man banging on our caravan door to tell us that our car had been broken into.

The passenger side door window had been smashed and Irene's handbag, which she'd left in the car, had been stolen. It contained my passport, credit cards and quite a lot of cash - disaster! Reporting the theft to the French police took several hours and in the meantime the discarded handbag was found. It still contained the passport and credit cards. The thief was interested only in the cash. What a relief. The problem of the broken window still remained so I drove back to Cannes where the nearest Ford main dealer was situated and asked them to fix the door with a new window. Not surprisingly, the foreman told me that they didn't stock new windows but he'd be glad to order one. He told me it would take five days. I wasn't happy but there was no alternative and, after all, if you're going to be stranded for five days there are worse places than Cannes.

After five days I went back to the dealership and sought out the foreman. It was immediately obvious from his blank expression that there was a problem - he'd forgotten to order the replacement window. I was livid. I asked to speak to the boss, who turned out to be a young woman who was the daughter of the owner of the business. My family and I had hung around Cannes for five days waiting for this window and had been badly let down, I told her. She spoke excellent English and apologised profusely, saying she'd try to resolve the matter. The storekeeper was summoned and asked if he had a left hand door for my model of Granada. When he said that he did, she told the foreman to remove the glass from the new door and fit it into my door. Problem solved. Why didn't the foreman think of that five days earlier?

We resumed our journey by driving into Northern Italy but, because of our enforced previous delays, we could only stay for a couple of days in the lovely Val d'Aosta area. The Black Forest area of

Germany was next but, as we drove into our chosen camp site, it was pouring down. I dashed through the rain into the reception cabin to register and pay for our spot and, on the way out, picked up an English language brochure describing the camp site. Once we were settled in and Irene was preparing our evening meal the children read the brochure. It said, "Welcome to the beautiful Black Forest. Here you will be wafted by the warm Mediterranean breezes and will be woken in the morning by the sound of birds singing. And you will enjoy it". We all thought this was hilarious as we could hardly hear ourselves speak for the rain battering on the roof of the caravan with loud claps of thunder being heard every few minutes. "You will enjoy it", spoken in a German accent, became a family catch-phrase for years afterwards. The rest of the holiday passed without further incident and we made the return journey home through France with lots of stories to tell of The Holiday From Hell. We all agreed that caravanning was not for us and I sold the van soon after.

Following two or three relatively uneventful holidays, we came to 1982 and Irene booked us to go for two weeks to the Spanish Mediterranean island of Menorca, in a small apartment in the resort of San Jaime. Ian and Lorraine were teenagers by this time and wanted to 'do their own thing', so there was only 9 year old Steven to accompany us. The apartments were built around a communal pool so we soon met our neighbours and Steven made friends with other children. The weather was very hot and we were having a great time. One or two of our friends from home had bought apartments in Spain quite inexpensively and it struck me that we could do the same.

I met with the management company who were building the complex of apartments and villas with a view to buying a two bedroom apartment. I was shocked when they quoted a price of £21,000 when I'd been expecting about half that amount. This seemed to be out of our reach as I was still only paying myself a modest salary. A few days later, I took a walk up the hillside, where all the beautiful detached villas were located and chanced upon one with a small handwritten sign which said 'A VENDRE' and showed a telephone number. On impulse, I noted the number, found a public telephone and made arrangements for a viewing of the villa. Irene and I loved what we saw and decided that we'd make an offer on our return to the UK, subject to our bank manager, Ron, coming up with an appropriate loan. He readily agreed to the loan and I gave myself a salary increase to fund the repayments. Our offer was accepted and we met up with John and Pamela Aitcheson, the villa owners, in a restaurant on Jermyn Street in London to complete the transaction. Although the decision was impulsive at the time, it proved to be a very happy one. We've enjoyed dozens of holidays with family and friends at our Menorcan house over the past 30 years or more and have seen its value increase dramatically. It's a great feeling to make an investment which gives a lot of enjoyment and makes money at the same time.

That same year I made a different but similarly profitable and enjoyable investment. Steven was attending the Junior School of Bolton School and two of his pals there were Roger Tonge and Stephen Warburton. Their fathers were David Tonge and John Warburton respectively. David and John shared a passion for cars, particularly old cars. One day David called at our house in a newly acquired 1926 Bull-nosed Morris and offered me a ride, which I jumped at. Next stop was John's house in Leigh, where I was shown his magnificent collection of vintage cars, all painted with John's signature maroon paint. Among the collection was a beautiful 1927 Rolls Royce 20 horse power open top tourer which John said he wished to sell in order to make room for and raise the cash for a Vauxhall 30/98 tourer.

It seemed incredible to me, as a novice in this field, that anyone would want to sell a Rolls Royce in order to buy a Vauxhall, but it turned out that in the 1920s the Vauxhall was considered to be the ultimate sporty grand touring car with a very impressive performance and was a very rare and desirable vintage car. I agreed to buy the Rolls and still own it over thirty years later, having completed many rallies, not to mention transporting my daughter and the daughters of many of my friends to church on their wedding days.

Old cars were very interesting to me but, unlike with David and John, they were never my primary interest, although I went on to acquire a 1913 Model T Ford runabout and an 1899 De Dion Bouton and had a lot of fun taking part in rallies, particularly the annual Gordon Bennett Memorial rally held in Ireland. Gordon Bennett was the wealthy proprietor of the New York Times, who was famous for sending Stanley to find Livingstone in Africa. He also sponsored the earliest car racing events in the early 1900s, which involved two teams of cars from each of Britain, France, Germany and the USA. The 1904 race held in Ireland (before partition) involved a fatal crash and the current Memorial Rally commemorates that event.

This was the time of the Rubik Cube craze and most youngsters quickly mastered the technique, whilst their parents remained mystified as to how to solve the puzzle. Our son Ian, who by now was in the sixth form at Bolton School studying 'A' levels in Maths, Physics and Economics, was no exception. The original Rubik Cube consisted of six sides, each with nine differently coloured squares, which could be rotated independently of each other in an ingenious configuration. Ian thought that it would be much more difficult and infinitely more interesting if the faces were 5 x 5 rather than 3 x 3 and set about trying to devise a design which would achieve that.

The trick was to allow all the pieces to move and rotate relative to each other whilst remaining locked together. Ian worked on his design for weeks and finally thought that he had a workable solution. I checked his design and agreed with him and at this stage we decided to apply for a patent in his name. Then I helped him to construct a 4x scale model of his design by casting resin blocks of the various pieces. This proved to be very time consuming, laborious work and it was impossible to achieve the accurate dimensions and curves which would be needed to prove that the design was viable. However, we managed to complete the making of more than 120 glass fibre resin blocks and assembled the giant 'Parkinson' Cube. Although it was as good as we could make it, it was still fairly crude but all the indications were promising that the design would work. I think that I was more excited than Ian as I was envisioning massive sales for this brilliant new development.

The next step was to make a proper working model in order to prove conclusively that the design was sound. I contacted a local engineering company, Velden Engineering in Bolton, who had CNC machine tools and who could work in plastic. Ian had prepared accurate working drawings for the six different components, which would go towards the final cube assembly. Velden quoted £2,000 to produce all of the plastic components which were needed for the final prototype and I asked them to proceed as quickly as possible. The Falklands War was in progress and Velden were working flat out producing shell cases in support of the British war effort, but they agreed to squeeze in our order and two or three weeks later Ian's components were ready. We couldn't wait to get them home to assemble the world's first 5 x 5 rotating cube and immediately set to work on this intricate task.

The first hundred or so components were quite easy to fit together, a bit like a three dimensional jig-saw puzzle. The last few, though, were more difficult, especially the corner pieces, which had to be forced somewhat. Finally, it was finished and a perfect 5 x 5 cube was lying on the table before us. With bated breath, I watched as Ian's practised fingers manipulated the cube by rotating first one side, then another. It worked beautifully. Then he got more ambitious and tried all different rotational combinations when suddenly one of the corner pieces became detached. Ian fixed it back in and tried the same manoeuvre again. The piece again fell out. During the next few days Ian took it apart and reassembled it and checked his design. Regrettably, he had to conclude that there was a flaw in the design which, in a certain position, allowed the corner pieces to become disengaged from the main body of the cube. He worked hard at rectifying the problem but was unable find a solution. Ian was disappointed, of course, but didn't seem too downhearted and was soon preoccupied with exam preparation and sports. My own disappointment was tempered by the fact that I had a son who was displaying an aptitude for engineering and design and who possessed the initiative to see a project through from conception to conclusion. These were qualities which he'd need in abundance if he chose to join the family firm in the future. And how many 17 year olds had a patent to their name?

Chapter 17 - More Acquisitions

By 1983 the company was very profitable and still growing quickly, but I felt that I needed help in actively monitoring the branches' activities. Peter Ashworth was doing a great job for us in Doncaster and I felt that he'd earned a promotion. He was appointed as Operations Director with responsibility for the performance of all of the branches, whose managers would report directly to him. He was replaced at Doncaster by Brian Swift, who had been my colleague at Pilkingtons and had first pointed out the Maritime advert to me. John Williams had also been a rock on whom I increasingly depended and he became a Director of the company that year, continuing to be responsible for our technical integrity.

At this time, whilst I was very satisfied with the progress which had been made, I was very conscious of my own shortcomings. I came to the conclusion that, although I had no particular talent for anything, nor did I have any significant weakness, and this gave me the confidence to embark on some ventures which, in hindsight, could be considered strange.

We had been important customers of Tangye, the hydraulic jack manufacturers, since the first days of LGH. I was a big admirer of their range of products, which had become central to our hire fleet. It was a big surprise for me to find out that Tangye were in financial trouble and their owners, Bookers Cash & Carry, were looking to dispose of the business. I contacted Bookers' CEO, Michael Caine, (not the actor) and arranged to meet him in London with a view to LGH acquiring the Tangye business. After seeing the accounts, I went to Birmingham for a visit to the manufacturing plant, which was very impressive. As an engineer, it was very exciting to have the opportunity to get my hands on such an iconic brand with a brilliant range of products. Because much of the machinery was old and heavily depreciated the balance sheet asset value was relatively low and I reckoned that, because the Tangye range was unique, there'd be an opportunity to raise prices and eliminate the trading losses which were being experienced. Mr. Caine and I agreed a price of around £1.0m and I arranged to meet Ron Gleave, my bank manager, to acquaint him with my plans and persuade NatWest to lend me the money to fund this acquisition.

Ron proved to be less than enthusiastic and warned me that such a big acquisition had the potential to ruin everything I'd worked for if it should go wrong. He pointed out that I had no experience in running a manufacturing business and this was in a totally different league to the Wilcox deal. I followed up our meeting with a letter in which I argued that this could prove to be a launching pad for greater things and wound up my letter with the following quotation from Shakespeare's *Julius Caesar*:-

> *There is a tide in the affairs of men,*
> *Which taken at the flood, leads on to fortune;*
> *Omitted, all the voyage of their life*
> *Is bound in shallows and in miseries.*
> *On such a full sea are we now afloat,*
> *And we must take the current when it serves,*
> *Or lose our ventures.*

Ron remained unimpressed by this and referred me to his colleagues at County Bank, the NatWest Merchant Banking arm, who had a look at my proposals before rejecting my application for a loan. I was desperately disappointed not to be able to complete this acquisition, which I'd come to regard as a personal challenge, but on reflection I think that the bankers were right on this occasion, as the balance of probability weighed heavily against a successful conclusion. One change that came about as a result of this interlude was that I sought the help of a larger firm of accountants than the local Bolton firm I'd used up to this time, and subsequently appointed Coopers & Lybrand (later PriceWaterhouseCoopers) to be our company accountants and auditors.

Having been thwarted in one acquisition venture, another opportunity arose soon after. I reckoned that what we were good at was the hire of non-operated plant in a specialist niche market. If we could find small specialist hire companies who had a good concept but poor management and/or customer service then we might be able to apply our superior computer based administrative systems to improve their performance. One such company, Tickhill Plant Ltd., was known to our Doncaster branch and we learned that their parent company, Geo Wills Holdings, a publicly quoted company, might be interested in selling to the right buyer. Tickhill specialised in the hire of tunnelling equipment, about which none of us knew a thing. The core offering was a range of tunnel shields up to about 12ft diameter. These were used to drive through the earth, cutting a tunnel. The spoil was removed by building a narrow gauge railway behind the shield and using small rail trucks to ferry it back to the start of the tunnel. For deep tunnels, compressed air would have to be supplied to reduce the seepage of water. Men working in compressed air conditions would have to enter and leave the work site through an air lock and decompression chamber in the same way that divers operate. Generators would also be needed to power the various equipment. All of this equipment was available for hire from Tickhill. They also had a number of winches, which our Doncaster branch would regularly rehire, as their rate was considerably lower than ours.

Having studied their trading accounts and balance sheet, it was obvious that they were making losses and their plant was old and heavily depreciated. However, this kind of plant would last for ever if it was well maintained and I didn't see it as a problem. The business operated from a decent sized freehold site of several acres on the outskirts of the village of Tickhill in South Yorkshire. My enquiries revealed that the demand for tunneling was likely to increase over the years as the nation's sewerage systems, many of which dated back to Victorian days, came under increasing pressure from population increases and the need to replace antiquated crumbling structures. This was an exciting opportunity and I formulated a bid which was accepted by the Wills board. I used a similar strategy to the Wilcox deal in spreading the payment over three or four years but in this case I left the existing manager, Peter Woolston, in charge.

On day one I went to Tickhill to get to know more precisely what we had acquired. I was impressed by the quantity and size of the plant assets but less impressed by the quality of the equipment. Maintenance standards were going to have to improve dramatically if they were going to proudly fly the LGH banner. As I walked round the workshops and offices, I stopped by the foreman's office to introduce myself. I had to wait as the foreman was on the 'phone to a potential customer and I listened with interest as the conversation went something like this: "No I'm sorry, we don't do wooden fencing. No, I've no idea where you'd get some, goodbye". After introducing myself, I asked him who the customer was and the foreman said, "No idea, just someone who wanted to hire wooden fencing. We don't do wooden fencing so I couldn't help him".

I told him that I'd just walked round the yard and seen lots of metal fencing available for hire. I also told him that he should have obtained the enquirer's name and contact details, found out the potential hire period and quantity required and offered to supply metal fencing as an alternative. It could have been Wimpeys needing tons of fencing for two years! Now we'd never know. I was both appalled and encouraged at this. If the company was handling enquiries so unprofessionally then there was massive potential for improvement with proper training.

I had recently started playing golf with my pals, Ray Garside and David Slane, so I was interested to see the registration number of

Peter Woolston's company car, which I now owned. It was GET 181N which was spaced to read GET 18 IN. Perfect for a golfer, and I thought it would look good on my car until Peter pointed out that although the car was the company's the registration number was his!

During the first few months of our ownership of Tickhill we worked hard at understanding the business and instilling our administrative systems and ethical standards into our new colleagues. Following the Wilcox model, we asked Geoff Ashworth and his marketing experts at ICA to revamp the image of the business. A new logo and colour scheme was introduced which went through the whole public image of the business, including signs, letter headings, business cards, vehicle livery and plant colour scheme. I later asked Brian Swift to take responsibility for both LGH Doncaster branch and Tickhill Plant, whilst retaining Peter Woolston to liaise with customers of Tickhill, particularly on the more technically demanding contracts. Brian quickly identified that there were three main activities at Tickhill which were only loosely dependent on each other, Tunnel Shields, Low Pressure/High Volume Compressors and Generators. Each of these plant groupings could be developed separately and collectively. He set about modernising and refurbishing our fleet of compressors and generators and, to make it easier to transport them and install them on site, he had the larger items mounted inside standard 20' long containers. With the containers painted in our livery, they made an impressive sight when on hire at construction sites.

It was still a great concern to me that we had no presence in London. Then, right out of the blue, I received a 'phone call from a Bill Wilson, who owned a lifting equipment engineering business called J. Wilkinson Ltd in the South East of London, in Woolwich. He wanted to know if I'd be interested in buying his company. This was October 1984 and the country was in the middle of one of the most bitter and damaging industrial disputes ever, the conflict between the

National Union of Mineworkers, led by Arthur Scargill, and the Conservative Government, led by Margaret Thatcher. The British economy suffered, inflation was high and unemployment reached unprecedented levels. Many businesses were suffering, including J. Wilkinson, and I started what was to become a protracted series of negotiations with Bill to try to agree a deal.

In the meantime, during the week before Christmas 1984, I received another 'phone call from an ailing London based lifting gear company. It was George Hegarty, chairman of our competitors East Ham Plant Hire Ltd., who I'd last met at our ill-fated Birmingham meeting in 1975. He told me that his company was about to fold and asked me if I'd like to throw my cap in the ring. I didn't know what he meant by this and thought he was asking if LGH could lend them money to get through a crisis. However, he explained that he meant that he would listen to any reasonable offer which could avoid the closure of the business.

I agreed to meet him at East Ham the following day and asked him to make an appointment for me to meet their bank manager. I travelled to London by train and by Tube to East Ham, where George picked me up at the station in his Daimler and, on the way to his office, he told me what a tough time they'd been having. When I looked round their premises I was appalled. It was a shambles! Plant was lying around all over the place in various states of repair and there was no semblance of organisation or tidiness, either in the workshops or offices. I also met with George Archer, the Managing Director, who tried to blame their demise on the Miners' strike, but it seemed clear to me that the main reason was poor managerial control. They were operating right at the limit of their overdraft and their bank was bouncing cheques. There was no money to pay the wages and, unless I could put a rescue package together, it was inevitable that receivers would be appointed within days.

It turned out that Hegarty and Archer were the biggest shareholders, but the previous owners had given away shares to ex-employees, cousins, uncles, aunts and others, totalling about thirty shareholders owning a total of 20,000 shares. The company was leasing its premises and owed its creditors about £50,000, plus wages due and unpaid PAYE and VAT, plus an overdraft of £100,000. This would be a big commitment to take on and I was, by this time, close to an agreement to buy Wilkinsons. I couldn't help but reflect on the irony of the fact that I'd waited for years to get back into London then two opportunities came at once.

However, it was a great chance to really assert ourselves as the leading lifting equipment hirers in the country and I wasn't prepared to miss it. I offered Hegarty and Archer 50p for each of their shares on condition that all of the other shareholders agreed to sell at the same price. I offered to continue their employment for six months, or until I could find a new manager. They agreed and I immediately wrote out an irrevocable sale contract which we all signed. I then went to see their bank manager, who was about to bounce several of East Ham Plant's cheques. I told him that within days I'd be the new owner of the business and gave him an LGH cheque for £20,000 to allow him to honour the uncleared cheques. I'd taken a big risk with this deal but I felt confident that, as with Wilcox and Tickhill, if we could apply our tried and tested administrative systems and regular managerial controls then we could turn the business round and have it producing a reasonable level of profits. We couldn't work miracles and there was no magic formula that we could apply apart from sound common sense and a keen desire to satisfy our customers before any other consideration.

The deal was completed within a few days and I asked Gordon Worswick to go down to London to oversee the transformation of East Ham Plant into a LGH branch. East Ham also had branches of their own in Ipswich and Norwich, which became LGH outposts too. We advertised the manager's job and appointed an experienced plant hire man, Kevin Mountford, to the position. I then informed George Hegarty and George Archer that their services were no longer required and I paid them the balance of their 6 months contract. The Daimler which Hegarty had been using was transferred to Atherton as my company car. A few days later I received a letter from a solicitor acting for Hegarty and Archer asking that we honour his clients' employment contracts with East Ham Plant Hire Ltd. The contracts had been drawn up by the company under advice from their solicitors some months earlier and were for a ten year term of office at a salary of £20,000 p.a. in Hegarty's case and £15,000 p.a. in Archer's case! A total liability of £350,000! I'd been conned. No wonder they readily accepted a ridiculously low offer to buy the company's shares.

I'd been set up and my own keenness to complete the deal meant that I hadn't gone through any due diligence procedures, nor had I asked them to indemnify LGH against any such claims. I contacted Barry Eckersley Hope. who was LGH's solicitor. and asked him to look over the claim with a view to finding a way to reduce the cost to the company. After a few days, Barry asked me to call in his office as he had some interesting news. He told me that, under company law, it was possible in a private company for Directors to give themselves contracts for up to five years without the approval of the company's shareholders. However, for a contract of over five year's duration, the approval of the shareholders was needed at a meeting convened by giving an appropriate amount of notice. According to the company's records, no such meeting had taken place and therefore the shareholders couldn't have given their approval. The ten year contract was consequently invalid and I couldn't wait to tell them to stuff their claim. If they hadn't been so greedy and had made their contracts for a five year period they'd have conned me out of £175,000. As it was they got nothing. Well done Barry Hope.

Meanwhile, negotiations to buy Wilkinsons, only a few miles South of East Ham, were grinding on, and were finally completed by April. Gordon Worswick had spent a lot of time with Kevin Mountford at East Ham (later LGH North Thames Branch) helping to introduce LGH systems and principles. He now transferred his attentions to Wilkinsons, which was now renamed LGH South Thames Branch. Bill Wilson was retained as branch manager and over the next few months he and Gordon worked well together and became good friends. From having no branches in London a few months earlier we now had two, together with the two small operations in East Anglia, in Norwich and Ipswich.

A few months earlier, I had recognised that Malcolm Jones' style of tough management would benefit some of the branches. He was promoted from Wilcox Chains to the position of Operations Director, with responsibility for the South and Midlands. Gordon Worswick reported to Malcolm and they decided to replace Kevin Mountford as East Ham's manager with a young 24 year old man called Paul Fulcher, who had been working for an East London tool hire business. It was a risky move to give such an inexperienced man the massive challenge of turning the chaotic East Ham Plant Hire into an efficient Lifting Gear Hire location, but Paul proved that he was more than capable of meeting the challenge. He went on to turn the East Ham location into LGH's most profitable branch and eventually became a valuable member of the Board. He ultimately took responsibility for the entire UK LGH branch network, the biggest operational job within the Group.

I remember Paul greatly upsetting me early in his LGH career by being the first person in the company to buy a mobile 'phone. Branch managers had discretion to spend quite large capital sums without reference to their Operations Directors and Paul chose to exercise this discretion by buying a brick-sized early Nokia mobile 'phone or £1,800. I was very annoyed because, as I pointed out to Paul, his

£1,800 decision would become a £36,000 decision for me when all of our senior management team decided they'd also like a mobile 'phone, following the precedent which he'd set. Paul eloquently argued that he'd be a much more effective manager if he could be out on the road meeting customers whilst at the same time keeping close contact with his staff back at the office.

Our daughter Lorraine had left school the previous year with better O level results than her Dad had achieved (not difficult) and had joined the business working as a clerk/typist at Atherton. Our elder son, Ian, had left Bolton School with good A level results in the same year and, after wanting to be a TV cameraman for most of his time in sixth form, he suddenly changed his mind and, much to my delight, decided he'd like to study for a Mechanical Engineering degree. His first choice University was Imperial College, London but his A level results didn't quite meet their requirements and he settled for an offer from City University, also in London. He spent the first year in Halls of Residence and passed six of the seven end of term exams. In order to proceed to year two's study it was necessary to pass all seven with a high average pass mark. The choice was to retake the failed exam in September and hope for a high enough mark to achieve the required average or take a year off and take all seven exams again next spring. Ian opted for taking a year out, which I thought was very dangerous. How could he expect to improve his results if he wasn't taking lectures?

Furthermore he wanted to stay in London and asked me to give him a menial job at the former East Ham Plant. He commuted daily from the centre of London to the East End, which was the opposite direction to all of the other commuters. Journeys to and from work were made on virtually empty trains, whilst the trains travelling in the opposite direction were packed. He obtained accommodation in an apartment on Frith Street, in the heart of Soho, opposite Ronnie Scott's Jazz Club. It turned out that this very apartment was where

John Logie Baird, the Scottish physicist, made the first ever transmission of a television picture. It struck me that if Ian was going to be staying in London, possibly for three more years, and Gordon Worswick was spending a lot of time in London in expensive hotels, it might make sense to buy a house in London for the use of Ian and the Company.

I made tentative enquiries but was deterred by the astronomical prices being asked. Who would pay £35,000 for a three bedroom terraced house in Chelsea? Those same houses that I refused to buy then are now selling for over a million pounds! What do I know about property? Ian made the right decision and, against all my expectations, managed to pass all seven of his exams the following year and resumed his studies at City University.

The miners' strike had ended in March 1985, with a crushing defeat not only for the miners but for the trade union movement in general. This followed the British victory in the Falklands War in 1982 and reinforced Margaret Thatcher's reputation as a formidable Prime Minister, not only in Britain but on the wider European and International stage. Britain gradually got back to work and the economy slowly improved. As a smallish hire company, I'd felt for some time that we were somewhat immune to the fluctuations of the economy. We were masters of our own fate and our own actions were much more significant in determining our success or failure than the wider economy. Also, it was true that in hard economic times companies would try to conserve cash which would encourage them to hire rather than spend capital on new equipment and we were only too happy to facilitate that policy.

Whilst all of this acquisition activity was going on in London, another interesting distraction was unfolding closer to home. Hillards, the Yorkshire based supermarket company, had identified the old Dan Lane Mill building in Atherton, part of which we leased from Leslie

Fink, as a perfect location for a town centre supermarket. Hillards' land acquisition manager, also called Leslie, was a very affable ex-RAF Spitfire pilot. He explained to me that they'd come to an agreement in principle with our landlords to buy the mill and surrounding land. The other tenants, of which there were about five or six, didn't pose a problem, as they were all on very short term leases which could easily be terminated. But as I'd secured a 77 year lease a few years earlier when we'd built the office extension then we had security of tenure and couldn't be evicted. It was now down to negotiating a fair price to compensate us for giving up this valuable lease.

The timing couldn't have been better for us, as we had begun to creak at the seams in both the workshop capacity and also, even more importantly, in what was now regarded as the Head Office and Central Administration facility for the growing LGH Group. I'd already been thinking about different options to cope with our inadequate premises but the costs involved were prohibitive, given the high costs recently incurred in the London based spending spree. The Hillards' approach gave us a wonderful opportunity to make a huge leap forward. We fairly quickly reached an agreement that the compensation would be £200,000, which I'd calculated would be what it would cost to replace what we already had.

Their offer was subject to the obtaining of Planning Approval for the town centre development. When the local public,, and especially local shopkeepers, became aware of Hillards' plans, there was great concern that the town would be ruined by this giant competitor on the doorstep. There had been recent publicity for a Southampton University study on the effects of out of town supermarkets on local shopkeepers. The report of the study indicated that disastrous results were frequent. At a public meeting to hear concerns in Atherton, Hillards argued their case quite eloquently and tried to persuade the people of Atherton that they deserved a proper supermarket (the nearest one at that time was in Leigh, about four miles away). I spoke briefly, to point out that the Southampton study was based on out-of-town developments, which dragged people away from town centres. This was a town centre development which could benefit local shops by bringing people into the town.

I started to search for potential re-location sites for LGH and found an old nut and bolt manufacturer's premises on Bolton Road in Atherton. Gorton and Blakemore were founded in Victorian times and were one of Atherton's many iconic nut and bolt manufacturers. They had closed down a few years earlier and their three acre, freehold plot with crumbling buildings was for sale. As most of our staff lived in and around Atherton it was important to stay in the area if possible, so this was perfect. I made an offer to buy conditional upon the Hillards deal being completed. I then invited Allen Brothers, the Wigan based builders who had built our Hamilton Street office extension, to tender on a design and build basis for a new 12,500 square foot industrial workshop building and a 6,000 square foot office building. The price turned out to be three times as much as the Hillards compensation, but we were getting three times the building area. Also, it was freehold, in a much better location, and it was new, custom-designed, state-of-the-art accommodation. But I had to raise the shortfall in funding.

We'd conducted hundreds of HP transactions during the fifteen years of LGH's existence, using Lombard North Central Finance, NatWest's finance arm. In that time we'd never missed a payment and had built up a good working relationship with their local Bolton office, first with manager, Ian McArthur, then later with his successor, Paul Baxter. LGH's record of growth in both turnover and profits was extraordinary and our balance sheet was very strong, especially in plant assets. Lombard understood the capital intensive nature of our business and agreed to lend us a substantial portion of what we needed to go ahead subject to a first charge on the buildings.

In the event, Planning Permission was granted for both the supermarket and our new workshop and offices and I immediately placed the order with Allen Bros. We agreed to vacate our Hamilton St. premises on 7th July 1985, which gave Allen Bros exactly six months to complete the work and get us into our new buildings. They had included a sum of £5,000 to cover the cost of demolishing the old buildings and clearing the site before building could commence. A demolition contractor approached me and offered to pay us £2,000 for the privilege of demolishing the buildings, provided he could keep the spoil. He promised to be in and out in a week and would leave the site flat and clear of rubble. It was a no brainer. I gave him the contract and Allens reduced their price by £5,000.

The demolition gang arrived on site on day one with three large lorries and immediately set to work stripping all the slates from the roof. There were thousands of them and it took two days to remove them all. I expected them to return on day three to start knocking down the buildings but they didn't show up. I wasn't too concerned but, when they failed to show for the rest of the week, I realised that I didn't have any contact details for the contractor. By the end of the following week it was obvious that they weren't coming back. They'd in effect paid me £2,000 for thousands of slates which were worth 50p each and hadn't fulfilled their part of the bargain. Furthermore, I now had to go cap-in-hand to Allens to reinstate the demolition part of their contract, having lost two weeks, which would prove to be critical by July.

We were now operating from twelve sites throughout the country, with a partnership in Holland and we also had wholly owned subsidiaries Wilcox Chains and Tickhill Plant. It was clear that our accounting department, which consisted of John Ashworth, was under considerable strain. I was expecting him to provide monthly reports for each operating location and was still meeting Ron Gleave every month to review the figures. We needed to recruit a qualified accountant who could bring increased levels of professionalism to this critical area and I consulted our auditors, Coopers & Lybrand, on the subject. They arranged a dinner to which Irene and I were invited and there we met a young qualified accountant called Simon Butterworth and his wife Elspeth. Simon had trained with C & L after university and had then held responsible positions in two different commercial organisations. I invited him to come to Atherton and subsequently offered him the position of Financial Accountant (Financial Director designate) which he accepted. His first job, after his accountancy responsibilities was to liaise with Allen Brothers on the progress of the new building work.

I was very excited at the prospect of moving into our splendid new buildings. So often in business we take premises which have to be modified to our needs. On this occasion, we'd been able to specify exactly what we wanted. Whereas previously we'd been tucked away in the corner of an old mill, now we'd be on a prominent main road position, shouting out our presence to the whole world. As July approached, it became increasingly obvious that the completion date was not going to be achieved. The two weeks lost at the beginning of the job because of my greed and carelessness were now shown to have been critical. I rang the Director of Hillards to explain the position and asked him to suggest a weekly figure for liquidated damages which his company would claim against us when we failed to move out on time. He said "I'm sorry Mr Parkinson, I don't understand what you're talking about. We have a contract which states that you will vacate our premises on 7th July. Our bulldozers will be moving in on 8th July to demolish the mill. Whether you're in it or not." End of conversation. That certainly had the effect of sharpening my thinking and I arranged an urgent meeting with Ken Fox, the CEO of Allens, to explain the position and to discuss what options were open to us. The only option was to step up the pace of work on site by drafting in extra manpower and working overtime at night and week-ends. There would, of course, be extra costs, which LGH would have to bear, making the £2,000 which I'd received from the rogue demolition contractor look like peanuts. In the end, the building was ready in time - just, and we moved in over the course of a weekend, with every member of staff playing a part.

The Atherton Branch and workshop building was separate from the Head Office building and we'd incorporated everything we needed for the most modern and efficient lifting equipment facility in the UK. There was a dedicated test house with facilities for both horizontal and vertical proof load testing. The vertical tester had been developed in-house by Dave Potts, who'd started with LGH some years earlier as an engineering fitter. I was concerned that our national trade body, the Chain Testers' Association of GB, didn't believe that hydraulic testing of machinery such as chain blocks, pull-lifts and Tirfors accurately simulated dynamic live load operating conditions. I took the view that it was better to make testing easier, even if the test was not exactly replicating working conditions, rather than have extremely difficult and potentially dangerous tests involving lots of steel or concrete weights.

Dave had responded to my concerns by designing a test rig which incorporated 20 tons of various sizes of steel weights located in an underground pit, over which a substantial gantry would be built. Each weight would have a lifting lug on top, which would allow any combination of weights to be selected and engaged within seconds, using a dedicated small computer to control it. It was brilliant. We immediately submitted a patent application and I authorised David to proceed from the design stage to producing a full size prototype working model. We called it the CVT, short for Computerised Vertical Tester, and the prototype was ready to be installed in our new test house. After quite a bit of refining, the tester worked exactly as hoped and we were able to apply live load dynamic proof test loads as easily and quickly as had previously only been possible with hydraulic simulations.

The Mark 1 test machine had cost about £20,000, excluding development costs, and we decided to offer them for sale at £25,000 each. I was very excited that the whole industry would be beating a path to our door and fully expected to sell many units. We made two more for our own branches in Doncaster and South Thames, but managed to sell only one other CVT. We seemed to be the only lifting equipment company in the UK prepared to invest this kind of money in testing equipment. I would modestly suggest that this was indicative of the difference between LGH and the rest of the lifting equipment industry in the country at that time, and was one of the reasons why LGH was able to go from a standing start in 1970 to being the biggest lifting equipment company in Britain within 20 years.

Atherton branch also housed a room designed especially for 'rumbling' chain. We owned a massive amount of chain, used mainly for chain-blocks, which would get rusty after being out on hire for a few weeks. We were always insistent that any equipment which was sent out on hire to a customer was clean, freshly painted, tested and, in the case of chain-blocks, with bright, shiny chain. This was achieved by means of rumbling the rusty chain in a rotating drum together with off-cuts of scrap leather and dash of paraffin and oil. This was a noisy, dirty process so it was good to be able to segregate it from the main workshop in a dedicated sound dampened room.

The maintenance workshop housed about a dozen fitters who each had their own specialities, including a hydraulics section which took care of our hundreds of varied hydraulic jacks. The plant storage area enabled us to neatly and efficiently store and pick a vast range of our lifting equipment available for hire. I loved having the opportunity to take customers around the branch, which never failed to greatly impress them. Never before had such a quantity and variety of lifting equipment been available for hire under one roof.

Hydra Services, in which I was a minority partner with Bert Leigh, had moved into our Bolton Old Road sausage works premises when LGH moved out in 1983 and subsequently followed us to Dan Lane Mill a few years later, as they continued their modest growth. They were also displaced by the Hillards development and I'd incorporated an additional 2,500 square feet in the new building for Hydra Services' use. It was good for LGH to have a specialist hydraulics firm next door and it was good for Hydra Services to have one of their biggest customers on the same site.

Chapter 18 - America Beckons

Despite all of the hectic activity in the UK, my thoughts kept straying longingly to the vast potential which I reckoned was waiting to be exploited in the USA. My first and, as yet, only visit in 1979 had fired my imagination and during that trip I'd tried in vain to find US companies who were doing the same kind of trade as LGH. After all, America virtually invented the rental concept and it was inconceivable that there was no American equivalent to LGH. I'd scoured trade directories and Yellow Pages but had found nothing remotely similar to LGH. What struck me during this crude research was how faintly amateurish and old-fashioned the plant hire companies' adverts appeared to be. Surely, I must be missing something. Either there was a legal impediment to hiring lifting equipment or I just hadn't looked hard enough.

The UK Department of Trade and Industry had started an initiative to encourage British companies to look overseas for expansion and were offering grant aid to help fund overseas market research projects. One of the conditions for receiving the grant aid was that the research must be conducted primarily by a professional market research practitioner. It was a tempting opportunity. I knew that Gordon Worswick had briefly used the services of a market research firm called Mass Marketing and was impressed by their senior partner, Dr Dan Park. At my invitation, Dan came to see me to talk about my thoughts regarding possible expansion into the USA. I told him that what really caused me concern was the sheer size of the country. The LGH branch model couldn't work with such vast distances between adjacent branches. Dan reassured me by explaining that the mid-West of the US, a triangular area bounded by Chicago, Detroit and Pittsburgh, was an area about the same size as the UK. This was the industrial heart of America, containing 70% of all of the USA's heavy industry. It wasn't necessary at this stage to think about the East Coast, the West coast, the Gulf coast - just concentrate on the mid-West. Now this I could get my head round! I asked Dan to prepare a market research program and submit an application to the Dept. of Trade & Industry for grant aid for he and I to conduct the US research.

Within a month or two we were off to Chicago from Manchester Airport. I was euphoric, but my enthusiasm was tempered dramatically when we disembarked at O'Hare International Airport. I felt dreadfully ill. I was running a high fever and Dan made sure we took a taxi to our hotel as quickly as possible. He ordered me to bed whilst he went out to find a pharmacy and bought some proprietary medicines. They did no good and I was too ill to take any meaningful part in the exercise for the rest of the week. We spent three nights in Chicago, two in Pittsburgh and two in Detroit, where Dan conducted a series of prearranged meetings and interviews with a wide variety of people. These included professional people such as bankers, lawyers, insurance brokers, real estate brokers and accountants, together with a number of senior managers from companies who might be regarded as potential customers. I was devastated to be missing the excitement but confident that Dan was doing a great job.

From the little I saw of it, I was very impressed by Chicago. It was a huge, thriving, throbbing modern city spread around the picturesque shore of Lake Michigan. Pittsburgh, too, was highly impressive, located as it is at the confluence of the Allegheny River and the Monongahela River, which together form the source of the mighty Ohio River. It's also the home of the Pittsburgh Plate Glass Co., with whom I was familiar from my Pilkington Bros. days.

From our schoolday Geography lessons we'd learned that Pittsburgh was home to America's steel industry based on abundant coal fields and iron ore. It was reputed to be dirty and heavily industrialised. The reality in 1985 was somewhat different and Dan and I found a city with a modern commercial downtown area with a pleasant feel to it.

When we made it to Detroit, though, our impression was totally different. This heartland of America's massive automobile industry felt depressingly run down to our European senses.

I was feeling less unwell by this time and Dan managed to obtain two prime tickets for us to watch the baseball game between Detroit and the Toronto Blue Jays that evening. There were said to be 85,000 people in the stadium and I couldn't help feeling that we were the only ones actually watching the game! Everyone was wandering around eating pretzels and burgers and drinking beer and chatting to their neighbouring spectators. When something interesting happened, which wasn't very often, everyone looked at one of the giant TV screens around the stadium. After four hours of excruciating boredom, the Blue Jays emerged as the 1 - 0 winners. And they have the audacity to call cricket boring!

On our return home Dan prepared his report, which he presented to me a couple of weeks later. The main points were that:

a. There was a large potential market for the hire of lifting equipment in the mid-west of the USA which was not being served by any hire company at present.

b. If LGH were present (or any other company providing this service) then the potential market would grow just because someone was providing the service and stimulating demand.

c. There were no legal or regulatory issues to worry about.

d. Chicago seemed to offer the best opportunities for establishing the first LGH business in America

e. Professional support was readily available and industrial premises were plentiful and not prohibitively expensive.

This was what I'd been hoping to hear and I now had to decide how we could establish a US outpost without breaking the bank. At this time there was an annual report on the UK plant hire industry called the Greene Report. This listed a great deal of financial and statistical information in league table format and allowed the practitioners in the industry to measure their performance against their peers. Although we weren't among the larger hire companies, we always featured near the top of the 'Growth' and 'Return on Capital' tables. I remembered having read in one issue of the Greene Report that no British Plant Hire company had ever succeeded in setting up a profitable American subsidiary. Several had tried but all had failed for one reason or another. This wasn't encouraging and I would have to tread very carefully.

If a subsidiary were to be established, the first decision to make would be whether or not to send someone from the UK to run the business. The alternative would be to hire someone locally and train that person in our methods and principles. The problem with that option was that it would be virtually impossible to find someone who had knowledge of the hire business and was familiar with the technical aspects of lifting equipment, together with the drive and' energy needed to establish a new concept and, at the same time, be prepared, as I had been in 1970, to jump in a van at a moment's notice to make a delivery. Above all this person would have to be trustworthy enough not to run off with our concepts at the first opportunity to start his own business once we were up and running.

Having considered all the options very carefully, for I realised that this was a major crossroads decision for my company, I decided that it would be wisest to send someone from the UK who was already well versed in our methods and whom I could trust implicitly. Only one of my colleagues met all of the criteria perfectly. Gordon Worswick had done a great job for us, initially as a sales representative but more recently in helping to successfully integrate both East Ham Plant Hire Ltd. and J. Wilkinson Ltd. into the LGH fold. He had the knowledge, skill, experience and personality to give the US venture every chance of success. I asked Gordon to meet with me. I told him of my plans and offered him the chance to emigrate to America and be the head of what would potentially be our largest and most profitable subsidiary. He was thrilled at the offer but asked for a few days to consider the implications. When he came back to me he was terribly dejected. His repeated absences from home due to his protracted stays in London had put his marriage under great strain and he and his wife Sue had just separated, with Sue having custody of their two young children. Gordon explained that if he left the country in these circumstances he would probably hardly ever see his children again. He wasn't prepared to do that and turned down my offer. Although I was bitterly disappointed at this, I could fully understand Gordon's difficult position and was sympathetic to the anguish he must have felt at turning down the chance of a lifetime. Having set my sights on Gordon for this job, I couldn't think of anyone else among my colleagues who had the perfect set of qualities required for this key role. Very often over the years, when faced with a decision with no clear cut correct answer, I would sit on the fence and delay making the decision rather than make a hurried incorrect move. This is what happened in this case and I sat on the US plans for more than four years before finally implementing a new strategy, which will be described in Chapter 23.

Chapter 19 - Real Ale

My earliest friend from our days as infants living on Peel Brow, Ramsbottom, was Colin Ingham. We were born a month apart at the beginning of the war and were inseparable as children until my parents moved to Padiham. Ramsbottom was a Lancashire mill town which nestled in the Rossendale Valley and Peel Brow was a very steep road of terraced houses about half a mile long on one side of the valley. Colin and I had little 'fairy' cycles which we rode everywhere. Colin was a stronger cyclist than I was and could cycle from the bottom of Peel Brow to the top, a feat which it was my ambition to accomplish. I never did, but ended up having three hernia operations at the local Cottage Hospital as a consequence of my efforts.

As I mentioned earlier, Colin met Janet Hargreaves in Padiham during one of his bike trips to visit me and they married a year earlier than Irene and I in September 1960. Twenty-five years later, it was their Silver Wedding Anniversary. Colin worked at British Aerospace at Wharton and by now they lived in Kirkham, near Preston. Irene and I were invited to their Anniversary celebration party but we'd already booked flights to Menorca for a holiday and were unable to attend, so we suggested that we'd like to see them a week earlier. Janet's cousin, Alan Parker, and his wife Maureen were from Padiham also, but now lived in Kirkham, so the three couples met at Colin and Janet's house.

The men decided to go out for a pint, as men do, and we left the ladies to have a good chat. Alan was keen on real ale and suggested going to the Eagle and Child at the nearby village of Wharles. He said they would have Moorhouse's beer, from Burnley, and he promised I would enjoy it. That turned out to be an understatement, as it proved to be the best beer I'd ever tasted. After the first sublime pint I couldn't wait to sink another one. If I hadn't been driving I would have happily stayed all night, it was so good. It made me wonder why all beer couldn't be so good and confirmed my conversion from gassy artificial keg beers to natural traditional real ale.

When I returned to work after our holiday in Menorca, I kept finding myself thinking about my experience of drinking the wonderful beer in Wharles and wishing that Moorhouse's was available in Atherton. Irene's nephew, Neil Atkin, was getting married in Burnley that week and I'd agreed to take his bride Susan to church in my vintage Rolls Royce. As I waited in my car outside the church for the young couple to emerge, someone gave me a copy of the Burnley Express to read whilst I waited. In it I read the obituary of a prominent local businessman, Alan Hutchinson, who had recently died. Mr. Hutchinson had many varied business interests, including cinemas, bingo halls, hotels, and he owned Moorhouse's Brewery. Back in my office a few days later I found myself at something of a loose end. I'm not what could be described as a tidy desk man but on this occasion I had nothing awaiting my attention. We'd settled into our new offices well and LGH was running like a well-oiled machine. In my moments of idleness, I found my thoughts increasingly drifting again to Moorhouse's. I guessed that, following Alan Hutchinson's demise, there might be a chance that the business could be for sale. On a whim, on a Monday morning, I picked up the 'phone and asked our telephonist, Judith, to connect me to Moorhouse's. The man who answered the 'phone turned out to be the brewer and he confirmed that indeed the business was for sale but if I was interested I'd have to move quickly as a decision would be made within the next few days. He agreed to see me immediately and I was in Burnley 40 minutes later.

The brewer showed me round the dilapidated Victorian premises and explained the whole brewing process to me. I'd never been in a brewery previously and found the experience fascinating. At the same time, the whole operation looked to be chaotic and disorganised. The offices were scruffy and untidy, the brewing plant was old and in poor condition, the advertising material and pump clips etc. were poorly designed and the handful of staff didn't appear to be highly motivated. The accounts, which I was shown, indicated that the business was losing money on sales of approximately 20 barrels of beer per week. (A barrel is a unit of measurement equal to 36 gallons which equals 288 pints). There were lots of negative indicators but the one positive indicator which outweighed all of the negatives in my mind was the undeniable fact that, for some reason, they could produce superb beer!

The brewery had been founded in 1865 by William Moorhouse to manufacture soft drinks such as Sarsaparilla and Dandelion & Burdock. The business went well and, within a few years, Mr. Moorhouse had premises built just off Accrington Road, in Burnley. The premises comprised a manufacturing area and offices, together with stables for the dray horses. There were also a few terraced houses either side of the factory to accommodate the workers. The day following my visit, Tuesday, I went over the figures again and calculated an approximate value of the assets which comprised the building, brewing equipment, vehicles, barrels and debtors less creditors. Mrs. Hutchinson's son-in-law was a solicitor called Chris Eddlestone, who was looking after the day-to-day needs of the brewery on a temporary basis. The family had asked Robert Sangster's Apollo Leisure Group to advise on the disposal of the various component parts of Alan Hutchinson's complex business empire. On Wednesday I 'phoned ALG to tell them I was interested in making a bid and arranged to meet two of their Directors for lunch at the Tickled Trout Hotel in Preston, on Thursday. During that meeting we discussed the deal in some detail and we reached an agreement for me to acquire the entire share capital of Moorhouse's Brewery (Burnley) Ltd. We met again on the following day, Friday, to sign the contract and pay over the consideration. From start to finish the whole process had taken only 5 days and I was now the proud owner of a brewery.

The following Monday, Chris Eddlestone and I met at the brewery to complete the formalities and to allow Chris to introduce me to the small group of staff. Being a consumer business, I thought that we could use as much publicity as possible so we invited the local newspapers to cover the story. I was interviewed by the Burnley Express and The Lancashire Evening Telegraph and Chris and I had our photographs taken toasting the future success of the business, with Moorhouse's beer of course. The Telegraph put the story on the front page with the story headed 'This is the man who liked the beer so much, he bought the brewery', in effect comparing me to Victor Kayam, the man who famously bought the Remington Razor company. The following day, Tuesday, the national dailies picked up the story and a few of them 'phoned me to confirm the details before printing in their Wednesday editions.

Radio Lancashire and Radio Piccadilly also covered the story and sent reporters with tape recorders to interview me. Then, on Wednesday, we hit the jackpot. Muriel came into my office at LGH in Atherton to tell me that she had a BBC TV producer on the line who wished to speak to me. He turned out to be the producer of Look North, a nightly magazine programme on BBC1 which aired at 6.30pm each evening. He asked me if the story about 'liking the beer so much I bought the brewery' was true and said they'd like to cover it on his programme. If I agreed, he had a cameraman, sound recordist and interviewer standing by and they could be at the brewery in an hour's time.

I cancelled several appointments and shot off to Burnley in double quick time. Although I'd no experience of this kind of thing, the BBC staff were excellent and helped me feel at case. They made several takes of each sequence and I always felt most happy with the first take. It was broadcast on Friday evening in an eight minute spot and they'd edited it very well. To get this kind of prime time exposure for a consumer product was priceless publicity and it had all happened because one local newspaper reporter had seen an unusual slant on what would otherwise have been a rather mundane business story.

The Moorhouse's acquisition followed a similar pattern in many ways to those of Wilcox Chains, East Ham Plant Hire and Tickhill Plant, in that the target companies were all badly managed businesses who were in imminent danger of going into liquidation. The main difference was that Moorhouse's was a manufacturing company dealing with a consumer product and was a business in an industry of which I had no knowledge at all. This lack of experience in the industry would prove to be very costly over the next few years. At this time, Moorhouse's had three core brands - Premier Bitter (3.6% ABV), Pendle Witches Brew (5.0 %) and Black Cat (3.2%) all being brewed on our 5 barrel brewing plant. If we brewed once per day for five days per week we could make 25 barrels per week, which equated to 900 gallons or 7,200 pints, but at this level we were losing money, so the simple solution was to either reduce costs by reducing staffing levels or increase sales.

There were only a handful of staff so reducing numbers was not really an option, and increasing sales was not too easy either. This was before the days of the Beer Orders of 1989, which allowed pub licensees to offer a guest beer sourced from other than the brewery owning the pub. Consequently, the doors of most pubs in the North of England were closed to our sales representative and it was necessary to look at clubs for the majority of our sales. These could be Working Men's Clubs, Conservative Clubs, Labour Clubs, Bowling Clubs, Night Clubs, Golf Clubs and so on. There was severe competition to sell to these clubs and the committees running them took advantage of this. Most clubs were anxious to improve facilities for their members, which involved capital expenditure. The big six breweries of that time, plus the many regional breweries, were flush with cash and hungry for growth, so they would lend large capital sums at uncommercially low interest rates to potential customers, in exchange for exclusive supply agreements. So, despite the fact that we were brewing wonderful beer, which was very highly regarded by the consuming public, it was extremely difficult to penetrate what was, in effect, a closed shop.

A particularly upsetting experience happened in a small West Yorkshire town only a few miles from Burnley. Our representative was jubilant because in the space of a few days he'd opened three new accounts in this same town. One was a Bowling Club, another a Labour Club and the other was a Working Men's Club. We provided pumps on each of the bars, together with cellar equipment for our casks plus assorted merchandising like bar towels and drip mats. Sales went exceptionally well and each week the clubs were ordering more of our beer as their patrons were trying it and acquiring a taste for it. Then, after a few weeks of very promising trading, we were contacted by each of the clubs in turn with the request to remove our pumps from their bars and retrieve our cellar equipment. We were dumbfounded, because sales had been going so well and it was obvious that the club members liked our product. Our prices were competitive and we hadn't let any of our customers down with deliveries. Why would they not want to continue selling our wonderful range of beers in their establishments?

The answer became clear during the course of the next week or two. This was the heart of Tetley's territory and their sales staff were extremely concerned to find that they were being outsold on bars where both their products and Moorhouse's were being offered side by side. The giant Tetley Brewery being outsold by the Burnley minnow Moorhouse's. That was not acceptable to them so they offered financial inducements to each of our three new customers in the form of grants or loans. The only condition attached to these bribes - get Moorhouse's off your bar! I was devastated as I came to realise that the Brewing industry operated like no other in my experience. Where else did a company offer to pay you or lend you money to buy their products? How could I possibly survive in this shark infested pool?

I decided that if I couldn't beat them, I'd join them. We started offering 'soft loans' as they were called. These were usually secured against property assets and personal guarantees from the directors of the businesses that were taking our loans. Interest rates were tied to sales values, so a customer who was selling a lot of our beer would pay lower interest charges. As Moorhouse's were making losses and trading at the limit of their overdraft, I arranged for LGH to provide the funds to make these loans. This strategy appeared to be working for a time, until two or three of the customers who had taken loans became insolvent and ceased trading. It was only then that we found that the property assets had already been pledged to a bank and we only had a second charge, which turned out to be worthless. The directors who had stood surety weren't worth a bean and couldn't honour their guarantees.

One particularly painful experience of this kind occurred when a would-be night-club proprietor called John Boast asked to see me. I invited him to my Atherton office to discuss his proposal to open a new night-club in Great Harwood, to be called Monroes, which would be themed after the Hollywood legend. I very much liked his concept and felt that a loan of £50,000 to gain exclusive rights to beer sales at the club would be an attractive deal. The loan would also be secured by a second charge behind the bank against the freehold premises. I had interviewed many people in my time but there was something about Mr. Boast which prompted me to ask a question which I'd never asked anyone before. I looked him in the eye and said, "Have you ever been accused of a criminal offence?". He shook his head and reassured me that he was clean in that respect and the interview continued on more usual business lines.

We eventually came to an agreement and I drew up a formal contract between Moorhouse's Brewery and Mr. Boast. Just before he signed, he turned to me and said, "With reference to your earlier question, Mr. Parkinson, about the criminal offence, I think I should explain that I was accused of an offence and had to stand trial, but I was acquitted". "Oh" I said, "thanks for coming clean. What was the offence, if you don't mind my asking?" "Murder" he replied, much to my astonishment. At my insistence he went on to explain that he'd served in the British Army and whilst on a tour of duty in Northern Ireland he'd 'had to kill a man'. He couldn't elaborate but told me that as a consequence he'd gone through a form of trial and had been acquitted. I was unsure whether I should be regarding him as a villain or as a hero but nevertheless completed the agreement and lent him the money.

When the opening night arrived for Monroes, Irene and I were invited, together with our friends, David and Carol Slane. It was a wonderful evening and the decor of the club was magnificent, with images of Marilyn all over the walls and Moorhouse's dominating the bar. After the first few months of excellent sales, orders from Monroes began to dwindle. Then they started paying their account later and later. We were concerned that things were not good with the business. I received a 'phone call at home from one of the brewery staff to tell me that the front page of the Lancashire Evening Telegraph carried the story of John Boast being arrested for armed robbery. He'd tried to rob an insurance brokers in Blackburn at the point of a sawn off shotgun! He was sent to prison for quite a long time and his night-club business folded, leaving Moorhouse's with a potential bad debt of about £70,000. We managed to recover a significant proportion of this eventually, through our second charge over the property.

The various 'soft' loans which we made were generally very poor and the losses which we accumulated in this respect, plus the trading losses which had continued to grow, meant that LGH was now owed about one million pounds by the brewery. It was looking like a disastrous investment from which it would be difficult to extricate myself. I couldn't sell the business because it was so clearly a poor commercial proposition. I couldn't just close it down because then I'd have to write off the loans and LGH would have to stand a big loss, which would adversely affect its balance sheet. It seemed that our only alternative was to increase our efforts to grow sales and try to achieve better margins.

We had replaced the old 5 barrel brewing plant and installed a modern 25 barrel plant. This meant that each batch of brewing produced 7,200 pints and it was more efficient because, as we cooled down one brew to start the fermentation process, we used a heat exchanger to recover the heat energy from the previous brew to heat up the water (or 'liquor' in brewing terminology) to start the next brew. We were also very meticulous in the milling of the malted barley. If the rollers of the mill were too close together then the resulting particles were too small and contained too much dust, which reduced the yield. If the rollers were too far apart then the malt particles were too large and the boiling water couldn't penetrate the husks during the mashing process, which also reduced the yield. A roller gap of 0.082" was found by trial and error to give us the most efficient extraction of sugars from the barley.

I had brought into the business a year or two earlier my brother-in-law, Malcolm MacDonald, as General Manager, and had replaced the original brewer with a young man called Robert Hill, who had the most refined palate of anyone I'd ever known. He was also passionate about the beer and keen to experiment with a variety of recipes to produce beers with different characteristics. During the next few months two unrelated events helped to cause a dramatic improvement in the fortunes of the brewery.

One murky November day, I was at the brewery for a meeting with Geoff Ashworth, who by now had started his own advertising and marketing company. I felt that our pump clips didn't stand out well enough when they were on a bar with competing brands. I wanted Geoff to redesign the clips so that they'd catch the eye of the customer who was unsure which beer to choose. At one point we were standing upstairs in the steamy brewery atmosphere and I was opening my heart to Geoff, who by now was an old friend. I told him of our financial difficulties and he asked me if I'd considered having a Moorhouse's pub. I told him that we'd thought of that option but the cost of buying a decent pub was way too high to contemplate for a struggling small brewery. We peered out through the steamy window which Geoff wiped and he shocked me by saying "Why don't you buy the building across the road and turn it into a pub?"

There was a block of three terraced houses across the road, the remnants of a row which had been partially demolished some years earlier. One of the units was a baker's shop whilst the other two had been knocked together to form a bookmaker's office, which had now closed down, with a For Sale notice displayed outside. This had been there for months and, even though it was right under my nose, I'd never noticed it. I was immediately excited by Geoff's suggestion and persuaded him to venture across the road with me in the drizzling rain to have a better look at the building. It was made of lovely Yorkshire stone and looked to be in an excellent state of repair externally. Even better, it was considerably lower at the back than at the front, which meant that there was almost certainly a cellar. We went round to the front again, which was on busy Accrington Road, and were more closely assessing its potential as a pub when a car stopped close to us and the driver wound his window down and asked if we were interested in buying the building. In one of life's amazing coincidences it turned out that he was the Estate Agent who was handling the sale of the building and had just happened to be driving past at the time that we were inspecting it.

He told me that they were asking £10,000 and I thought he meant that price for each of the two units which had been joined together, but no, that was the price for both units. I immediately told him that I'd have it and asked him to send someone with the keys to allow us to look inside. We bought the property and then went through the lengthy process of obtaining not only planning permission to turn the building into a pub but also a new licence for the sale of alcohol. The planning approval was quite straightforward but we were warned that the licence approval would be virtually impossible to obtain without going through a lengthy and expensive appeal. The chairman of the Burnley licensing magistrates was an elderly lady called Nellie Hargreaves, who had been chairman for as long as anyone could remember. She had never ever granted a new licence we were told and would be unlikely to start now.

Within a hundred yards of our proposed pub site were three other pubs, all of them owned by Bass. Many years earlier, Bass had bought out the substantial Massey's brewery, which had been successfully operating in Burnley for over a century. They owned most of the pubs in Burnley, which became Bass's after the takeover. I prepared a persuasive story for Nellie, emphasising the fact that Moorhouse's was now the only brewery in Burnley, we were employing local people whose livelihoods depended on the success of the business and this would be our first pub, which would give the people of Burnley more freedom of choice. In the event. Ms. Hargreaves granted the application at the first time of asking and we were free to change the shell of the bookies office into Burnley's newest pub.

We engaged a professional bar fitting company to do the work and, for £90,000, they transformed the cellar into a proper beer storage area, fitted out the bar with integral seating and tables and chairs and converted the upstairs rooms into a comfortable flat for the pub manager's use. Whilst the work was in progress, the Burnley Express announced the pub's impending opening to the people of Burnley. They also quoted me as saying that we would offer a prize to any reader who could suggest an appropriate name for the new pub. I'd not said any such thing but it was a good idea and generated a trickle of suggestions. One idea was to call it Nutter's Bar, after Alice Nutter, one of the infamous Pendle Witches who were hanged for witchcraft. Good idea, but not entirely appropriate. I felt we'd probably attract the wrong sort of customer with a name like that. Another letter, which was several pages long, suggested that we call the pub The General Scarlett, after General James York Scarlett, who led his troops to a famous victory against overwhelming odds in The Charge of the Heavy Brigade. This was clearly an elaborate spoof. I'd never heard of General Scarlett and neither had anyone else to whom I spoke on the subject. Nor had I heard of the Heavy Brigade, which must have been a play on words referring to the tragic Light Brigade so eloquently remembered in Tennyson's famous poem. The letter had been written by a Mr. Hornby, a history teacher at Burnley Grammar School, who was well versed in local history. Every word he'd written turned out to be true, to my amazement, and we were delighted to name our first pub after Burnley's most famous son. Mr. Hornby's prize was to have the honour of naming the pub and pulling the first pint of Moorhouse's ever to be sold in one of the brewery's own pubs.

The second event was very fortuitous and involved an Act of Parliament which could have been drafted purely for our brewery's gratification. There had been a feeling for a long time that the big six breweries, Allied, Bass, Courage, Grand Metropolitan, Scottish & Newcastle and Whitbread, were using their market dominance in a way which was prejudicial to the interests of the consuming public. The Competition Commission investigated the industry and concluded that the vertical integration of the main players was indeed harming healthy competition. In other words, they didn't like the biggest brewers owning virtually all the retail outlets in the form of pubs and, in 1989, issued what became known as the Beer Orders. This restricted the number of tied pubs which could be owned by a brewery to a maximum of 2,000 and, furthermore, the large brewery landlords were instructed to allow their tenants to source a guest ale from a brewery other than their landlord. This was a dramatic and far-reaching change to the industry and I must admit that, if I'd been the owner of one of these big six, I'd have been very unhappy to see the commercial advantages I'd worked hard to achieve for over a hundred years wiped away at a stroke. But I wasn't one of the big six, I was little Moorhouse's, working away in a corner of East Lancashire trying to compete with the giants. This was a massive opportunity to open doors which were previously closed and, if our products were good enough, we could massively increase sales. This is exactly what happened during the 1990s and, in addition, we added five more pubs to our tied estate and the business became profitable for the first time in many years. So much so that the one million pound debt was paid back to LGH over the next few years and the Moorhouse's brand became very well known, not just in the North West but much further afield.

Chapter 20 - Family Matters

Our elder son, Ian, was still studying Mechanical Engineering at City University in London, living in an apartment on Frith Street in Soho. Disappointingly, he failed one of his seven second year subjects and, on this occasion, because it was a second failure, no re-sits were allowed and he had to leave University with nothing to show for his three years of effort. He told me that, although he was bitterly disappointed that he hadn't obtained a degree and felt that he'd let his parents down, he didn't regret a moment of the time he'd spent in London and felt a better person for the experience. I was pleased to hear him turn a potentially disastrous result into a positive feeling and his return to the North gave me the opportunity to bring Ian into the family business. After a year or so of working in different departments and becoming familiar with all aspects of the business, I gave him the job of opening a new branch in Leeds. This went well. The business in Leeds grew satisfactorily and gave Ian valuable experience at grass roots level. Carol Slane's role in sales had grown and she was now offering support to all of the branches in the North. One day she called on Ian at his office in Leeds. She wasn't wearing her glasses as she didn't need them for driving and, as she got out of her car to enter the LGH premises, there was a cardboard cut-out of a man holding an electric drill, advertising the trade of the company next door. Carol didn't realise the cardboard cut-out wasn't a real man and said to him "Is that a gun in your pocket or are you just pleased to see me?" Then she realised her mistake and looked round in embarrassment to see if anyone had witnessed her faux pas. Too late, Ian and a colleague had been watching through the window and Ian never let Carol forget this incident. There were many other Carol stories like this. For example, when she came into the office in a hurry and sat down on a telephone engineer who was working on his hands and knees under her desk. Or when she drove out of our car park with her handbag on the top of her car. Or when she was at the golf driving range showing Irene how to use the ball dispensing machine and forgot to place the basket under the chute where the balls came out. There were a hundred golf balls all over the floor. Carol's exploits would justify a book of their own, but for all her dizziness she excelled at selling and represented the company brilliantly. She was subsequently promoted to the position of National Sales Manager.

Ian's younger brother, Steven, was still at Bolton School, studying for A levels. His interest in computers had never waned from his work with the old Wang machine. He now had access to the school's computers and started giving informal lessons in computer science to younger pupils. He felt that the security system of the school's own computer-based administrative system was very weak and expressed his concerns to the teacher in charge of this, but he refuted Steven's fears. A few days later, in order to prove a point, Steve hacked into the school's system and was able to access all of the school's confidential data. Just as he achieved this and had files displayed on the screen, the Master in Charge came into the room and caught him red-handed. He was reported to the headmaster and I was summoned to school to hear what the Head had to say. Despite Steve's assertions that he was trying to help the school to improve their security systems, he was suspended for a week and barred from the computer room for several weeks. At that time there were no formal classes in computer technology at Bolton School and no-one from School had ever taken A level computer science until Steve entered and without ever taking a class in the subject gained an A grade pass.

Steve's A level studies were disturbed significantly at this time because of a medical condition. As he'd grown older, it had become increasingly obvious that his jaw formation was not normal. In the vast majority of people the top jaw protrudes beyond the bottom jaw and the top front teeth lie outside the bottom front teeth. In Steve's case, the opposite was true and, by some fluke of genetics, his bottom teeth extended beyond his top set. For the three or four years that we had been aware of this condition, Steve had been seeing a consultant at Royal Bolton Hospital, who finally suggested that we might consider corrective surgery. He explained that both the bottom and top jaws would be severed from the skull and the bottom jaw would be replaced 6mm further back., The top jaw would be replaced 6mm further out, making a relative adjustment of 12mm (1/2") which was what was required. Following the operation the jaw would be wired shut for a 6 week period whilst the healing took place. There was a possibility that Steve would lose all sensation in his lips.

It sounded horrific and, after discussing the ramifications that night at home, Steve said that he didn't want to go through all that and we wholeheartedly agreed with him. A few days later, on a vintage car rally, I met up with John Warburton, the dentist from whom I'd bought my old Rolls Royce some years earlier. I told John of Steve's predicament and he was very interested, saying he'd like to see my son at his surgery. We made the arrangements, John took plaster casts of Steve's upper and lower jaws and a few days later came to our house with his models. He demonstrated to Steve how his jaw looked now and then re-positioned the models to show how his jaw would look after the operation if he chose to have it done. John explained how the condition would probably get worse and, though there was no cosmetic disfiguration at the moment, this could happen over time. Furthermore, he said, Steven's biting and chewing ability would be seriously affected to such an extent that he would almost certainly suffer from stomach and digestive problems in future.

If it was John's intention to shock us into action, he certainly succeeded. He told us that this branch of medicine was known as maxillo-facial surgery and we were fortunate that two of the most skilled surgeons in this field were working at Withington Hospital, just a few miles away on the outskirts of Manchester. He offered to arrange an appointment for Steve to see the medical partners and, after the briefest of family conferences, we agreed.

Following the initial consultation, arrangements were made for the very complex and precise surgery. Every dimension of Steve's skull and jaw were measured and models were made. Finally, after all the meticulous planning, the big traumatic day arrived for the surgery. The operation took six hours and went perfectly to plan, but when we saw our son afterwards in the intensive care unit we were horrified to see that his head was full of bruises and was seriously swollen. Over the next few days, the bruising reduced and so did the swelling, but he was unable to talk because his jaws were wired tightly shut together. I don't know how he tolerated this, which would have given me claustrophobic attacks. But Steve accepted his situation with great equanimity and, when he was allowed to come home after a week or so, he had to carry a pair of wire cutters with him everywhere so that he could cut his wires in case he vomited. He found that the worst feeling was when he tried to yawn, which is impossible with your jaws wired tightly together. He learned to speak through clenched teeth and tolerated his unfortunate situation without complaint for six weeks, feeding exclusively on liquids taken through a straw. He resumed school for his critical A level studies a couple of weeks after the surgery. We were very proud of his courage and determination throughout this period.

Chapter 21 - Megalift

I always made a point of seeing all of the mail received at LGH's Head Office. Whatever was not addressed to a particular individual member of staff would be brought into my office each morning by Muriel, after she had sorted it into some logical order, and together we'd allocate action points. I might annotate some of the correspondence with my instructions or suggestions. An item of mail arrived one day which would have been easy to throw in the waste basket, but something caught my attention. The letter was from a Wirral based company who specialised in buying plastic sheets from America and reselling in the UK and Europe to end users of this type of product. The owner of the business was called Mike and, on his travels to the USA had met an American businessman who owned a company called Lift Systems, located in the Quad cities of America's mid-West. The businessman, Gary Lorenz, was looking for a European company to market a new development they'd called the Four Point Lift System, which was a remarkably unimaginative name for what I thought was an exciting new lifting concept.

Basically, Gary had developed a huge hydraulic telescopic ram which could lift up to 100 tons through a height of twelve feet. They coupled four such rams together with large steel beams and a single hydraulic pump to power all four rams. The whole assembly could lift up to 400 tons, but the fascinating part was that each pair of rams could be controlled independently, allowing the operator great flexibility when lifting heavy loads. I immediately saw the hire possibilities for such a device and responded positively to Mike's circular letter, which I found out later had been sent to just about everyone in the UK's lifting equipment industry. LGH was the only company to show any interest.

I met with Mike a few days later. He wasn't able to give me much more information as he'd never actually seen the equipment, but he offered to accompany me on a trip to Moline to meet Gary and see the Four Point Lift System in operation. The deal was that Mike would pay for the trip if LGH subsequently placed an order with Lift Systems. We arranged to fly to Chicago and stay for three nights. Mike was also a squash player so we agreed to take our squash gear with us and try to get a game in Chicago. We flew from Manchester a week later for my third trip to the USA and, having checked into our hotel, thought that it would be good to have a game of squash that evening before starting work the following day.

We obtained a copy of the Chicago Yellow Pages and were delighted to find about a dozen squash clubs listed. I 'phoned the first one and explained that we were newly arrived visitors from England and asked if they had a court available later that evening. The very friendly receptionist offered me a court at 8.20 p.m. then asked for my name and membership number. When I reiterated that we were visitors and were not members, her attitude changed and we were frostily told that it would not be possible to play at their exclusive members only club. Mike and I 'phoned every club in Chicago and received the same rebuff every time. I was getting more and more frustrated until at last I rather rudely told one of the receptionists that I thought that their hospitality was incredibly poor and emphasised that if the positions were reversed and one of their members was visiting England we'd go out of our way to ensure that they could play at our club in a friendly and welcoming atmosphere.

Having failed to get a game of squash, we hired a car the following morning and drove the 165 miles to Moline from Chicago. Gary and his senior team welcomed us and, before any demonstrations, took us for lunch on a converted Mississippi paddle boat moored at a jetty on this massively wide river. After lunch, I was treated to an amazing demonstration of the Four Point Lift System's sheer power and versatility. I was convinced that we had a potential winner as a hire proposition, but the price was astronomical compared to the usual values of our hire plant. The biggest value piece of plant that we currently owned in LGH was a 5 ton diesel winch worth about £10,000, although the replacement value of some of Tickhill Plant's fleet would be considerably more. Gary was quoting $140,000 for a complete set of four-point hydraulic gantries, which was made more difficult to justify by the alarming drop in the value of the pound versus the dollar. From a position where a pound would buy two dollars we were now seeing the pound sinking to almost parity with the dollar. I decided I needed some time to think about the proposition and Mike and I returned late that night to Chicago.

The following day, still determined to have a game of squash, Mike 'phoned another Chicago based contact of his who was a member of the very exclusive and expensive East Bank Club. His contact readily agreed to introduce us as guests to his club and met us there for lunch. What an eye opener this was for me. The club contained four indoor tennis courts, two swimming pools - one on the roof of the skyscraper which housed the club - a 400 yard indoor running track, ten squash courts, 6 badminton courts, ten handball courts, aerobic work-out rooms, two or three different gymnasia, restaurants, snack bars and the most magnificent changing and showering facilities I'd ever seen. Americans have a totally different attitude when it comes to putting a value on their leisure activities. Mike's friend was quite happy to pay $10,000 joining fee and $1,000 per month membership fee for this facility. But then he expected nothing but the best, and he certainly got it. The place was buzzing with activity and this was true from 6.00 a.m. to midnight every day. Mike and I thoroughly enjoyed our hard-won game of squash and I left America the following day once again fired up by the massive potential for my business, which was very evident, but still with no idea how to exploit this opportunity.

On my return to Atherton, I was excited at the prospect of being the first European company to offer a Four Point Lift System for hire, but I tried to temper my enthusiasm by involving two of my most senior branch managers in a market research exercise. I asked them to come to see me at Atherton, explained the principles of the new hydraulic gantry system to them and furnished them with Gary's catalogues and technical data sheets. I gave them a week to seek out the biggest potential customers for such a piece of equipment and conduct a market research exercise to estimate the potential value of hire revenue earnings. A week later they presented me with their report in which they concluded that there was little or no market in the UK for a 400 ton capacity hydraulic gantry. I was devastated. This was not what I wanted to hear. I wanted to know that the biggest industrial machinery movers and bridge builders and construction engineers would be clamouring to use this brilliant new tool. In the face of this conclusion from two of my most respected managers, I couldn't risk £120,000 of the company's money on such a speculative investment and I reluctantly sat on the idea for the time being. Then, after a few weeks, right out of the blue an ex-employee, Bob Hamilton, came to see me.

Bob had been one of my first staff in the early 1970s and had subsequently been instrumental in growing our machinery moving department. When the work in this activity dried up as a result of the miners' strike in 1984, Bob had left us to join Sparrows Crane Hire as a sales representative in their heavy lifting division. He'd just been made redundant and was looking for a job. This was perfect. Bob had exactly the experience and credentials to head up a new department with the Four Point Lift System as the focal point. I told him about this huge new hydraulic gantry and he could immediately see the way it could be marketed to his many contacts in the heavy lifting industry. I offered Bob the chance to start this new venture and sent him to Moline with the authority to buy a Four Point Lift System configuration and asked Gary Lorenz to give him a course of instruction in the use and technical aspects of the equipment.

When Bob returned to the UK we had a few weeks to wait until our new addition arrived. Neither Bob nor I liked the cumbersome name which Lift Systems had bestowed on the apparatus and we had a brain-storming session to try to think of a more appropriate name. Among many names proposed, Bob suggested Megalift. This immediately had connotations of huge strength and size and was perfect, but would it be available to register as a Trade Name? I asked our patent agent, Andrew Beeston, to try to register the name and we were in luck, there was no prior application so it was ours. From then on we always referred to the Four Point Lift System hydraulic gantry as the Megalift. Over time this word also became a verb in a similar way to the Hoover.

When our Megalift finally arrived from the States, Bob set to work training two or three of the fitters from Atherton branch in the methods of utilising the considerable hydraulic power now available to us. The first order was handled with some trepidation but we needn't have feared. Bob planned the whole procedure meticulously and it was carried out flawlessly like a military operation. This first job involved turning over a machine weighing 60 tons inside a building with very little headroom and then lowering it into a previously prepared pit. There was no room to use a mobile crane inside the building and the only other option would have been to take the roof off the building and use a massive mobile crane located outside. This alternative would have been horrendously expensive but, using Megalift, we were able to do the job quickly and safely for only a few thousand pounds. The customer was delighted, Bob was thrilled and I was relieved that this new investment showed all the signs of being successful.

During the next twenty years the original Megalift was supplemented by the addition of more units, some smaller and some larger but all working on the same principle. It was involved in many jobs, some extremely spectacular and complex. One job which Bob undertook stands out particularly in my mind. We were asked to pick up a 45 ton machine from a workshop in Manchester and transport it to Italy, where it was to be off-loaded and installed in a factory on an island. Megalift picked up the load in the Manchester factory and placed it on a low loader. Megalift was then disassembled and loaded onto the same low loader and Bob and his team accompanied the machine on its journey to Italy. When they came to the bridge which connected the river island destination to the mainland it was clear that the bridge could not support the weight of the low loader carrying the machine.

Bob hired a small mobile crane to unload our Megalift, re-assembled it under the bridge and used the hydraulic rams to provide extra supports for the bridge, allowing the low loader to cross safely with its precious cargo. Megalift was then transported across the bridge, where it was used to unload the machine and install it in the factory. A great example of versatility and ingenuity working together to perform what seemed an impossible task. Megalift's importance to the company grew over the years, as it not only generated a reasonable return on our original investment but many of the jobs which we undertook were very newsworthy, particularly in the technical magazines, and our reputation as experts in the use and application of lifting equipment was enhanced as a result.

One regret that I had regarding Megalift was that I missed the opportunity to secure a sole distributorship agreement for the whole of Europe, which I could have easily obtained at the time of buying the first unit. Some of our larger customers who were regular users of our Megalift decided it would be more economical to own their own Four Point Lift Systems and placed orders directly with Gary Lorenz, thus cutting us out of the equation. If we'd secured a distributorship agreement, at least we'd have had the consolation of earning commission on each sale.

Chapter 22 - Honours

Irene and I were thoroughly enjoying our Menorcan house and had invited many friends to join us from time to time. In 1985 we asked our bank manager Ron Gleave and his wife Aileen, who had become good friends, to join us with our younger son, Steven, for a couple of weeks in the sun. Aileen, who was about sixty years old at the time, used to swim, but hadn't swum for several years. She was keen to use the pool but had lost confidence. Steven was an excellent swimmer and, at the age of twelve, appointed himself Aileen's swimming coach. He patiently helped her to build up from a few hesitant strokes to, within a few days, swimming twenty lengths with confidence. She was thrilled at her achievement and I was proud that my son had been so kind to an older person. Three years earlier, Steve had swum in the Bolton Town Junior swimming championship, representing Bolton School against all the other junior schools in the town. He was a year under age and came third in the boys' backstroke race. I told him that the following year he'd still be eligible for this event but the two lads who'd come ahead of him would be seniors by then. I said that I'd arrange for him to have coaching and we'd go to Atherton Baths every week for training. He looked dismayed and said, "Do I have to?" When I replied "No, you don't have to, but if you want to be a winner then you do have to." he said that he'd think about it, but we never did the extra training and the following year he was runner up!

One day on this same holiday, I was sitting by the pool reading my favourite book. Ron asked me what I was reading and I told him that it was a collection of Somerset Maugham's short stories and was a Clitheroe Royal Grammar School library book which I'd inadvertently failed to return when I'd left school 29 years earlier. I joked that the accumulated library fines would, by now, amount to a small fortune. Ron suggested that, to assuage my pricking conscience, I could write to the school and send a donation to the school library fund. This simple suggestion would have far-reaching consequences. When we returned home after the holiday I acted on Ron's suggestion and wrote a letter to the school addressed to 'The Headmaster' as I'd no idea who had the job at the time. I enclosed a cheque for £100 and expected that it would be the end of the matter. However, a couple of days later I received a 'phone call from a Roy Adams, who was acting head on a temporary basis. Roy had taught me Geography for only one year of my time at Clitheroe and was very keen on keeping accurate records of old boys. He had been delighted to receive my letter, as I was one of only two boys from my year for whom he had no information.

I could hardly believe it when he said he could remember me, and went on to prove it by describing me as a spectacle-wearing scruffy thin kid whose nickname was Bunnocks. For a teacher who'd taught thousands of boys, I thought that it was a remarkable feat of memory. Roy was very interested to learn how my life and career had progressed since leaving school and, as a car enthusiast, was especially keen to talk about my old cars. He was also a knowledgeable fan of cask-conditioned beer and was incredulous to find out that I owned Moorhouse's Brewery.

At the end of our discussion he invited me to attend that year's Old Clitheronians' Reunion Dinner, to be held in November. When I told him that I'd be delighted, Roy went one step further by suggesting that we make a big effort to make it the Reunion of the Class of 1951, the year I entered school, and together we'd attempt to cajole as many as possible of my class to attend. In the event, we managed to persuade seventeen of my erstwhile classmates to attend and it was wonderful to see them all again after so many years. Following my highly publicised acquisition of Moorhouse's Brewery a few months earlier than this Reunion Dinner, I was given the singular honour of being invited to be the following year's President of the Old Clitheronians Association. There were no onerous duties involved in this position save making a short speech at the dinner and attending one or two school functions such as Speech Day. Making a speech to entertain 250 of my peers was something completely outside my previous experience but I was determined to give it my best effort.

When I saw the list of my predecessors it was obvious that I was way out of my depth. One was a professor and immediately before him was a Barrister, who was a Queen's Counsel and had become an MP. Before him was a previous Headmaster of the School. What was I doing in this illustrious company? They all made speeches for a living. Just because I'd bought a failing Brewery didn't make me an entertaining after-dinner speaker. Filled with a feeling of utter inadequacy I worked hard on my speech and managed to pluck from the darkest reaches of my memory some amusing incidents from my school life involving teachers which all of the Old Boys would remember. I was also able to tell a few stories about my business life, mostly against myself, which everyone seemed to find entertaining. Although I was unable to eat my meal because of nerves, the speech itself seemed to go well and I received a very warm and generous ovation at the end. What a relief! The following year I had to make another speech as retiring President, which would be shorter and less important. I was a little over-confident as a result of the success of my first effort and as a consequence didn't prepare as diligently as I could have. This resulted in a very average performance which taught me a hard lesson. You have to work hard to succeed in endeavours for which you have little talent.

As LGH grew ever bigger on the national lifting equipment stage, I felt that it was important for us to play a part in the wider administration and regulation of our industry. The company had been accepted as a member of the Chain Testers' Association of GB during the 1970s and I had been elected to serve on the Executive Committee of this important body. The membership comprised about eighty companies throughout the UK with some members, like ourselves, having several branches. The Committee met four times a year, usually in Tewkesbury or some other Southern location, and there was an Annual General Meeting attended by senior representatives of all members. The highly competent Secretary, later Chief Executive, was Derrick Bailes, who efficiently guided our deliberations in an increasingly complex world that was witnessing growing influence on our National Technical Standards from Brussels. Although this work was time consuming and I wasn't naturally suited to committee work, it proved to be an important link which helped me to keep my finger on the pulse of the industry and allowed me to get to know all of our major colleagues and competitors. I felt great pride to be elected as Chairman of the CTA in 1986 for a two year term of office.

During the term of my Chairmanship the name of the Association was changed to The Lifting Equipment Engineers' Association, which more accurately described the activities of the membership in these modern times. Thus I was the last Chairman of the CTA and the first of the LEEA. The influence and size of the LEEA has continued to grow dramatically and now, under Chief Executive Geoff Holden, there are over eight hundred members with over 500 overseas members from 57 countries. The Association monitors the professional and technical standards of the lifting equipment industry, not only in the UK but, increasingly, internationally. It audits applications from would-be members to ensure that these standards are maintained, publishes technical guidance and sits on various standards committees, as well as conducting instructional courses and examinations in a wide range of lifting related subjects.

During my time on the Executive Committee there was a general consensus that it would be a good idea to have an Annual Golf Competition for members. One of the older committee men volunteered to organise the event but, after two years, nothing had happened. Then someone else volunteered and again nothing was done so, at the AGM in 1994, I said there would definitely be a golf tournament the following year and I would organise it. It was held at the Golf Club of which I was a member, Shaw Hill, near Chorley, and was a great success, with over 20 members from all over the country meeting in an atmosphere of friendly rivalry, competing for the trophy which I had donated, The LGH Cup. Whose was the first name on the trophy? Wouldn't you just know it! The original trophy has now been replaced by a bigger and better trophy now called The Bill Parkinson Cup, and I'm proud to have been able to get my name on it a further three times. The golf event has become a firm annual fixture in the LEEA's calendar and regularly attracts more than forty competitors with member companies taking turns to stage the event.

Chapter 23 - America Here We Come!

By early 1990, our UK based LGH branch network was thriving and gradually expanding. The business model was sound and capable of generating a growing stream of profit, but cash flow remained problematic because of the demands of capital expenditure when investing in large amounts of new plant to support the growth . I had no qualms about borrowing more funds from the bank. We had a great relationship with NatWest, who saw that we had a sound balance sheet and a wonderful track record of consistent growth in both revenues and profit. The few acquisitions we'd made had all turned out to be sound investments and we felt that we were walking on water. I was confident that any reasonable request for further funding would be positively received by the bank.

It was against this background that my thoughts increasingly drifted across the Atlantic and I re-read the Market Research Report that had been prepared by Dr. Dan Park in 1985. Over four years had passed and I still hadn't acted on the clear signals that there was a potentially lucrative market to be tapped. I was still stuck on the idea that the most suitable candidate for the job of getting us up and running in the US was Gordon Worswick. Then I had an idea which now seems so obvious and simple that I can't believe it didn't strike me earlier. Gordon didn't need to go and live in America, he could visit on a temporary basis, set up the business and monitor the performance from the UK.

I met up again with Gordon to put this suggestion to him and he was as excited and as enthusiastic as I was. I offered him a Board position with the title Overseas Development Director and an incentive-based remuneration package. We discussed the plans in considerable detail and formulated our strategy. We had to decide on a name for the business. In America they don't use the term 'lifting gear', which is our generic term for all kinds of lifting equipment. They say 'hoisting equipment', 'rigging equipment', 'jacking equipment' etc. Nor do they use the word 'hire' in this context. They say 'rental'. So we considered 'Hoisting Equipment Rental' as a potential name and other variations. In the end, we came back to our UK name of Lifting Gear Hire, taking the view that American construction workers and engineers would understand what the company's business was and would recognise the Englishness of the company, which we thought would be no bad thing. A huge advantage of this decision was that our logo and corporate image could be used by the new business and sales literature could easily be modified for the new market.

Because Gordon wouldn't be staying permanently in the US it meant that he'd have to recruit a local to start up and manage the business. This would be THE key task, as the first employee would have to be prepared to get his hands dirty, as I had done twenty years earlier, then drive the delivery truck and be able to do a good selling job on potential customers. Plus, he'd have to demonstrate many more qualities if and when the business grew.

I visited Ron, our bank manager, and put our American dream to him, supported by budget profit & loss accounts and cash flow projections, which secured loan capital of £100,000 to fund the project. We'd readily agreed that Chicago would be the location for our start up and Gordon flew there from Manchester in early March 1990. He disembarked from the plane, having never been to the USA before, and within a few weeks had achieved tremendous progress. He rented an apartment to act as his temporary headquarters. He registered the company name, found and appointed accountants to act for us, found and appointed lawyers to help with the legal intricacies of setting up a business in a foreign country and, most importantly, started advertising to recruit our first American employee.

The adverts attracted quite a lot of applicants, which Gordon whittled down to about ten possibles, whom he interviewed. From these he prepared a short list of three whom he planned to see again. Each of these three candidates had a very impressive CV, which Gordon faxed to me for my opinion before interviewing them again. He told me that his favoured candidate was Pat Fiscelli, a Chicagoan of Italian parentage. Pat had previously had an excellent career in industry but had more recently failed in his own fork lift truck business. I was doubtful that he would settle for working for us if he'd had his own business and might be tempted to take our ideas to have another go on his own. When I expressed these reservations to Gordon he told me that Pat was the outstanding candidate and, despite what I said, he wanted to offer him the job. I'd trusted Gordon with this very important project and it would have been foolish of me to veto one of his early key decisions. So Pat Fiscelli became our first US employee in what was arguably the most important appointment which we ever made.

Gordon and Pat found a small industrial unit to rent in Bridgeview, South of Chicago, and set up agreements with manufacturers and suppliers of lifting equipment. A car was procured for Pat, and a delivery truck. Stationery was ordered in the image of the UK model and sales literature designed specifically for the local market. Office furniture and industrial racking was ordered and telephone lines were installed. Signs were erected and the truck sign-written. They arranged appointments with dozens of potential customers and Gordon coached Pat in how to sell the concept of hiring lifting equipment, which was totally unknown to the people they were seeing.

They devised a leaflet called Ten Reasons to Rent and that became a cornerstone of the message they were delivering. These two charismatic men, working together as a team, must have been formidable, but they were meeting tremendous resistance. Engineers couldn't see why you'd want to rent a chain block or a hydraulic jack when you could buy one for $100. But what if you wanted ten jacks for only two weeks and what if the manufacturer was quoting six weeks' delivery? The two men worked tirelessly, building up an impressive list of contacts, but the 'phone was stubbornly refusing to ring. Chicago was alive with new construction activity and there was lots of heavy industry all around the huge city, but no-one wanted to hire lifting equipment! Then, after a month, the first small order. A week later, another. The trickle started and, in a very similar way to our UK experience in 1970, the business gradually developed. Pat worked like a demon and, as revenue slowly expanded, he grew in confidence. After three months, as originally planned, Gordon came back to the UK but, before he left the US, he had set up reporting procedures so that he could tell what was happening in our Chicago business at all times and could talk to Pat regularly by 'phone. Apart from the decision to start my own business in 1970 this was probably the key event in my business life, to which I'll return later.

Chapter 24 - Delegation

In my forties I was extremely active socially and in sports activities. I was a member of two squash clubs and played team squash every Thursday night for Horwich Leisure Centre. I played squash and badminton every Monday night with my closest pals and played snooker, darts and dominoes every Tuesday for Atherton & Tyldesley Botanical Gardens Club. Wednesday was reserved for duplicate bridge in St. Helens and Irene and I went out every Friday night with our friends, David and Carol. I'd usually have at least one game of squash at week-end. One day, Irene became very upset and pointed out that she was hardly ever seeing me. I was treating our home as a hotel. She was having to raise three children like a single mother and she'd had enough. She gave me an ultimatum that I'd have to change or our marriage was over.

When I considered what she'd said and examined my own lifestyle it was obvious that her claims were fair. It was clear I'd have to modify my activities drastically. I quit one of the squash clubs, gave up club bridge and gave up playing team snooker. This still left me with my team squash on Thursdays and my Monday night out with my mates, which seemed to satisfy Irene that I'd made an effort to meet her demands whilst leaving me with some competitive sport, which I loved.

Then David quit smoking and, in order to do something positive with the money he was saving, decided to buy himself a set of golf clubs and take up the game. Ray Garside and another friend, Mike Cooney, also fancied the idea of playing golf and the three of them started going to Municipal courses on a Saturday morning. They were really enjoying their new sport and invited me to join them. I'd played a bit of golf at Whalley GC as a youth when we lived in Padiham but I'd not been very competent at the game. I had an old set of clubs in the garage, which I'd used about once a year when I was invited on corporate events, but I'd grown to detest the game because of my lack of ability. I was reasonably good at most games and sports but golf was so technically difficult that I gained no satisfaction from it. However, my mates seemed to be having such a good time that I reluctantly started to join them.

We called ourselves The Four Musketeers and we had a little trophy we played for once a month in a competition called The Musketeers Monthly Medal - that got our competitive juices flowing. After a year or so, the four of us joined Shaw Hill Golf & Country Club, near Chorley, where we were able to be assessed for handicap purposes. It became increasingly clear to me that I was using my pitching wedge on virtually every hole. I wasn't good enough to be hitting the putting surfaces with my approach shots and would regularly have to use my wedge, usually with disappointing results. I determined that if I was ever going to improve at golf then I'd have to learn to use this club much more effectively. I was fortunate that we had a large garden and it became my habit, when I came home from the office, to spend half an hour each night in the garden, practising my pitching and chipping shots.

After a few months of this practice, I became much more accurate with these shots and could regularly play my pitching wedge shots close to the flagstick from up to 80 yards away. What a difference this made to my overall game - over the next three years my handicap came down to 18, then 15, then 12, where it stuck for the next twenty years. The wives of our friends, Carol and Kath, together with Irene, also took up the game and it became the increasingly important epicentre of our sporting and social life.

The first eighteen hole round of golf Irene and Kath ever played happened to be at Gleneagles in Scotland, one of the most famous golf resorts in the world. This was at the end of March 1990, a time when Ray and Kath's wedding anniversary and my 50th birthday happened at about the same time, so we decided to splash out on a mini-break. As a result of this experience, Gleneagles became one of my favourite places in the world, not just for the golf but for the excellence of the hotel, all the other facilities and the magnificence of the surrounding countryside. I thought this was the extent of my birthday celebrations, apart from a night out with friends back home in Atherton, but Irene had other ideas. The 6th April was a Friday and, as we prepared to leave the house to go for a drink and a meal with Carol and David, cars started to arrive from everywhere, with old friends from every period of our past life back to infanthood. Irene had arranged a surprise party for me at our house and had managed to contact and invite virtually everyone, friends and family and colleagues, who had significantly touched my life during my first fifty years. It was an amazing and memorable occasion for which I'll be grateful to Irene for the rest of my life.

Although my business life was giving me tremendous satisfaction, I'd recently turned fifty and was ready to step back and not be too involved with the day-to-day operations. It was clear that for the company to continue to prosper it would be necessary to have a talented, hard-working and experienced senior management team with professional leadership. With John Williams, Malcolm Jones, Peter Ashworth, Gordon Worswick and Simon Butterworth already in place as trusted directors of the company, I needed someone who could tighten up the organisation and report performance accurately to me. Simon had brought a new level of professionalism to our accounting functions, with all facets working very efficiently in an increasingly complex international organisation. He was hard working, intelligent, reliable and always worked with a calm air of authority. I invited him to take on the role of Managing Director whilst I'd become Chairman. I told him that he'd be responsible for every aspect of the Group's activities and ultimately for achieving budgeted revenue and profit targets. His remuneration package included a profit-based bonus element.

In fact, all of our staff, almost from day one, had an element of profit-related bonus built into their salaries. I'd always been keen to ensure that all staff, whatever their function in the company, had a vested interest in seeing the business succeed. This was especially true of the staff who had direct or indirect dealings with customers. A surly or unhelpful delivery driver, for example, could easily alienate a customer who was otherwise happy with our service. I remember, years later, when Simon gave a talk at one of our Annual Management Meetings. The talk was entitled 'You are a towel' and described a customer's experience at a magnificent five star hotel. The reception procedure was smooth and efficient, conducted by smartly dressed, bright, attractive, polite staff. The porter was very effective in accompanying the guest to his room, ensuring that his luggage was delivered safely. The room was immaculate, with superb furnishings, a magnificent bed and lovely views from the window, which was draped by rich curtains. But when the guest used his bathroom he was horrified to discover that there was a soiled towel on the rail. The chambermaid had forgotten to change it. All of the efforts by the management and staff and the huge investment in the property were brought to nothing by this small error of the lowliest employee in the chain. The customer would only ever remember the dirty towel. It was a great story, told well by Simon, with a memorable punch line that strongly reinforced our long-held principles of excellence in customer service.

I'd seen many business owners of my acquaintance take a similar step to the one I had just taken, but when it came to the crunch they just couldn't let go. I was determined that this would not happen in my case. For one thing, I trusted Simon's work ethic and integrity and was able to face the fact that he wouldn't get it right every time, just as I'd made many mistakes and errors of judgement. I quickly got used to the idea of having a loosely structured working environment which didn't require me to have strict office hours - .some would say it had always been like that. I retained Muriel as my Secretary/PA and she helped to deal with issues of a routine nature and brought to my attention those matters which needed my input. Muriel was also accepting wider responsibilities by taking charge of the administrative functions of the whole Group, not just in the UK but also overseas. I was very happy with the new arrangement and felt very comfortable with my new role as Chairman, except for the fact that I was a very poor Chairman, at least as far as organising and conducting Board Meetings was concerned. I was always more comfortable in a small informal group meeting than a structured formal Board Meeting with an Agenda and Minutes and votes etc. Votes? What? This was my company and I wanted to have the last say. But I also recognised that my senior colleagues had achieved their positions because they excelled in what they did and if I emasculated them by denying them the right to contribute to the decision making process then they would quickly become disillusioned and demotivated. I learned to accept that I would sometimes be outvoted, but it didn't happen very, often.

Chapter 25 - Even More Acquisitions

We had learned that buying an existing lifting equipment business was the quickest way to penetrate a new geographical area, but it could also be fraught with difficulties. We would instantly gain premises and workshop equipment, offices, vehicles, customers and, most importantly, experienced staff. However, most lifting gear engineering businesses offered the traditional services to their customers such as repair, testing, merchanting and small scale manufacturing. At that time, not many of them were very concerned with offering a hire service. I think the prevailing philosophy was that companies would rather complete one transaction for a thousand pounds than many transactions at twenty pounds each. The cost of manually producing hundreds of invoices per month for relatively small amounts would be prohibitive to most companies, whereas our computer-based systems handled this task easily.

We weren't interested in buying highly successful companies (not that there were many of those in our industry) because we'd have to pay a large premium and would then find it difficult to improve on what we'd bought. The idea was to buy struggling firms in locations where we weren't already represented, then move in with a team of our own experienced people to transform the target firm into a model LGH branch. Such an opportunity presented itself during 1991, when we were contacted by Jim Martin of A.Martin & Son from Bristol. The whole transaction was completed smoothly and quickly to everyone's satisfaction. Jim saved the jobs of his employees who would doubtless have lost their jobs when the business inevitably went under. He gained a cash payment for his family's assets and secured a job for himself with a progressive company; we gained a new branch in a City that held great appeal to us. We hit the ground running in our excellent freehold premises and LGH Bristol Branch became a significant contributor to our Company's performance.

For some years, we had been the biggest UK customers for the Tirfor winch, an ingenious type of manual winch with capacities ranging up to 3 tons and which was operated by using a reciprocating lever rather than the more usual rotating principle. They were perfect for hiring out and we owned hundreds of them. Tirfor's UK depot was in Sheffield and their Managing Director was Gilbert Simm, one of the best known characters in the lifting equipment industry. Tirfor's parent company was the French owned Tractel Corporation who had wider interests in a variety of industrial lifting and pulling products. One day, I received an invitation from Gilbert for myself and Irene to attend the Manutention Exhibition, the French Mechanical Handling Exhibition to be held in Paris. The tickets and the hotel would be reserved for us but we should make our own travel arrangements. We flew to Paris De Gaulle Airport and met up with Gilbert and the other guests at our hotel. We found that among the other guests were none other than Dennis Tattoo, my erstwhile boss at Coubro, who had set me on my business career by sacking me, and his wife Yvonne. I hadn't seen Dennis since my Coubro days and he was clearly embarrassed to see me here. I was now the owner of the biggest and most successful business in our industry and he was working for John Scrutton, trying to keep afloat what had once been a successful business but which was now struggling. The other guest was Darrell Pickup, with his wife Annie. Darrell owned Northern Industrial Marine Ltd (NIM) a successful winch hire business which was one of the few which could effectively compete against us in their specialist field.

After spending an exhausting day at the Exhibition, we were invited to be the guests of the French owner of the Tractel organisation at the famous French restaurant, Le Doyenne, on the Champs-Élysées. This probably remains the best and most expensive restaurant at which I've ever eaten. It was magnificent and the food was delectable. I was sitting next to Yvonne and half way through the meal she turned to me and said, "Bill, why ever did you leave

Coubro?" I nearly choked before telling her calmly, "Well Yvonne, it was because your husband fired me". She was mortified and I presume Dennis received a tongue lashing for not having prepared her for this potential embarrassment. I found out later that someone else had asked him why he had let Bill Parkinson go and he replied, "You can't keep the best guys". Why couldn't he just admit that he'd made a mistake? A mistake that gave me the biggest break of my life. At some point during the meal, Gilbert disappeared and didn't return for about half an hour. I didn't think too much about it at the time but I later found out that Gilbert's French boss was expecting Gilbert to pay for the meal whilst Gilbert was assuming that his boss was paying. Neither had brought cash, cheques or cards and would be unable to pay the considerable bill. Gilbert had to dash back to the hotel to secure some means of payment.

The following day was free so Irene and I used our first visit to Paris to visit the Rodin Museum on a freezing cold day. When we arrived at the Charles De Gaulle Airport that evening it was snowing and all flights were cancelled. We checked back in to our hotel, met up with Darrell and Gilbert and their wives and decided to make the best of it by going out on the town. Darrell and I agreed that, as Tractel had been so generous in inviting us, we'd stand the cost of the night out and the extra night in the hotel. When we eventually got home we couldn't believe it when we received a bill from Tirfor for the whole cost of the trip. We'd presumed, as we'd been invited, that Tirfor would be standing the cost.

Darrell and I regularly kept in touch and we'd meet occasionally at trade functions such as the LEEA AGMs. His Head Office and main location was at Alfreton in Derbyshire, but he also had a large engineering facility on the banks of the Tyne, in Newcastle, at Walker. This was where NIM designed and built a wide range of winches, from diesel and petrol to electric and hydraulic. NIM had also acquired a winch business in Glasgow which had been started by my old employee, Peter Ashworth. NIM's business involved designing, making, repairing, selling and hiring anything related to winches. They were the undoubted national leaders in this field and we were frequently competing against them, often unsuccessfully, for winch hire business. When Darrell approached me in 1992 to ask if I'd be interested in buying his business it was too good an opportunity to miss. The problem was, the timing was wrong.

We were at the limit of our overdraft and loan arrangements due to a succession of acquisitions and new branch openings. I really only wanted Darrell's winch hire business. I wasn't interested in the manufacturing and merchanting side of the operation, but he was adamant that it was all or nothing. I very much wanted this business, which I felt would confirm us as the pre-eminent supplier in our industry, and Darrell's Sales Hub at Alfreton was handling massive enquiries which we never even saw. I had to have it, but how could I complete a transaction which I couldn't afford?

Simon Butterworth and I worked out a proposal which we put to Darrell and he accepted. I offered Darrell a million pounds for his business. This would be paid in a special issue of dated, convertible, redeemable preference shares in LGH Group. In other words, on a certain date in three years time, Darrell would present his new shares, for which LGH would pay him £1,000,000. If LGH could not honour that agreement then Darrell had the right to convert his shares into Ordinary Shares equivalent to 10% of the issued capital of LGH. I was gambling 10% of my company on being able to write a cheque for one million pounds in three years time.

We sat down together in my office and agreed all the main points of the deal, which we wrote on one side of an A4 sheet of paper. We passed this to our lawyers and accountants, who prepared a formal sale and purchase contract running to dozens of pages, and arranged a completion meeting in Manchester for the day before Irene and I were due to go to Menorca on holiday. The meeting was attended by myself and Simon, together with our representatives from Coopers and Lybrand and our lawyers, Eversheds. Darrell was there with his accountants, KPMG, and two lawyers, one of whom, a lady, had prepared an agenda and was acting as the chairperson.

The agenda comprised about twenty items that needed to be resolved before the deal could be signed off. The chair announced that we'd start with item one, which was non-contentious, and proceeded to outline a small problem. Then our lawyer responded with a highly technical argument which I didn't fully grasp. Then KPMG expressed their opinion with particular reference to the complex tax issues which could affect this item and, of course, our accountants had to show that they weren't just along for the ride. More than half an hour had passed and all we'd heard was professional accountants and lawyers trying to score points off each other at £120 per hour each - and this was supposed to be non-contentious! I caught Darrell's eye across the room and inclined my head towards the door. We asked to be excused and in the corridor outside we agreed to take control of the remainder of the meeting. On our return to the room I announced that from then on only Darrell and I would be allowed to speak unless a professional advisor was invited to give an opinion. They were all stunned but it worked beautifully. It was a difficult meeting with tough compromises to be made, but in the end we completed a good transaction for both parties within two or three hours. It was the biggest and most complex deal I'd ever made.

Following the acquisition of NIM, which Darrell liked to call a merger, he joined our Board and his wide experience of our industry proved to be valuable. He had a few eccentricities and was not universally appreciated by all of my colleagues. He always answered the 'phone with the phrase 'Ayyup' and was pretty blunt and forthright in his opinions. The extra revenue which the NIM business generated was valuable to our group and we worked hard to increase

LGH's business with the great many new customers with whom we were trading. The biggest problem we encountered was in measuring the performance of this complex operation, which was working from locations in Alfreton, Glasgow, Aberdeen, Newcastle and London in a wide range of activities ranging from hire and manufacturing to merchanting and repair and testing. Where we at LGH measured performance by location, there was no such differentiation at NIM. All sales went into one 'pot' and similarly all costs were lumped together. It was impossible to know which aspect of the business was making a positive contribution and which section might be making losses. Simon and his accounting team worked hard to rectify this situation and, having done so, it became clear that the manufacturing division presented a massive potential problem.

Housed in a collection of freehold buildings extending to over 60,000 square feet on the banks of the River Tyne at Walker, NIM Engineering, as we'd renamed this division, was responsible for designing and making a wide range of winches. Over the years, Darrell had bought the rights to most of the now defunct British winch manufacturers, including Thompson's and Colt's. When I bought my first Thompson winch for £800 in 1970, I never imagined that one day I'd own the Thompson brand. As an engineer myself, I was incredibly proud of the workshop capability we now possessed. We had large fabrication facilities incorporating overhead cranes up to 50 tons capacity and a machine shop with a collection of machine tools including large lathes, radial arm drills, milling machines, surface grinders and shapers etc. There was hardly anything which we couldn't make. Whereas, fifty years earlier, every town had its own engineering company with this kind of capability, by the nineties many of these companies had closed down. I figured that this would become an increasingly valuable resource. To recreate from new the facilities which we had in Newcastle would have cost many millions and I was keen to see this unique resource start earning its keep.

It became clear that the main problem we faced was keeping the workshop full to capacity to generate enough revenue to cover the high overhead content at the site. The workshop staff were skilled, the technical staff and design team were experienced and the sales department seemed competent and well-connected, but often we'd have five reasonable months' trading followed by a disastrous month, during which any previously generated profit would be more than wiped out.

Our own LGH and NIM Hire businesses were good customers of NIM Engineering and it made sense to time our winch purchase orders to meet lulls in demand from external customers. Stuart Wild, who had been one of Darrell's key staff, was Director of NIM Engineering and Colin Midson, one of LGH's most successful branch managers, had been given the responsibility of running the NIM Hire and Sales businesses in Alfreton. Unfortunately, Colin and Stuart were always falling out and Colin was always looking for reasons to source his hire fleet winches externally, rather than keep the business within the LGH family.

The NIM acquisition helped us to grow considerably in the early nineties but the NIM Engineering losses caused us great concern and a disproportionate amount of senior management time was spent in dealing with these problems. Looking back, I'm still not sure whether this was a good deal or a poor one in the whole scheme of things but, after the critical initial three year period, I was just about able to write out Darrell's coveted cheque for £1,000,000 in exchange for the LGH Preference Shares he'd been given. It was a close call, but I was very relieved to avoid the spectre of losing 10% of my company.

Chapter 26 - Domestic Matters

Our daughter, Lorraine, was married in 1988, to Gordon Warke, a Merchant Seaman from Bolton with whom she'd been courting for a couple of years. I offered Lorraine my 1927 Rolls Royce as her wedding car, but she turned down the offer, scoffing that she wouldn't be seen dead in that old banger. However, a few weeks before the wedding she changed her mind and said that she'd love to be driven to church in this beautiful old car. I arranged for my friend David Tonge, who was responsible for me buying the car in the first place, to drive Lorraine and me to church. David turned up in a beautiful maroon coloured chauffeur's livery, complete with peaked cap and shiny calf boots. When the other members of the family had left home for the church it was a very poignant moment, to be left alone with my daughter on her last day living with us, and we both shed a tear. After the wedding, at St. John's, Atherton Parish Church, David drove Lorraine and Gordon to the Pack Horse Hotel in Bolton town centre, where the reception was held. The manager of the Pack Horse had kindly agreed to replace his usual beer on the bar with Moorhouse's Premier Bitter, which the brewery supplied as free issue, and we all had a wonderful time. The newly-weds had bought a nice semi-detached house at Bromley Cross in Bolton, close enough for Lorraine to commute to work in Atherton. Gordon continued his career in the merchant navy (later the Royal Fleet Auxiliary) for many years thereafter, a situation which Lorraine accepted with great equanimity.

Our elder son Ian's work, running our small Leeds branch, was going well. In 1990 he moved in to live with his girlfriend Jayne and her young daughter from her first marriage. He continued to commute to Leeds each day from his home in Tyldesley. Occasionally, during the school holidays, Steve would travel to Leeds with Ian, sharing the driving duties on the busy M62 motorway. It was great to see Steve becoming involved in the business and the two lads worked well together. One day, Irene and I were horrified to learn that there'd been a massive accident on the M62 on the way to Leeds, involving Steve's car and a fully laden 29 ton coal truck. Steve had been driving in the outside lane of the very busy motorway and was overtaking a car in the centre lane. The driver of this car hadn't seen Steve's car and pulled out into the outer lane, pushing Steve's car into the central reservation barrier, from which he bounced out of control across all three lanes, hitting the massive coal lorry so hard that it knocked out the lorry's front axle. Miraculously, everyone emerged without a scratch. We could so easily have lost both of our sons in this amazing accident, but fate smiled kindly on us all.

Three years later, Ian came to see me to say that he'd like to resume his academic studies by taking a three year BSc course in Business and Management Studies at Salford University. It would mean leaving his Leeds job and require the company to continue paying his salary for three years, but I was delighted and readily agreed. This time he excelled himself by gaining a First Class Honours Degree. We were immensely proud of him and even more proud when, a year later he gained an MSc in Operations Research from Lancaster University. I was only sorry that my mother, who placed great emphasis on education, did not live long enough to see her oldest grandson gain this distinction. She would have been thrilled.

Steven meanwhile left Bolton School in 1990, but was adamant that he didn't want to attend University. He was intent on setting up his own high tech business with a partner friend of his, David Spink, who lived in Arbroath in Scotland. They had developed some cable connections for computers, which they were making and selling, and were convinced that this would form the cornerstone of a business venture. Twelve months later, the two boys were still tinkering with these cables, without seeming to make much progress. They'd formed a business called Zig-Zac Computers and had great hopes of emulating the likes of Bill Gates and Steve Jobs. I was reluctant to dampen Steve's ambition, but at the same time I wanted him to be realistic about the future. He was a bright, well-educated young man and I didn't want to see him frittering away the best years of his life on a fruitless venture. I told him that we'd be prepared to support him for another twelve months if he could convince me that Zig-Zac had a reasonable chance of success. Otherwise, he should get a job, either with LGH or elsewhere or alternatively, go to University.

After thinking about this for a while, he changed his mind about his previous aversion to University and told us that he'd like to study Computer Science, but not in the UK. He wanted to study in the USA, where he believed the best courses were offered. He had to go to London to sit the SATs (Student Aptitude Tests) required by all American Universities. He obtained good grades and applied to both UCLA and USC. He was offered a place at USC (University of Southern California) who wrote to me to ask if I was prepared to support my son to the extent of $25,000 per annum for the next four years. I had to complete a form to the effect that I agreed to this and was surprised a week or two later when my bank manager friend Ron 'phoned me to say that he'd had a letter from USC asking if I was good for $25,000 per year.

Steve took up his place at USC, in September 1993, at the age of twenty, two years later than most students. We had a holiday in Orlando with our friends the Slanes and the Garsides in October. At the end of our two weeks in Florida we flew to California to be with Steve for his 21st Birthday. He'd only been in Los Angeles for a month but had already become familiar with the city and was eager to show us the sights - Hollywood, Malibu Beach, the Getty Museum and, of course, the magnificent USC campus, whose sports field was none other than the LA Olympic Stadium. We left him in LA with a feeling of satisfaction that our younger son was in a fine place which would stand him in good stead in the future. The next three months caused us to change that view dramatically, as LA dominated the international news headlines. First there were riots of disenchanted and aggressive black youths in the ghettos of LA. Then there were massive bush fires which destroyed many houses around Malibu, followed by enormous mud slides which caused extensive damage. But the biggest disaster of all came on 27th January 1994, just four months after Steve had gone to LA.

I'd gone home from the office to have my lunch on that day, which I remember well. As usual, I'd switched on the TV to catch up with the lunch-time news. The big story was that Los Angeles had been hit by one of the most intense and most damaging earthquakes ever. The live pictures of collapsed buildings, roads and bridges with fires raging across the city were horrifying to Irene and me, as we imagined our son lying trapped under a pile of rubble. We sat glued to the TV set for the next couple of hours, when the 'phone rang. It was Steve, calling to tell us that he was OK. It was 4.30 a.m. in LA when the 'quake happened and Steve told us that he was thrown out of bed with the intensity of the tremor. Most 'phones were out of action but he'd found a public 'phone which was still functioning and he joined a queue of students who were all ringing home to assure their parents that they were OK. What a relief! We found out later that this was the biggest earthquake ever to hit an urban area and it proved at the time to be the most expensive natural disaster to ever hit the USA, with a cost of $20 bn. Things seemed to settle down after this series of catastrophes and four years later Steve graduated with a good degree in Computer Science and Engineering.

Irene and I used Steve's graduation as an excuse to visit California again. This time we made a carefully planned excursion lasting four weeks. First we flew to San Francisco, where we spent a few days of most enjoyable sight-seeing. Then we hired a car and drove to Yosemite, the huge, wild National Park. We stayed for two nights at a small bed and breakfast lodge just outside of the park boundary and found that we had to drive twelve miles to the nearest town to find a restaurant. This area was so quiet and remote that we made the twenty-four mile round trip without seeing another vehicle. We then drove to the Monterey Peninsula via Gilroy, the capital of garlic farming in the USA. On the coast we stayed in a lovely motel in Carmel, famous for the fact that Clint Eastwood had been the Mayor there. The other distinction of Carmel is that it has no traffic lights or roundabouts. Every intersection is a four-way-give-way. In other words, when you approach a junction, you have to stop and allow any vehicles which were there before you to proceed first. It works perfectly and encourages polite behaviour. There are no chain restaurants in Carmel, only owner managed establishments. No McDonalds or KFCs. Also, it is next to what is arguably the finest group of golf courses on the planet. Apart from the famous Pebble Beach and exclusive Cypress Point, there are four or five other world class venues.

I was desperate to have a game at Pebble Beach and achieved this by getting up before dawn and putting my name down with the starter, who managed to squeeze in an extra four ball. I played with three American men and Irene drove my buggy cart. After 16 holes of incredibly demanding but enjoyable golf, Irene told me I'd taken 90 strokes to this point. That meant I'd have to take no more than nine shots for the last two holes, including the formidable eighteenth if I wanted to break one hundred. I managed a three and a six to finish with a gross score of 99, which might not sound that great but it gave me tremendous satisfaction.

The following day, heading south, we drove down the Pacific Coast Highway, US1, through what is known as the Big Sur. The road is dramatic, with ravines and bridges and tunnels, the wild Pacific coast on the right hand side and lots of opportunities to watch basking seals on the rocky shore. We were headed for Santa Barbara, but passed through a small village called San Simeon, famous for being the location of the Hearst Castle. William Randolph Hearst was a publisher and newspaper proprietor who became one of the wealthiest men in America. He bought a fifty mile stretch of California coast and built his ostentatious castle, where he entertained the world's rich and powerful and famous, such as Winston Churchill and Marilyn Monroe. He was said to have imported wild African animals, including zebras and giraffes, which were allowed to roam wild on his vast estate. It's rumoured that the descendants of some of these animals still roam wild in the vast forests in the area. Mr. Hearst's grand-daughter, Patti, achieved notoriety following her kidnapping in 1974 by the Symbionese Liberation Army. She was apparently brainwashed by her captors, became sympathetic to their cause and joined in their criminal activities. Our visit to the Hearst Castle was most interesting and showed us what can be achieved by the use of unlimited wealth. That evening we spent a pleasant couple of hours on the beach, gathered around a campfire with a dozen or so other tourists, both American and European.

Next stop was Santa Barbara, where we were surprised to see young mothers in bikinis roller-blading at high speed along the wide promenade, pushing their infants in special high performance three-wheeled prams (strollers). A far cry from the leisurely walks with the coach-built Silver Cross prams of our children's day. Our hotel concierge told us about a recently opened brew pub/restaurant in town. That was too good an opportunity to miss, as the chance to drink beer other than the bland Bud or Miller American lager was rare. When we arrived at the site we were very impressed by the lay-out, displaying all the brewing equipment through a large glass window behind the bar. On the bar was a glass jar showing the different roasting levels of the malts being used and a further display of various hops. I couldn't wait to try one of the several beers on offer, which I presumed would be cask-conditioned. What a disappointment. The beer had been pasteurised, filtered, chilled and carbonated to create a product just like all of the other available American beers.

When I introduced myself, the barman said he'd bring the owner to meet me. The very likeable young man who came to greet me told me that his parents had put up the money to fund his dream of owning a brew pub. He said that he'd quickly realised that the real profits were to be made in selling food and the novelty of having a brewhouse on site was the 'hook' which brought the customers into the restaurant. When I asked him how he'd learned to brew beer he said that the Texan firm who had designed, made and installed the brewing equipment held a course at their workshops in Texas, which he had attended at the outset. The course lasted a whole week! I resisted the temptation to tell him that the two senior brewers at my brewery had spent four years each at the Heriot Watt University to gain a degree in Brewing Technology and had then trained as assistant brewers for several years before finally taking charge of the brewing process. No wonder the American beer left a lot to be desired.

At this time there were probably less than one hundred breweries in the USA. Now, as I write this in 2015 I'm told that there are over 4,500. There has been a massive explosion of interest in flavourful, hoppy beers to fuel this growth in the micro brewing industry. Americans, however, remain steadfast in their taste for freezing cold beer. They just can't seem to understand the subtle benefits of cask-conditioned (real) ale served at cellar temperature.

Steven was graduating the following day and we excitedly made our way to the massive USC campus in Los Angeles, which was all decked out for the various outdoor ceremonies, each faculty holding its own function. It was a beautiful day, with marquees erected all around and bands playing well-known tunes. Steve was part of the Engineering Faculty and the whole ceremony was orchestrated immaculately to ensure a smooth passage for the hundreds of graduating students in their caps and gowns. A truly memorable day, which filled us with pride.

The following day Steve joined us for the remainder of our epic Californian trip, as we left Los Angeles, making our way further south to San Diego, where we had a wonderful three night stay. Then we gave up the hire car and flew to Las Vegas for another few nights, taking in a couple of shows and a helicopter flight to the Grand Canyon. Steve flew back to LA to pick up his old car, which he'd previously packed with all of his worldly goods, and drove to San Francisco. That became his home for the foreseeable future. We returned home to England full of wonderful memories of a great trip.

Chapter 27 - Sports Sponsorship

I describe in Chapter 11 our first venture into sports sponsorship with the Lifting Gear Hire Lancastrian Squash Tournament. During our Lancastrian involvement, I met and became friendly with a young promising squash professional who was of Scottish parentage but lived locally in Oldham. He was Chris McManus, who had already represented Scotland but was keen to make the next step up onto the professional squash circuit. He needed to gain some world ranking points and felt he could achieve this on the Sunshine Tour based in South Africa. I agreed to sponsor him for this six week long trip by paying for his expenses. In return Chris agreed to give me as much coaching as I wanted and to wear the LGH logo on his clothing. After a promising start in the first two tournaments, he suffered an unfortunate accident on court when he fell and sprained an ankle. That was the end of his Sunshine Tour but we kept in touch after that and he gave me a fair bit of coaching to fulfil his side of the bargain.

Because I was keen on squash myself, it was natural that I'd be inclined in this direction and we also agreed to sponsor the North West Counties squash leagues, involving hundreds of clubs and thousands of players. I felt that it was appropriate for my company to be associated with what was then a very high profile sport with a high percentage of its participants being senior or middle management men and women.

During our Monday night squash and badminton evenings at Howe Bridge Leisure Centre, my friends and I would regularly find ourselves playing badminton on a court next to three young boys about thirteen years old when we first saw them. They had a coach called Brian who would feed them with certain shots - drop shots, smashes or overhead clears. The boys never played games against each other and would only play these practice routines, so we couldn't judge their ability. Because there were five or six in our group it meant that we took turns to sit out and when I was sitting out I'd often help Brian and the boys to pick up the dozens of shuttlecocks which were littered around the court. We only used plastic shuttles, but these boys were using feather shuttles, which were very expensive. I was appalled at how badly worn and damaged their shuttles had become and mentioned this to Brian, who told me that they couldn't afford new ones.

After we'd known them for a couple of years, and watched them develop both physically and technically, I asked him how good the lads were. He told me that two of them, Chris and Andy, were off to Germany the following week to represent Great Britain at the under 16 European Team Championships. Two weeks later, we learned that team GB were runners up, but Chris and Andy were the only undefeated men's doubles pairing at the event. Brian later told me that they received no financial support from anyone and the boys' parents had to pay for the hire of the practice court and for his coaching services, not to mention the shuttles.

I asked him if a thousand pounds per year from LGH would help. He and the boys were very appreciative of that small gesture and agreed to wear LGH logos on their sports shirts whenever possible. Like many teenage boys, Andy discovered girls, which distracted him from badminton, but Chris Hunt went on to become a very successful professional badminton player, winning the mixed doubles gold medal and men's doubles silver medal at the 1994 Commonwealth Games in Victoria, Canada. He also twice won the European Championships Gold Medal partnering Simon Archer in 1994 and 1998.

Chess prodigy Nigel Short lived only a few hundred yards from us in Low Green, Atherton and was in the same Bolton School Sixth Form class as our son Ian. After Nigel left school he became a professional chess player and I thought it would be good for Atherton's best company to be associated through sponsorship with the town's best chess player. I arranged to meet Nigel in a local pub one lunch-time and outlined my suggestion that he could wear my company's logo on his blazer pocket, in return for which we'd be prepared to pay him £5,000 per annum. I thought he would find this an attractive offer but I totally underestimated the earning power of a grand master chess professional. Nigel graciously declined my offer. In addition to tournament prize money and newspaper column writing, the world's top players were all signed up to play in the German Bundesliga, not at football but at chess. Most of the German cities had professional chess teams in a highly competitive league and Nigel would fly to Germany each week to take part in these well paid matches.

At the time of this lunchtime meeting, I was keen on playing backgammon and had taken my board with me to the pub in the hope that Nigel would give me a game. He told me that a lot of the professional chess players, including himself, liked to play backgammon for relaxation and he was pleased to play me. I was thrilled to beat him 2 - 0. Nigel went on to have a brilliantly successful career, becoming British Champion several times and the only British player ever to play in the final match for the World Championship. This was against Gary Kasparov in 1993, a match televised live by BBC, when Nigel was heavily defeated. Pity, he would have looked good with our logo on his blazer pocket.

A few years earlier, when we were still living in Lancaster Avenue's cul-de-sac, we frequently saw our neighbour's son, Adrian Marsh, bring his show-jumping horse into the avenue. The children would gather round to stroke this lovely animal, named after a local beauty spot called Anglesarke. My office was still at Hamilton Street when Adrian came to see me asking if I'd be interested in sponsoring his horse. He said it could be re-named Lifting Gear Hire's Anglezarke. I didn't think that this had any kind of memorable ring to it and when he said that he'd want £5,000 per year for the privilege I nearly fell off my chair. I told him that I couldn't justify that amount even if he had a chance of appearing on TV with the horse at one of the big show-jumping events. Adrian tried to convince me that this was a very special horse and would almost certainly be on TV in the near future. I didn't believe him and in any case I wasn't particularly interested in show-jumping and couldn't see a valid case for associating my company with this activity. Three weeks later we were at home on a Saturday afternoon when a buzz went round the avenue that Adrian was on TV. We switched on and watched enthralled as our young neighbour took on and beat the best show-jumpers in the world, including Harvey Smith, to win the prestigious Calor Gas Championship. David Vine was commentating and within five minutes of the results being declared he announced to the world that following his victory Adrian and his father Roy had accepted a massive offer to buy Anglezarke, which became Capt. Mark Philips' horse for the Mexico Olympic Games. Roy used the funds to buy a farm in the local rural village of Culcheth, where Adrian went on to have a successful career as a breeder and trainer of show-jumping horses.

By 1991, Lifting Gear Hire Ltd was a well-known local company and we were approached by an attractive young lady who introduced herself to me as the Commercial Assistant of Leigh Rugby League Football Club. At the time, Leigh were a Second Division club and were our closest professional sports team, their Hilton Park stadium being only three or four miles away. Many of our staff and customers were avid Leigh supporters and I felt that it would be good to have a close association with the club. I agreed to meet their Chairman, Tony Cottrell, who'd recently led a consortium to acquire the club. We negotiated a three year shirt sponsorship deal which included bonuses for achieving promotion and appearing on TV. Alex Murphy had been coach at the club, but was replaced by Kevin Ashcroft at the beginning of our first season's involvement.

My early life in the Burnley area had given me no exposure to Rugby League, my interest being in football up to that point. However, Irene and I started to attend all of the home games with reserved seats in the Directors' Box and we soon became keen fans, as the team performed heroically that season, gaining promotion to the First Division whilst proudly wearing their cherry and white Lifting Gear Hire shirts. John Stringer, the Commercial Manager, and Kevin Ashcroft, arranged to celebrate by taking the players to Tenerife for a few days as a reward for their tremendous achievement. They invited me to join them and I jumped at the chance to get better acquainted with the players and management of the club. The trip turned out to be one of the most amazing experiences of my life. To be in close proximity for five days and nights to fifteen crazy, young, fit, testosterone-fuelled young men with unlimited access to alcohol and girls was a total revelation. It was a blast which, for ethical and moral reasons I'm prevented from recalling. The fact that we escaped from Tenerife without serious injuries and without anyone being arrested is a miracle which I'll never fully understand.

During the close season, there was a club board-room shake up. Tony Cottrell left, to be replaced by a mystery Irishman called Tim Maloney. I was invited to join the Board, along with a rugby savvy local businessman, Dennis O'Halloran. It was decided to replace Kevin Ashcroft as coach and we received an application for the job from an Australian, Steve Simms. Tim, Dennis and I interviewed Steve at the Greyhound Hotel and offered him the job. His first match in charge early the following season was against the formidable St. Helens, at home at Hilton Park on a miserable, cold and rainy November day. Saints were one of the star teams of the First Division but we achieved one of the upsets of the season by beating them in a scrappy, low scoring game.

Later in the season we had the return fixture at Knowsley Road in a televised game. Sky TV's Eddie Hemmings wanted to interview a Leigh director on the pitch before the kick off, on live TV. Tim was very reluctant to appear in public, for reasons which we only discovered later, and Dennis was strangely reticent on this occasion. That left me and I duly obliged. Saints were riding high at the time and had won many consecutive matches whilst we were bottom of the league, struggling to make any headway in the first division since our early shock win at the beginning of the season. Eddie put the question to me, implying that Leigh were looking like lambs to the slaughter, but I confidently reminded him that we were one of the few teams to have beaten Saints that season and I saw no reason why we shouldn't repeat the result. We received one of the most comprehensive beatings in the club's history and I was later the object of some ribald comments which rightly questioned my knowledge of the game.

The following year, the club was suffering from considerable turmoil from lack of leadership and acute shortage of funds. Denis and I were kept completely in the dark and had little input into the day-to-day running of the club. Tim was extremely secretive and paranoid about appearing in public, which was a strange way for the Chairman of a professional sports club to behave. He was in business as a wholesale potato merchant and the rumour around the club was that he had swindled a Manchester market trader who had put out a knee-capping contract on him. This was not the kind of situation with which I wished to be associated and I became increasingly uncomfortable.

I thought that one way out of the problem would be for me to buy control of the club and seriously considered that option. Ultimately, I took the view that the potential risks were virtually unlimited and I really didn't know enough about either the game of Rugby League or the management of a professional sports club to have a reasonable chance of making it work. That summer we took a holiday in Menorca and whilst there spoke to our daughter Lorraine at home. She said that the local paper was full of the news that Dennis O'Halloran and I had resigned as directors of the club amid allegations of financial irregularities. Dennis and I were livid to have our good names tarnished in this way and the newspaper published a retraction and apology the following week. It transpired that Tim Maloney had absconded, it was rumoured, to either Ireland or America. We never saw him again. The club was taken over by Mick Higgins, to whom Tim had passed his shares before disappearing. A very exciting but also distressing chapter of my life was over.

Chapter 28 - Failures

I've probably given the impression that the growth of the LGH Group was seamless and straightforward, but along the way there were many obstacles to overcome. For instance, we had more branch locations than any competitor, we had many more items of plant, our maintenance standards were better than anyone else and we had more technical staff, more sales personnel and more transport vehicles, so how could a competitor possibly touch us? The only way was to compete on price.

Our hire rates were based on the capital cost of the plant with the historic utilisation figures factored into the equation. Our successive computer systems gave us the most comprehensive information relating to utilisation data, which was vital in determining a hire rate that was reasonable for the customer, competitive within the industry and profitable for our company. If the calculations suggested that the hire rate for a particular item of plant should be say, £20 per week, then that was the price charged by all of our branches. We would only discount this rate in the case of long-term hires or large quantity orders. However, our competitors were not in possession of the detailed management information which was available to the LGH team and were usually not entirely reliant on hire revenue in their businesses. They would ask themselves the question 'Is it better to have a piece of plant sitting on the shelf at £20 per week than out on hire at £5 per week?' Many of our smaller competitors resorted to price cutting and we had to hold our nerve and remain confident in our standards in the face of this worrying trend.

Alf Lewis, of Capper Pipe, our first and one of our best customers 'phoned, me one day to tell me that he'd had a visit to his North-West office from a small lifting equipment hire company in the Midlands, 100 miles away. Alf had been told by this company that they would supply all of his hire needs at 40% below LGH's rates and they'd deliver free of charge. I knew that it was not possible to fulfil this promise and make a profit but Alf had no alternative but to give them the work. We lost a contract worth over £85,000 per annum to a competitor who clearly had no idea what they were doing. Twelve months later, Cappers called in the receivers and the Midlands lifting company also went bust. In the end we were saved from a large bad debt which we would inevitably have suffered if we'd still been trading with Cappers.

Another trend which adversely affected our bottom line was the reduction in average length of hire for our hire contracts. Whereas in our early days customers would leave equipment on hire for months and sometimes even years, by the 1990s computer systems for contract management had become more sophisticated and our customers became much more cost conscious. They were able to monitor their expenditure on hire very effectively. The days of hiring out a piece of equipment and counting the money coming in for months on end were over forever.

As a fairly high profile businessman, at least on the local stage, I was approached regularly by would-be entrepreneurs who tried to interest me in an assortment of business ventures. One such proposal came from one of my Horwich Squash Club fellow members, Gordon McVean. Gordon worked as a salesman for a power tool sales company in Horwich, whose owner wished to sell up and retire. Gordon told me that he and a colleague, Patrick, who managed the administration and internal sales office, were keen to buy the business. Both Gordon and recently married Patrick owned their own houses and had secured offers of second mortgages which they would use to buy the business, but they were still £50,000 short of the required amount. I met both young men in my Atherton office and was particularly impressed by Patrick, who seemed bright, knowledgeable and ambitious. They outlined their excellent plans for growing the business, which had a valuable Hitachi main distributorship, and offered me 20% of the business if I'd put up as a loan, the £50,000 capital which they needed to complete the deal. I spent a few days considering the proposal before deciding that it would be a useful diversification and completed with the minimum of delay, making sure that the legal formalities were put in place. One of the conditions of my loan was that I was to be given full access at any time to the management accounts of the business.

The young men went ahead with the acquisition of their former employer's business and made great progress in growing sales during the first few months. The management accounts appeared to be healthy but cash flow was always a problem, as stock levels needed to be high and suppliers usually had to be paid before customers met their obligations. Then, a few months after they'd started in business, Gordon 'phoned me to ask if he and Patrick could come to see me urgently. I was about to go on holiday the following day and was extremely busy with last minute tidying up of my desk. However, I told them that I could spare 15 minutes and they arrived in a great state of excitement.

They told me that they'd secured a very large contract to supply all of the power tool requirements for a large locally based engineering and construction group. Their problem was that the contract required them to significantly increase stock levels, for which Hitachi were insisting on cash with order. The business needed another £25,000 to fund this expansion and I was the only option. The opportunity was immediate and the decision couldn't wait until I returned from holiday. That gave me five minutes to make up my mind. Although I wasn't comfortable with the proposal, I negotiated a further 10% shareholding for the additional loan and made out the cheque. The following few months were very busy for me and I had no time for the small tool sales business, which I presumed was performing as planned. After about twelve months, Irene and I, together with our children, went away for an annual early November week-end to a remote hotel at Shap, in Cumbria, with a big party of friends. Whilst there I received a telephone call from Gordon to tell me that his partner Patrick had been found dead in his car on Rivington Pike, a local beauty spot. The exhaust pipe of his car had been connected to a tube, which had been led through the window in what was almost certainly suicide.

The next few days proved to be very distressing, as the circumstances behind Patrick's death became apparent. The boot of his car was found to contain dozens of betting slips for increasingly large stakes, amounting to many tens of thousands of pounds. Unknown to Gordon or me, Patrick had a history of gambling addiction and was a member of Gamblers Anonymous, who were under the impression that he was cured. As the facts were unravelled and we called in accountants to examine the company's records, it was clear that Patrick had been systematically robbing the business by writing out cheques payable for cash from the company's Royal Bank of Scotland account. All of the amounts of these cheques were multiples of eleven. i.e. £550, £2,200 or £4,400 etc. It transpired that Patrick was making 'Yankee' bets on horse racing.

If you pick four horses in different races and back them in a Yankee this makes eleven separate bets - six doubles, four triples and a quadruple. If all four horses win then the returns are massive. This was Patrick's secret vice and, unfortunately for him, his chosen horses rarely won and his losses mounted at an alarming rate. In less than twelve months he lost over £120,000 of the company's money. The inevitable result was that the company folded with large debts and all investors, including me as the largest creditor, lost their money. The most disturbing aftermath of this affair from my perspective, apart from the death of a bright young man, was that RBS had allowed him to draw virtually unlimited amounts of cash from the company's account without ever questioning this. Most companies operate on credit and rarely use cash for large transactions. That alone should have rung alarm bells at the bank. Not only this, but the company bank mandate clearly called for two signatures on every cheque, with Gordon and Patrick both being required to sign. In my opinion RBS were clearly responsible for having allowed the account to be drained illegally and were also indirectly responsible for allowing a young man to be exposed to irresistible temptation which led to his tragic death.

The bank's response to this assertion was that, at times when Gordon was absent on business or holiday, it had become normal practice to allow cheques to be processed with just Patrick's signature. I thought that this was a weak response and discussed the possibility of taking legal action against RBS with the liquidator of the business. It was estimated that such action would cost £50,000 to mount and the liquidator could not fund this. He said that he would release the rights to the action to me as the largest creditor if I had the appetite to take on the bank. My solicitor advised me that the case against the bank looked reasonable but I should consult a barrister on the matter. He set up an appointment for me with a London based QC who specialised in this kind of case and I travelled to Lincoln's Inn to meet with him, armed with all of the documentary evidence which I could find, including copies of all of the paid cheques with just Patrick's signature, amounting to a value of over £120,000.

The barrister advised me that the fact Gordon had agreed to only one signature being valid when he was not available would weaken my case somewhat, but he still felt that we had an 80% chance of success. I had to decide whether to risk a further £50,000 to potentially win £120,000 with a success possibility of 80%. It seemed like a good bet but money at LGH was tight, as usual, and I didn't have to decide immediately. The more I thought about it the more convinced I became that RBS would not let this go to court. A case involving the death of a young newly married young man and the bank's alleged incompetence leading to a huge gambling spree would be sure to attract massive media attention which the bank would be very keen to avoid, whatever the merits of their defence. They'd be sure to offer a settlement and I resolved to pursue the case as soon as I had the required resources.

A year went by, and then another. Although the possible action entered my consciousness occasionally, it ceased to be a high priority. By the time I determined to pursue the case my lawyers advised me that the statute of limitation had expired and it was no longer possible. It remains a huge regret, especially bearing in mind my future relationship with RBS, which I'll recount later, that I did not pursue this action.

My sister, Joan, had a son, Kelvin, before she married Malcolm MacDonald, who was now managing Moorhouse's Brewery. Kelvin had been in the Army as a career soldier, as a cook in the catering corps. One of his more enjoyable jobs had been to accompany the Army ski team on training trips to the Alps to ensure that they were well fed, which gave Kelvin the chance to hone his skiing skills as well. When he was demobbed, one of his ex-officers was now responsible for recruiting civilian staff for the Government and he offered Kelvin the chance to be the chef at Dorneywood, the Chancellor of the Exchequer's country residence just outside London. Kelvin jumped at this wonderful opportunity, which included living accommodation at Dorneywood. The Chancellor at the time was Nigel Lawson who, after a change of Government, was followed by John Prescott. Kelvin's duties were not very onerous as the politicians would only use the facility occasionally and this gave him the time to write a syndicated newspaper column called Kelvin's Kitchen and to offer outside catering to the local gentry. He was also called upon to work at No 11 Downing Street from time to time when the need arose.

After keeping this job for a few years, Kelvin decided that he'd like to be like his uncle Bill and run his own business. He was in his early thirties and had recently married an attractive and bright Russian girl called Natasha. Kelvin came to see Irene and myself, together with my parents, his grandparents, to try to raise the money for a proposed restaurant enterprise in London. His credentials appeared to be impeccable and we were all keen to help him on his way, confident that his ideas were sound and his ambition keen. Irene and I invested £50,000 in his venture and his grandparents came up with a similar amount, as did Joan and Malcolm. He also raised considerable amounts from various friends and contacts in the London area. He secured rented premises just south of the Thames on Southwark Bridge Road, near the Globe Theatre and the Tate Modern Gallery. Amid a flurry of publicity, the doors of Bankside Restaurant were opened. There had been massive expenditure on fitting out the premises with dining furniture and professional kitchen equipment, which had exceeded the capital expenditure budget considerably. Nothing but the best was good enough for Kelvin. We attended the impressive opening night and afterwards followed the progress of the business through the receipt of regular monthly trading statements.

The first full month of operation happened to be December and business was fantastic. Local companies booked Bankside for their Christmas parties and the restaurant made excellent profits. The following months, however, told a different story and, despite offering excellent food in a lovely setting at affordable prices, the restaurant failed to achieve its budgeted levels of turnover and profit. Kelvin remained bubbly and optimistic and assured all of his shareholder investors that he had plenty of ideas to improve the performance of the business. A second year went by with a similar story. December was incredibly profitable but the rest of the year saw losses exceeding the gains made in that one month. Then Kelvin hit us all with a bombshell as he embarked on another round of fund-raising in order to open another restaurant to be known as Bankside 2 on Throgmorton Street, in the financial City area of London.

Kelvin had secured the basement kitchen and dining room of the old offices of the giant American Bank, Merrill Lynch, which were located opposite the Bank of England and close to the Stock Exchange building. I was very disturbed by this action. Firstly, Kelvin was opening a second restaurant before he had ever made a profit at the first, which I thought was irrational and dangerous. Secondly, the investors in the first restaurant had every right to believe, as they had originally been encouraged to, that any subsequent Bankside developments would be as subsidiaries of the original establishment, not a separate business. Thirdly, it was Kelvin's plan to take the main chef and some of the staff to the new restaurant at the expense of the original Bankside. And fourthly, Kelvin's own time would be seriously diluted by trying to run two businesses when he couldn't even get one right.

Despite these reservations, Irene and I invested a further £50,000 in the new venture. I firmly believe that you make your own luck in life, but I had to admit that the two Bankside businesses were hit by unfortunate occurrences within a short time of each other. In the first place, the original Southwark Bridge Road premises were flooded when a main sewage outlet burst, so the restaurant had to be closed for months and then be subject to a very thorough and expensive clean-up operation. The subsequent insurance claim proved very difficult and took over a year to settle. Bankside 2 suffered an even lengthier disruption when Throgmorton Street was closed to traffic for several months to facilitate a massive construction project, which led to a catastrophic loss of trade. The inevitable consequence of these events, coupled with inexperienced management, was that both businesses became insolvent and the investors were left nursing their losses.

As the LGH Group of businesses grew, not only in revenue terms but also in the number of locations and the number of staff employed, I became increasingly concerned that it was becoming more difficult to instill our core values on the newer locations and their management and staff. I was no longer selecting new managers and in some cases I rarely saw them. In order to try to unify the company's aims and strategy we held an annual Management Meeting which served the purpose, amongst other things, of allowing me to meet and maybe exert some influence on our management team, who numbered over eighty at one point.

It was our practice to use a hotel within easy reach of our Atherton Head Office for our meetings. On the occasion which I now recall we had entirely taken over the Kilhey Court Hotel, near Standish. On the second and final day of our gathering, I took a stroll in the grounds of the hotel after lunch and came across a man practising chipping golf balls. I engaged him in conversation, as fellow golfers often do, and then I queried his presence at the hotel which my company had reserved for our exclusive use. He introduced himself as Trevor Bladen, the owner of the hotel who, together with his partner, had recently bought the property from the receiver after the previous owners had gone bankrupt. When I told him that I was also a keen golfer he told me that he was in the process of building a new golf course a couple of miles away in Standish, which he'd be pleased to show me if I was interested.

The initiative for this development had come from Morris Homes, a housebuilding company who had won planning approval from Wigan Council for a large housing development in Standish provided they'd build a golf course on part of the land which they owned. They delegated the task to Trevor and his partner Richard Bradshaw, who would be charged rental for the use of the land. I jumped at the chance and excused myself from the meeting for the next hour whilst taking Trevor in my Land Rover Discovery to the construction site which was where the new golf course was being created. We drove around the site and Trevor pointed out all the features, indicating where tees and greens would be positioned and describing the intended hazards, such as ponds and bunkers. It was fascinating to see the act of creation and to try to understand the thoughts of the designer as he juggled with the complexities of trying to make a golf course both a difficult and fair challenge within the confines of a finite piece of land, using terrain which had been there forever.

As we drove back to the entrance of the site on Rectory Lane I spotted a man laying a brick. I asked Trevor what would be built there and he explained that it was to be the clubhouse. This was too good to be true. I had a camera with me and suggested to Trevor that the momentous occasion of the laying of the foundation stone of the new clubhouse should be captured for posterity, with himself in the picture. He was delighted with the suggestion and happily posed for me. He was incredulous when I asked him whose beer he'd be selling on the bar of the clubhouse, until I explained that I owned a Brewery that would be delighted to supply him. It was a subject to which he'd given no thought at all so he was receptive to my suggestion. I asked him what membership options would be available once the course was open and he told me that there would be Silver, Gold and Platinum categories, with differing benefits. The Platinum Membership was the most expensive, giving ten years' of full benefits. I suggested a reciprocal deal. I'd purchase Platinum Membership and in return he'd put Moorhouse's Beer on the bar. He only thought about it for a minute then held out his hand and we shook on it.

After the course opened, about a year or so later, I'd meet up with Trevor occasionally at the club and we became quite friendly. One such day, we talked over a drink in the clubhouse and Trevor gave me a share tip for a company, which we'll call ABC Ltd. I'd received share tips in the past and rarely acted on them, but on this occasion I took Trevor's tip seriously and the following day I 'phoned my stockbroker and instructed him to buy for me £5,000 worth of ABC Ltd.'s shares. With the intensity of my business life, or maybe just sheer forgetfulness, my ownership of these shares and the fact that Trevor had tipped them completely slipped my mind until twelve months later, when I was walking on Son Bou beach in Menorca with Irene and our friends Ken and Christine Fox. Ken was chief Executive of Allen Brothers, who had built our original Hamilton St. offices and later our Atherton Branch and Head Office. This was at a time when mobile 'phone ownership had become the norm and I happened to have mine with me at the time. It rang and when I answered it my stockbroker said, "Are you sitting down?"

He asked me if I remembered telling him to buy shares in ABC Ltd following a tip and he laughed when I said that I'd no recollection of the trade. He explained that my £5,000 investment was now worth over £53,000 and asked me what I'd like to do, if anything. I was stunned at this windfall and perplexed when I was unable to remember who'd given me the tip. I instructed my broker to sell the shares immediately. This stroke of good fortune indirectly led me into one of the worst investments I ever made and ultimately cost me over one million pounds!

A year or two later, I received a 'phone call from Trevor Bladen, who asked me if I'd followed his advice to invest in ABC Ltd. I was thrilled to discover at last the identity of my benefactor and thanked him for sharing it with me. He told me that if I'd held on to the shares for another two months I'd have made an additional profit of £25,000, but if I'd held on for six months more the value of the shares would have dropped back to where they were originally. But the main purpose of his call was to ask me if I'd be interested in investing in Standish Court Golf Club.

He explained that the three original owners, himself, Richard Bradshaw and Patrick Dawson, the course designer, wished to restructure the ownership and management of the club and introduce additional capital. Patrick would give up his 33% shareholding and three new shareholders would be brought in, each contributing £50,000 for 20% of the shares. Trevor and Richard would also contribute an additional £50,000 each and reduce their holdings to 20% each. So there would be five equal partners in the business, which would have £250,000 of additional capital. Ordinarily, I think that I would have probably declined this opportunity but, as Trevor's advice had led to me making a substantial profit, I felt that it would be churlish to turn him down now.

The other two new investors turned out to be a local businessman called Ian and a young golf professional called Mike, whose parents had funded his share purchase. Mike became the manager of the business, reporting to a Board consisting of the other four investors. We four directors all had our own businesses to run and saw the golf club as an interesting diversion which wouldn't take up too much of our time and effort. We expected Mike to run the club as a Pay & Play facility, with a core membership who would contribute annual fees.

The course itself, whilst not long, presented an interesting challenge for golfers of all standards and was kept in reasonable condition by the very capable small team of green-keepers. After about eighteen months of this new regime, it became apparent that things were going wrong. Losses were accumulating at an alarming rate and it was obvious that we were neither attracting enough golfers on a regular basis and nor charging enough for a round of golf. Decision making at Board level was a shambles, as we were rarely together at the same time and it was clear that we needed to change things drastically.

At one of the rare Board meetings at which we were all present, I became exasperated and on a whim offered to buy out my fellow Directors for considerably less than they'd invested originally. They all accepted gleefully and I went home that night and told Irene that we were the proud owners of a golf club. She went mad and questioned my sanity, explaining that we needed a problematic golf club like a hole in the head. My previous track record of turning round ailing businesses like Wilcox Chains, Moorhouse's Brewery and East Ham Plant Hire had given me the confidence to feel that nothing was impossible.

My first task was to recruit a manager to replace Mike, and I found a young, likeable golf professional called Blake Toone who came with excellent references. Then I met with Dale, the head green-keeper and his brother, Lee. I was conscious that the standard of turf on the fairways was not as good as I would have liked and Dale explained that, with his present inadequate mowing equipment, it would be impossible to improve the quality of the sward. I asked him to make out a wish list of the equipment he'd need to present a course of which we could all be proud.

We had two other serious problems. Just before my acquisition of the business we had suffered criminal vandalism to eight of the greens on the back nine holes of the course. The police had investigated but could not name the culprit. Weed killer had been spread in several banana shaped arcs across each of the damaged greens, which had totally killed the grass. Even worse was the fact that the weed killer used had seeped down through the soil, where it would remain for a long time. This weed killer could only be obtained by professional gardeners. The only corrective solution would be to dig out the poisoned soil and returf the damaged areas. I gave the job of carrying out this work to David Siddall and his sons, who had done a lot of landscape gardening for me at home over many years and in my opinion were the best in the business. Fortunately, I was able to claim the cost of this remedial work against our golf club insurance policy.

The second serious problem was that the drainage of some of the holes on the course left a lot to be desired. In particular, the signature 15th hole, with spectacular views of Rivington Pike and the West Pennine hills, would become a quagmire following heavy rain. There was a pond to the left of the green, fed by a small stream, and the outlet went through a culvert under the railway line which had been built 150 years earlier in early Victorian times. This pond would overflow after heavy rain and flood the green, which would remain under water, sometimes for days on end. I was told that this area had always flooded, even before the golf course was built. It was obvious that the culvert was not allowing sufficient flow of water to deal with heavy rain and I asked Dale and Lee to investigate.

They dug down to the culvert and removed the paving stones which enclosed it to discover a mass of tree roots which had gradually found their way into the culvert over many years. Once these were cleared away we never had any more problems with flooding. That still left the problem of poor drainage on the fairway of the 15th hole, so I called in three professional drainage companies to assess the problem and asked each to give me a quotation for carrying out the required work. I chose the company who seemed to offer the best solution and instructed them to start work as soon as possible.

It was November and I was keen to get the work completed during the quiet winter season so that our best revenue earning months wouldn't be disrupted. I was dismayed when the contractor told me that it would be impossible to start work before June as the wet, boggy conditions would mean that his heavy machinery such as excavators, trench diggers and dumper trucks, would cause irreparable damage to the golf course, not only on the 15th hole but also three other fairways over which they would have to travel. I discussed the problem with David Siddall, who was still working on the damaged greens, and he told me of a machine which he'd read about called a Softrak. This had rubber tracks, which caused less damage to the ground over which it travelled. That sounded as if it could be the answer and I immediately contacted the manufacturer of the Softrak, a company called Loglogic, based in Devon. They told me that they weren't aware of anyone who offered Softraks for hire but they'd be happy to bring a demonstration machine to Standish for us to try out. I agreed to this and borrowed a trench-digging attachment from Deane Golf Club. This fitted to the Power Take Off drive of the Softrak and we successfully cut a trench without damaging the surrounding turf.

The problem was that we'd need two such Softraks, one to cut the trench and a second unit to catch the spoil and take it away for disposal. I placed an order for two of the machines at £25,000 each, bought a trencher for £11,000 and set up a new company called Sports Turf Drainage Ltd. I engaged an engineer, John Holdbrook, one of my long-standing Monday night squash and badminton pals, who had recently lost his job, to run the embryonic business, starting with the difficult 15th hole at Standish.

I was confident that if we could solve the problem of carrying out drainage work in sensitive areas in winter then we'd find plenty of work for the machines at sports facilities all over the country. I knew of many golf courses which were experiencing drainage problems and we could supply a neat solution for them. The work progressed exactly as planned and a herringbone pattern of drains was laid down the whole length of the 15th fairway, with exceptional results. Drains of this type don't usually show immediate benefits. The surrounding land needs to develop fissures which allow the water to 'learn' the way into the new drains, but we were delighted with the improvement, which continued to get better over time, and so were the club members.

I mentioned earlier that I asked Dale for a wish list, and he furnished me with three sheets detailing his requirements. The first sheet was headed Essentials, showing items such as a five gang fairway mower at £35,000, a tractor at £27,000 and various other mowers for tees and greens. The total value of the items on page 1 was £120,000. The second page described equipment which would be good to have available and would make the green keeping staff's job easier and quicker, but it wasn't essential in Dale's view. The third sheet showed plant which would be considered a luxury to own by any but the very top clubs in the country. I agreed to all of the items on page 1 but reminded Dale that within a few months I'd expect to see a significant improvement in the standard of presentation of the golf course.

Lombard North Central helped with the finance to purchase these items. During this first year a massive amount of work and' expenditure took place and the results were most encouraging. Members were giving me complimentary comments about the improvements to the course and I became hopeful that we'd soon see an increase in the bookings of tee times as word got around that Standish Court was a wonderful golf venue which represented great value for money. This increased demand would allow us to increase prices to a level which would show a return on my investment. Three problems prevented this from happening.

In the first place, the local golfing population had become accustomed to paying only £10 or £12 for a game of golf and anything more than that was considered to be extortionate. Secondly, there were two Municipal courses within a few miles of our venue, Haigh Hall owned by Wigan Borough Council and Duxbury Park owned by Chorley Borough Council. These were excellent courses, heavily subsidised by their respective Councils for the benefit of the local population. Haigh Hall were offering a round of golf and a three course meal for £12.50. Duxbury Park had similarly ridiculous offers. How could we possibly compete with those offers and still make a profit?

The third problem was completely outside my control - the weather. In Britain, golf is a seasonal sport, played almost exclusively in spring, summer and early autumn. Members' clubs have a guaranteed income each year from their membership fees, but a Pay and Play facility like Standish Court relies on green fee income from players who come for a game with their pals when the sun is shining. Unfortunately, during my first two or three years as owner of the club, the sun hardly ever seemed to shine in Standish and our revenue earnings fell dramatically whenever it rained. The manager, Blake, became despondent and left us to become a driving instructor (car driving not golf driving). He was replaced by Stuart McGrath, another golf pro, who assured me that he was full of ideas to transform the fortunes of the business. It didn't happen, however, and the losses continued to mount. To add insult to injury, our landlords, Morris Homes, applied swingeing increases to our rent under the terms of the original lease. I found myself regularly having to provide funds from my own pocket to keep the business going. After eight years of determined effort, producing a cumulative total of over a million pounds of losses, I gave up the battle and, after unsuccessfully trying to sell the business, I called in the receivers. I personally paid off all of the creditors of the business with the exception of Morris Homes, who I felt had overcharged the ground rent for years.

Stuart approached the landlords, agreed a new lease and took over the business. I questioned the wisdom of this, bearing in mind that he was fully aware of the huge losses I'd suffered, and he told me he thought he could do things differently. If that were true, why didn't he do things differently when I was paying his wages? In the event, Stuart's reign lasted only about twelve months before he was forced to call it a day, and soon afterwards the lovely green fairways and manicured greens became overgrown with weeds. What a shame. Then the clubhouse caught fire and was totally destroyed and the whole facility is now derelict and overgrown. No doubt it won't be too long before Morris Homes get their wish and build a thousand homes where once a golf course lay.

As a footnote to this horror story, I'm happy to say that the Sports Turf Drainage business went on to be a success story, in a small way. John Holdbrook stayed with the business after the successful drainage job at Standish and prepared beautiful sales catalogues describing how golf clubs could now deal with their drainage problems without disrupting the playing season and without inflicting irreparable damage to their hallowed turf. He sent a copy of this catalogue to every golf club in the North West of England, expecting an avalanche of enquiries for this revolutionary new drainage method. Amazingly, we didn't receive a single enquiry. Many other golf clubs were also struggling financially and couldn't justify non-essential expenditure. However, just as I was thinking that I'd have to sell the Softraks as second hand plant, we received an enquiry from a forestry contractor who said he'd like to hire one of our machines for a few weeks. We set a hire rate of £400 per week without operator and gradually the number of hire enquiries started to increase. Marcus and Graham, the owners of Loglogic, would also refer potential customers to us and the hire business grew to such an extent that I had to buy more Softraks. John Holdbrook had left the business after receiving a good job offer and I continued to run this new hire business in my spare time, with help from a local Plant Hire contractor called David Ellis, who stored, repaired and delivered my machines. A few years ago, the five Softrak machines were transferred to Rotrex Ltd, our UK based winch hire business, who continue to successfully hire out Softraks.

During the late 1990s, Irene and I were in Chicago visiting our US business, which was making steady but not spectacular progress.

Taking a break from meetings, we visited the downtown area of this wonderful city and had a stroll down one of the world's iconic shopping streets, Michigan Avenue. It was winter and bitterly cold in the windy city, so we ducked into a Barnes & Noble book store, where we could have a coffee and get warm. I wandered round the store, checking out the vast array of books from crime thrillers to travel guides, sports instruction to medicine, when a book caught my eye for some reason. It was called The Complete Hormone Promise. I took it from the shelf and carried it to the seating area to have a closer look while I drank my coffee. Its contents were a complete revelation to me and I couldn't put it down until Irene persuaded me that it was time to move on. I bought the book and continued to read it that night in our hotel room.

The book explained that, as we get older, our hormone-producing glands become less productive and, by the time we're fifty, we're producing less than half the hormones we made in our twenties. Hormones are the body's chemical messengers and are vital in ensuring that all of our bodily functions are working effectively. The authors of the book argued that we should counteract this natural decline by supplementing our diet with hormone products such as DHEA, Melatonin, Pregnenolone etc. This would counter the effects of ageing to a certain extent and could lead to a healthier, more active and longer life. It was a compelling argument which fascinated me and when I visited an American pharmacy I noticed that all of these hormone products were displayed on the shelves and were available without prescription. I bought a few bottles of these hormones, determined to try them when I returned home, even though the book advised that before taking hormone supplements a patient should be evaluated by a doctor who would administer blood, urine and saliva tests to determine the exact hormone deficiency and prescribe the correct 'cocktail' for each particular patient.

Another Monday-night friend of mine was Alan Greenhalgh, whose wife Molly was suffering from what they thought was ME. I told Alan about the book, as I knew he'd be interested. I lent it to him and, after reading it with the same kind of fascination I'd felt, he mentioned it to his doctor, whom I'll call Dr. A, who also wished to read the book. After a few weeks Alan told me that his doctor wished to meet me to discuss a business proposition, which intrigued me. We arranged a meeting at Dr. A's General Practice surgery one evening and I was surprised to find two other men present. One was Ron, a motor body repairer businessman, and the other was Mr. Patel, a pharmacist.

Dr. A's proposal was that we set up a new company called Chronobiology Ltd., trading as the Complete Hormone Clinic. We would advertise our unique services in the quality press such as County Magazines to attract reasonably well-off clients who wished to improve their quality of life and life expectancy by taking expensively procured hormone supplements. He, as the doctor, would apply the tests to determine the patient's requirements and Mr. Patel would apply for a licence to import the products into the UK. As UK law only permitted hormones to be supplied against a prescription, Dr. A would privately prescribe the hormones and the prescription would be filled by Mr. Patel's pharmacy. The patient would pay for the hormones at a price which afforded a handsome profit. The business would operate from rented rooms on Chorley New Road, an area where many prestigious professional offices were located. We would each own 25% of the new company, which was expected to be very profitable according to the projections. Dr. A would supply his medical expertise on a part-time basis and would be paid on a pro rata basis for his time. whilst the other three partners would each contribute £25,000 to supply the initial working capital needs of the business.

The business was set up as discussed and employed Doreen, Ron's wife, as a part-time receptionist/telephonist. For a time, everything seemed to be going to plan. We each received a monthly management report which showed the number of patients seen and the value of hormones prescribed. The beauty of this business was that the patient had to pay £120 or so for the initial consultation and evaluation and then a monthly fee for his or her supply of hormone pills. The pills were not available from any other pharmacy and, once a patient was convinced of the benefit of the treatment, we would achieve an indefinite stream of revenue. It was beautiful. We were bringing wonderful benefits to our patients and making good profits for the business. Our customers in the main were healthy, well-off, middle aged, well educated people from the North West who wanted to remain healthy and were prepared to pay reasonable amounts to gain an edge in life's lottery.

However, Dr. A was a medical practitioner, not a businessman, and all of his instinct and training led him to want to treat sick people and make them better. The business gradually gravitated away from being a money-making exercise to being a clinic which would treat all manner of sick people who could benefit from hormone treatment, whether or not they could afford the exclusive services we were offering. Inevitably, the revenues of the clinic declined and Dr. A was drawing more in his salary than we were earning from patients. Ron and I regularly reminded him that he had a responsibility to the shareholders to run the clinic responsibly as a business, with the primary aim of making money. Dr. A repeatedly assured us that he'd do that in future but it didn't happen. After a couple of years we were forced to close the doors on what could have been a very interesting venture. I'd had visions that we'd have Complete Hormone Clinic surgeries in every major town and city in the UK and I'm still convinced that it could have happened with the right motivation from our medical practitioner. I couldn't help thinking that nipping into Barnes and Noble on a freezing winter day in Chicago had resulted in completely unforeseen consequences. On such turns of fortune are business empires created. But not on this occasion.

One of our steadier hire items was a range of products called machinery moving skates. A machine which had to be moved would be jacked up using hydraulic or mechanical jacks to a height of a few inches. The set of four skates would be positioned at each of the four corners before the jacks then lowered the machine onto the skates. A Tirfor or other pulling device would then haul the machine to its required position. We had almost exclusively used a make of skate called Verrolec, but recently a newer British design had been launched by a likeable engineer called Bob Pooler. Bob was successful in convincing LGH to stock his products and I got to know him quite well. Unusually, Bob's hobby and passion was flying light aircraft and one day he asked to see me to put a business proposition to me.

He explained that there was quite a big disparity between the US and the UK in the cost of light aircraft. They were about 30% cheaper in America and he had a chance to buy a second-hand twin engined six seater Beechcraft Baron for £75,000, which would sell easily in Britain for over £100,000. The problem was that he hadn't access to that kind of money. If I'd fund the initial purchase, Bob would organise everything and we would split the profit. It seemed easy so I agreed, with further provisos: between the time we bought the plane and subsequently sold it we would hire it out on a charter basis and I'd get half of the revenue, and I would also be entitled to the free use of the plane for eight hours per month with Bob as the pilot. I drew up a legal agreement which also gave me a charge over the plane if Bob, for whatever reason, failed to repay the £75,000 loan capital within a specified time scale. The loan also carried interest charges which I thought would encourage Bob to sell the plane quickly. Bob went ahead with the purchase and had the plane flown from America to England using a professional delivery pilot via

Iceland and Greenland. He obtained the necessary Certificate of Airworthiness but didn't seem to be in a hurry to sell it.

He was very happy to fly around in his own personal plane for a few months whilst keeping his part in the bargain of flying me on business trips to Aberdeen, Amsterdam, Milan and other destinations. It was wonderful to have a very smart private plane and pilot at my disposal, but the original objective of making a quick profit was not being met. I started to put pressure on Bob to find a buyer as soon as possible. I reminded him that interest charges were building up and I needed to recover LGH's £75,000. Then he hit me with the news that the recent recession in the UK had seriously damaged the market for second-hand aircraft. Not only had he failed to sell at a good profit as promised but it was now looking unlikely that he could even recover the original purchase price. Eventually, after a lot of pressure from me, he found a buyer and took a hefty loss. He paid by cheque to LGH part of what he owed in capital and accumulated interest charges. We took the balance in kind and Bob was supplying us with 'free' machinery moving skates for a few years after this venture. It was like playing at being millionaires for a few years, with the use of a private plane, but the novelty soon wore off and I realised that small aircraft, even a sporty Beechcraft Baron, were not very fast; most journeys could be made more quickly and considerably more cheaply by scheduled flights from main airports.

This chapter has been somewhat painful to write, as the recollections I've needed to make have reminded me forcibly of my own fallibility, not to mention stupidity, naiveté and gullibility. However, I console myself with the thought that I've managed to have many more winners than losers in my career to date, and all of the losers have been manageable at the time of their impact. My main businesses were never threatened with failure as a result of these adventures. I love Rudyard Kipling's poem *If* and, in fact, I had a framed print of it on my office wall for years. But I could never put myself in the position which he advocates in the verse which goes:-

> *If you can make one heap of all your winnings*
> *And risk it on one turn of pitch-and-toss,*
> *And lose, and start again at your beginnings*
> *And never breathe a word about your loss.......*
> *You'll be a Man, my son!*

Chapter 29 - Grandchildren

The 1990s were significant to Irene and me, not only for the excitement of starting a US business and seeing dramatic growth in our UK businesses but also because this was the decade during which our family grew.

Our first grandchild was born to Ian and Jayne in 1994. Much to my delight, he was a grandson. I was even more delighted when they did me the honour of naming him William. Then, in 1996, it was Lorraine's turn to become a mother. She and Gordon became the proud parents of our first grand-daughter, named Bethany. Then, a year later, it was Ian and Jayne's turn again, when their second son James was born. Our third grandson, Conor, was born in 1999 to complete Lorraine and Gordon's family.

Steven, our younger son, moved to San José in California and has not married. He has now become an American citizen but it's looking increasingly unlikely that we'll have any American grandchildren any time soon. Ian and Jayne separated in 2005 and subsequently divorced. This was a harrowing time for all the family, especially the two boys, who have now grown into fine young men.

All four of our grandchildren passed the Bolton School entrance examination and took up their places there. As I write this, William is working for his father, using his computer skills in various projects for our companies and attending college part time. His brother James is in his final year at school, where he is preparing to take A level exams and hoping to gain a University place later in the year. His cousin Bethany is just completing her first year at Liverpool University, where she's studying Psychology, and her brother Conor is preparing to sit his GCSE exams this summer.

We're thrilled to have four wonderful grandchildren, who are a credit to their parents. Ian and Lorraine are devoted, caring and loving parents who have the children they deserve.

Chapter 30 - Steady Growth

With a solid and experienced management team in place within the LGH branch network, we were able to maintain a consistent growth in revenues up to the millennium. Excluding the non-LGH subsidiary companies and overseas operations, our revenue grew steadily from £3,770,000 in 1985 to £19,699,000 fifteen years later. This represented an average compound growth rate of over 12% per annum which, although not matching our earlier exponential growth rate, was quite acceptable, given that we were operating in what was now a mature market with many competitors.

It proved much more difficult to maintain a similar growth in group profits. Some of our subsidiary companies, especially NIM Engineering were incurring heavy losses. Tickhill Plant, which we sold at about this time, was also under-performing, and the anticipated investment in the nation's sewage infrastructure failed to materialise. Our Group profits plateaued at between £1.5m and £1.8m per annum, which was very frustrating, as I felt that we were working very hard to stand still and, in business terms, if you're standing still you're really going backwards.

Chapter 31 - Suspended Access

In July 1997 we were offered the chance to buy a small London based business called Kobi Maintenance Ltd. Everyone has seen what are popularly called 'window-cleaners' cradles' on high-rise buildings in cities. These cradles, the hoists which move them and the roof-top beams which support them are called 'suspended access equipment'. The safety standards for this type of equipment are necessarily very stringent to minimise the risk of accidents to the operators, who use the cradles to access the exteriors of high buildings for maintenance and cleaning purposes. Kobi offered a very specialised inspection and maintenance service aimed at suspended access equipment.

After a thorough evaluation, we bought the business, which was nearly breaking even at the time. We were encouraged by the fact that there was a close affinity between lifting equipment and suspended access equipment. We were very familiar with the engineering principles and could readily appreciate the legal requirements. When we bought the NIM business from Darrell Pickup in 1992, we also acquired a young graduate management trainee called Anton Lavery. Anton had been involved in various projects within our business for the past five years and had acquitted himself very competently. The Kobi acquisition gave us the opportunity to let Anton prove his worth in the cut and thrust of running a business and he took up the position of manager.

The basic trick to maximising results in this business was to sign up customers to a rolling maintenance contract in order to reduce reliance on one off jobs. The work for customers on the contract terms could be scheduled to ensure that the maintenance staff were continuously occupied and, as one job was completed, another job started. Anton proved to be particularly adept in scheduling the work effectively and also in winning new business. The new addition to our widening business portfolio was soon generating healthy growth in revenues and profits.

One of our London based branch managers was Colin Midson, who had succeeded Paul Fulcher as manager at North Thames. This branch seemed to be a golden chalice, bringing good fortune to all who managed it, and Colin was no exception. He'd achieved excellent results and, following the NIM deal, we offered him the chance to move to Alfreton and take charge of the substantial NIM Sales and Hire operation. We had placed the Kobi business under Colin's umbrella and Anton reported to him. Colin and Anton were very ambitious, which of course I encouraged, and they soon saw the limitations of restricting our suspended access activities to the maintenance and servicing aspects only. The possibility of also offering to design, supply and install the equipment was looking increasingly appealing and lucrative. Instead of servicing a cradle for a few hundred pounds, we could be selling and installing the full kit for tens or even hundreds of thousand pounds. When they found a New Zealand based company called Farra Engineering, who were looking for a northern hemisphere distributor for their state-of-the-art suspended access equipment, it seemed that the circle was completed. Colin prepared a business plan, which he presented to the Board. It promised massive rewards and stunning growth opportunities. It was a compelling argument which wouldn't, it seemed, require much by way of capital investment and we tentatively gave Colin the support to enter negotiations with Farra.

Farra's M.D., Eoin Orr, came to the UK to meet us and assess our capability for fulfilling the demanding role of selling their superb range of equipment, which was completely different in concept from the existing crude hoist and cradle designs. Farra had brought suspended access into the high tech era by incorporating highly sophisticated, computer controlled, retractable swinging cantilever arms into their designs. They could be fitted to virtually any high rise building, whatever the profile, and could even be fitted to sloping roofs. They were considerably more expensive than conventional cradles, but the technical advantages were tremendous. We were very confident that we could successfully sell the Farra cradles and, with the amount of new construction work evident all around London, we couldn't wait to get started.

We renamed Kobi Maintenance as NIM Suspended Access and signed an agreement with Farra, which gave us the distribution rights for the whole of the northern hemisphere, excluding Hong Kong, which was already covered by another distributor. We appointed Paul Coleman, an experienced suspended access designer, to manage this side of the business and, together, he and Anton approached all the architectural and design consultancies and construction companies who were active in the city.

It was slow at first, but they managed to gain a few enquiries for this new technology. We expected it to be difficult because there were no reference sites to show to potential customers, and this proved to be the case until, eventually, by cutting margins to the bone, they clinched the first order. This was valued at £150,000, which was one of the biggest single orders which we'd ever received. Only NIM Engineering had occasionally secured larger contracts. Paul designed the installation to the customer's specification and liaised closely with the Farra design team. The order was placed and, when the finished package arrived from New Zealand, we hired extra men on a temporary basis to supplement our own fitters, who would be responsible for the installation on the roof of the customer's new building.

It was a big learning curve for Paul and Anton and the installation team, who had no experience in this new technology, and there were inevitable over-runs in time and cost terms. When the job was finished we had a very satisfied customer and a superb reference site to show to subsequent potential clients. However, we were also left nursing a hefty loss on this first contract. I wasn't too concerned about the loss as I was confident that, now they had experience, the team's performance would dramatically improve and, furthermore, now that we could demonstrate the superb specification of the kit it would not be necessary to offer discounts on the price.

Unfortunately, my optimism was soon to be destroyed, as we continued to win contracts and continued to incur alarmingly large losses. The management team of Colin, Paul and Anton apportioned blame everywhere but themselves. They accused customers of changing specifications at the last minute, Farra of failing to manufacture in accordance with designs, installation engineers of failing to understand the technicalities of the equipment and a host of other problems outside of their control.

Some of the contracts they were obtaining were very large by our standards, with an average value of over £250,000 and the largest, at Canary Wharf, worth over £500,000. It seemed that the larger the contract the bigger the losses incurred. It took us two years to realise that these losses were endemic and wouldn't be eliminated without major surgery. To our consternation, there was a string of new contracts in the pipe-line which we had won in competitive bidding processes. Orders had been placed with Farra with lead times of up to a year. Also, we were committed to continue maintaining the equipment which had already been installed for at least a further two years. It wasn't possible just to close down the operation and walk away licking our wounds.

Earlier in this business, before we'd become aware of the extent of the losses, Colin, Paul and Anton had made a presentation to the Board which was a proposal to open a subsidiary company in the USA to serve the huge suspended access market there, particularly in New York and Chicago. Their enthusiasm for this new venture was infectious and they were confident of building a business in the USA which would soon dwarf the parent company. The fact that LGH already had a presence in Chicago and other American cities would undoubtedly help to get the new project off the ground quickly. Thankfully, my fellow directors and I urged caution and we promised to support the proposed American venture only when they had proved that they could run the UK venture profitably.

We had no option but to close down this business, as the extent of the losses was seriously affecting the Group results. The closure had to be carefully phased so that we could complete our contractual obligations whilst minimising costs. Colin resigned in order to start up a competing hire business in London and Paul and Anton were made redundant. We were finally able to close the door on what had been a very difficult episode in our company's history. The original suspended access maintenance business is now called Rotrex On Site and is still one of our Group of businesses. It continues to trade successfully in London under the capable management of John Aytoe, who I'm sure will never suggest to me that we should get involved in the installation business!

Chapter 32 - Health Issues

Apart from my serious car accident in 1973 and Steve's jaw problems in 1989, our family had been remarkably healthy. However, in 1999, whilst on holiday in Menorca, Irene discovered a small, firm but squishy lump in her neck. On our return home we arranged to see a general surgeon in the local private Beaumont Hospital in Bolton. Within a couple of days he had removed the lump, which was an enlarged lymph node, and sent it for a biopsy report. This revealed that Irene was suffering from non-Hodgkin Lymphoma, a type of blood cancer.

There are thirty five different non-Hodgkin Lymphomas, with different symptoms, characteristics and effects. We were told to expect that, in addition to the small lump which had been surgically removed, there would almost certainly be another tumour, possibly on an organ such as liver, lung, kidney etc. Extensive tests and scans didn't reveal the existence of anything more sinister and the decision was taken not to administer any treatment. How can you treat a condition which can't be detected? Irene was assigned to the Christie Hospital in Manchester, the north-west's pre-eminent specialist cancer facility. She continued to have regular monitoring under Christie's Dr. Welch, who saw her at our local Royal Bolton Hospital. She was regularly given a clean bill of health and it seemed that she'd been incredibly fortunate not to have developed more serious symptoms when, in 2008, another lump was discovered, low down in her neck, near the collar bone.

Again, the lump was surgically removed and now Irene was placed in the care of specialist Lymphoma Oncologist, Dr. (later Professor) Cowan. He explained that this time it would be necessary for Irene to receive treatment. The favoured option was a course of chemotherapy, with all of the dreaded complications and side effects. We were resigned to this when Dr. Cowan told us of an extensive clinical trial of a revolutionary new treatment in which the Christie were one of the leading research hospitals taking part in the trial. He explained that Irene's medical profile and diagnosis exactly fitted the patient requirements for the trial. He gave us plenty of semi-technical reading matter explaining the principles of the new treatment, which had been given the nick-name The Magic Bullet.

In essence, the patient would receive an intravenous drip containing a chemical called Rituximab. This had a strong affinity for cancer cells, to which it would attach itself. Then, a week later, the patient would receive another intravenous drip, this time containing a radioactive chemical which had a strong affinity for the Rituximab. Thus the radioactive chemical would be directed only to the body's cancel cells, where it would hopefully do its job by killing the cancer cells without affecting the vast majority of healthy cells. After carefully reading all of the information, we came to the conclusion that this was an amazing opportunity to be at the cutting edge of medical science and Irene was incredibly lucky to have such a chance. She joined the trial as one of eighty such patients at the Christie. In Irene's case, the treatment was wonderfully effective and the spread of Lymphoma was halted in its tracks, without the usual side effects associated with other treatments. The clinical trial received widespread publicity at the time, including TV coverage. The drugs involved are extremely expensive and the drug manufacturers supported the very high cost of the clinical trial. Now, with the benefit of being able to evaluate the results of a large number of trial patients, I'm not sure whether or not the Magic Bullet will be widely available.

Now, six years after undergoing the revolutionary Magic Bullet treatment, Irene's lymphoma has returned, this time in the form of diffuse large B-cell lymphoma, which is more aggressive than the original follicular variety. This time she will have to undergo chemo-therapy and, as I write this, she is about to start her treatment. It's a fifteen week course which will clearly affect our lives, but the prognosis is good for a complete recovery and Irene is optimistic and in good spirits.

Chapter 33 - Banking Woes

My old bank manager and friend, Ron Gleave, had retired from NatWest some years earlier and subsequently died where he would have probably chosen - on the golf course. We then experienced one or two different managers, none of whom became involved in our business until NatWest decided to transfer our account from their Atherton Branch to the Manchester City Regional Office, at which point Steve Hall was appointed as our 'relationship manager'. The transition was seamless as far as we were concerned and we established a good relationship with Steve, built on regular meetings between him and Simon.

In the late 1990s, NatWest made some ill-advised forays into areas of business of which they had little knowledge, such as insurance - a bit like our venture into suspended access installation. Investors lost confidence in the bank and their share price collapsed. The much smaller Royal Bank of Scotland, which at the time could do no wrong, mounted an aggressive and hostile opportunistic take-over bid which, after an intense battle, was successful in the year 2000. For a time, there was no noticeable change in our banking relationships. For over thirty years, as I grew my business, the bank had always supported us, safe in the knowledge that our term loans and overdraft facilities were secured by a strong balance sheet full of valuable capital assets such as plant and freehold buildings, not to mention several million pounds worth of debtors, representing the amounts owed by our customers. Then in the summer of 2003, Simon received a 'phone call late one Friday afternoon from Steve Hall, who was on holiday at the time, to inform him that he, Steve, had been relieved of the responsibility of acting as our relationship manager and our account would henceforth be administered by a department of the bank called Specialised Lending Services (SLS). We could expect a visit from them on Monday morning. At the time we had no idea of the massive and horrible consequences which would result from such a seemingly innocuous modification of our relationship with the bank.

As I made clear in the previous chapter, the losses incurred by our ill-fated venture into suspended access installation had affected our Group profits. In addition, NIM Engineering was still performing erratically as we prepared to sell this business. This was also not helping our overall results, although they nevertheless remained in the black. When companies arrange borrowings with their bankers they have to agree to 'covenants' which introduce conditions upon which the bank consents to make the agreed loans available. These covenants have to be approved by the borrowing company and can involve such items as profitability, liquidity, nett asset value, interest cover etc. We were deemed to have breached our interest cover covenant, which gave the bank the option to take us out of the mainstream banking regime and put us under the SLS umbrella. The interest cover term meant that we had to generate profits which were at least equal to a certain ratio (say three times) of the annual interest charges made by the bank against our borrowings. So, this was fair enough, we were in breach of the covenants and the bank were perfectly within their rights to make this change. What we were not prepared for, though, was the brutal way in which these new hatchet men would try to decimate our business.

Over the course of the next few weeks the SLS staff, led by a man called Andrew Bruce, effectively rewrote our balance sheet and revalued our assets in a massively negative way. Our main assets were our plant equipment. We had over 50,000 items of beautifully maintained lifting equipment which had cost £21 million and would have cost over £30 million to replace. Mr. Bruce said that in a forced sale in an auction this plant, in his view, would only bring £250,000 maximum. He was a banker, what did he know about lifting equipment? And why judge the value on the basis of a forced sale? We had no intention of selling off our equipment in any kind of sale, especially a forced one. There was no argument, no negotiation. At a stroke he'd devastated our balance sheet.

Our American business was performing very well at that time and was a significant asset, as a wholly owned subsidiary, on our balance sheet. In Mr. Bruce's view, because it was located in a foreign country, it was worthless from his perspective and its value was removed from our balance sheet. The rewritten balance sheet now showed that we were technically insolvent, which triggered a sequence of measures from the bank, made possible because of their very questionable manoeuvring. First, they recalled a £500,000 term loan which had been agreed a year or so earlier. The loan was set up to last for seven years with an interest rate tied to the Bank of England base rate (i.e. 2.5% over base). Their manipulation of our balance sheet gave them the right to arbitrarily cancel this loan agreement on which we were reliant and which we'd been confident would be in place until maturity.

I was stunned that they could do this and had to mortgage my house in order to raise the money to pay off this loan. I'd spent years paying off my mortgage and now, at the age of over sixty, I had a bigger mortgage than ever. The next bombshell came when they cancelled our agreed £1.2 million overdraft facility, giving us only a few days to comply. I should stress that in over thirty years we'd never exceeded our overdraft facility without the prior approval of the bank, had never missed a single payment to their Lombard North Central finance house, which had handled thousands of HP transactions for us over the years, and had never missed a loan repayment or interest payment deadline. The only way we could quickly raise the cash required to repay our overdraft was to 'sell' our debtors.

Every company that, like us, sells on credit is owed several weeks or months worth of turnover. The bank would arrange what they called Invoice Discounting, whereby they were deemed to own the debt and would advance a percentage of the value to us at comparatively punitive interest rates. This had always been an option for us to raise funds in the past but I'd always resisted because I felt that the increased administrative effort and increased interest costs were not justified. Now, though, we were left with no option. Then, this greedy, heartless bunch of villains told us that in order for them to continue to 'support' us then they would require an equity stake in two of our most valuable freehold properties, the Atherton site and our Alfreton property called Gryphon Works. This meant that at maturity, in ten years time, RBS would be entitled to 10% of the value of these properties at that time. Barefaced robbery!

Finally, they required a massive personal guarantee from me to complete their watertight arrangements. I well remember attending a meeting in the SLS offices in Manchester and had to sit there listening to this know-all banker, who'd never had his hands dirty in his life, telling me that the business which I'd painstakingly built up during the past thirty years was worthless. I was livid, smashed the desk with my fist and shouted at him, "I'm not sitting here listening to this crap." I dashed out of the meeting, never to return. I left Simon to conclude the painful business. I'm sure that if I'd stayed I'd have strangled the RBS man with my bare hands. Our first instinct, of course, was to leave RBS and find another bank who were more sympathetic to our cause. However, within banking circles there seemed to be a code which said that once you were in SLS no other bank could take your account. So we were stuck with RBS, whom I grew to hate with a vengeance. One final condition that RBS imposed was that they insisted on appointing a non-executive director to our Board to report to them at our expense!

The next two years were extremely difficult as we continued to grow the business within a framework of limited financial resources whilst presenting a calm and untroubled face to staff, suppliers, customers and competitors. Simon handled the strained relationship with the

SLS people very professionally and, after two years of this severe discipline, we were returned to the conventional banking regime. This episode hurt me very much and for a time I became very disillusioned with the whole procedure of running a business. It was only a few years later, following the banking collapse of 2008, that I realised that all of these harsh measures which were implemented by RBS in 2003/4 were as a direct consequence of their problems, not ours. They were systematically squeezing every penny they could from their customers, using every subterfuge at their disposal. Following the collapse of the banking system, the Government conducted a review, which was particularly critical of Fred 'the shred' Goodwin, RBS's CEO. I, for one, shed no tears.

Chapter 34 - For Sale

Our elder son, Ian, had been working hard in the business, utilising his unique combination of talents to excellent effect. He was particularly strong in technical areas relating to the application of computers and mobile devices. He had developed an intranet based system which ensured that each branch and subsidiary company in the Group could communicate easily and economically with each other. Customers too, could be involved in this revolutionary communication method. He also developed a sales reporting system based on the Blackberry mobile device. Up to that point, sales representatives had made hand-written weekly reports to their branch managers, with copies going to Carol Slane as National Sales Manager. Following Ian's development of the Blackberry-based system, the representative would input his report after every sales call and the data would be instantly downloaded to a data base, which prepared and stored invaluable sales information. On similar lines, he also developed a site inspection reporting facility, also based on the hand-held Blackberry device. This saved a massive amount of time in both the recording of inspection data and the production of voluminous inspection reports, which often contained the records of hundreds of items of a customer's lifting equipment.

Once we'd grown to about twenty branches, it became more difficult to evaluate the best options for the location of the next branch in our inexorable march towards global domination. If we looked at a map of the UK showing all of our existing branches, there were gaps which were looking very inviting. But if it was possible, because of cash and management resources limitations, to open only one branch, would it be better to open in Nottingham or Port Talbot, Oldham or Crawley, Hull or Coventry? It was always a matter of opinion, until Ian designed a mathematical model to analyse available data from the industries that were our main customers.

The model measured many parameters and, using a mathematical technique known as 'multiple regression', assigned a numerical value to the potential of each town in the UK which was more than 25 Km from an existing LGH branch. Ian then produced a 'hit' list of these towns, which gave our Operations Directors the most accurate guidance when planning a new branch. I remember discussing Ian's work in this sphere with the Sales Manager of a competitor, who had about eight branches, and he said, "Ah, we don't bother with all that scientific stuff. We just look where you've got a branch and then open up close to that".

It's not always easy being the boss's son or daughter. To promote Ian ahead of some of his colleagues could have caused resentment and he was always conscious of the need to justify his position by producing exemplary and innovative work. When the opportunity arose, it was not difficult to appoint him to a Board position, where his keen analytical logic proved to be a great asset to many of our deliberations. When I decided to retire as Chairman of the business on my 65th birthday, in 2005, it was easy to hand over this most senior management role to Ian, who at the time was 39 years old. I asked all of the Head Office staff at Atherton to gather in the general administration office, where I made a little speech to thank everyone for their contributions to the success of the company, then I invited Ian to become Chairman of the Group, which by then consisted of 34 LGH branches, wholly owned subsidiaries in Holland and Germany, ten branches of LGH Corporation in the USA and several wholly owned subsidiaries, altogether employing about 550 staff. Ian responded with his own short speech, in which he thanked me for having the confidence in him to appoint him to such a responsible job then said, "I've only one more thing to say Dad. Will you please move your car out of my parking bay?"

Although our banking arrangements were now back on a conventional footing, the severe financial constraints under which we had been working for the previous three years had made things difficult for the UK branch network. Capital expenditure had been cut to a minimum and pay rises had been sparse. There were also signs that some competitors were getting stronger and more aggressive. Allen Bros., the Wigan based building company who had designed and built our Head Office building, and Atherton branch, had some years earlier started a tool hire business which they called Speedy Hire. It had a single branch in Wigan, mainly serving their own building company's needs. Allen's had become a publicly quoted company with access to investment funds from the stock market and, when their design and build company encountered problems, they put much of their resources into building up the Speedy Hire business.

They achieved rapid growth by a combination of opening new branches and pursuing an aggressive acquisition strategy. They actively and deliberately diversified into lifting equipment hire, but I was confident that they couldn't compete with us. However, they proceeded to go for our customers with offers of hefty discounts, then started to poach some of our key senior staff. First, Philip Prince our Marketing Manager, was enticed away and then Tony Longmire, our Technical Director, joined them. The really worrying news, though, was that they opened up a branch close to our Crawley Branch in South London. They made all of our staff there offers they couldn't refuse and we lost everyone to Speedy, from the manager to the driver. Then the same thing happened at Hull. This was war!

Unfortunately, I had to accept that it was a war that we were ill-equipped to fight. Our trading losses from the suspended access debacle and our NIM Engineering problems, followed by the RBS treatment, had left us with a weakened balance sheet, which meant that we had no chance of aggressively battling a company with almost unlimited resources. Before I retired, Ian and I had discussed the options and had reluctantly agreed that the best way to save the company and the jobs of our staff would be to sell the UK business whilst some value remained.

Chapter 35 - The Sale Process

We appointed Manchester based specialist Mergers and Acquisitions professionals, Rickitt Mitchell, to help us to sell the UK LGH business. With a lot of input from Simon and Ian they prepared a portfolio describing the unique business, with lots of current and historical financial data. Matthew Bridon Smith, one of their senior partners, was responsible for our account and he would guide us through what was a very painful experience for me. It felt as if I was selling my offspring which, in effect, I was. Matthew rigorously researched the UK industrial scene to find potential buyers and eventually drew up a list for our consideration. I was not surprised to see Speedy figuring prominently on this list. Not only had they demonstrated keen ambitions to develop their business into the lifting gear field, but they had been aggressively buying competitors in other specialist areas such as power generation, scaffolding, portable accommodation and more. They had the resources and the ambition to complete the deal. I didn't particularly like their business and some of their senior management behaved more like London barrow boys than reputable businessmen, but I had to admit that they presented the best chance of obtaining a reasonable price for our business.

Ian and I arranged to meet Speedy's CEO, John Brown, and Andrew Simpson, their Financial Director, for lunch at Standish Court Golf Club. When I told them that we were contemplating selling the UK business they seemed genuinely amazed as they were resigned to facing a long battle with us for a decent share of the lifting equipment hire market and here I was offering them the opportunity to become market leaders immediately. However, as they had become our main competitor and a deal with them was far from certain, we were reluctant to let them have sensitive information which wasn't already in the public domain. Ideally, we needed to have two or three other companies, preferably PLCs, to show a serious interest, so we could have a competitive bidding process. Ashtead (A Plant) and HSS had previously made approaches to us and we were hopeful that they would show some serious interest but, for various reasons, this proved not to be the case and we were left trying to negotiate a good price from Speedy without the benefit of a stalking horse.

Increasingly, Ian was taking the leading role on our side during the talks, with Matthew Bridon-Smith providing support in the form of statistical and financial information, whilst hinting to Speedy that other bidders were waiting in the wings. There were several potential stumbling blocks to overcome. One of our most significant UK subsidiaries was NIM Winches, which operated from Alfreton with branches in Aberdeen, London and Glasgow. This was a very successful winch hire business with significant off-shore revenues and a buoyant on-shore trade, based mainly on the utilities industries such as telecoms, electricity distribution, gas and water. We owned some of the biggest winches available for hire anywhere in the world, including several 100 ton and a 200 ton capacity winch. Three of our 100 ton winches had been used by the Dutch salvage company, Mammoet, in 2000, to help recover the stricken Russian submarine Kursk from the bottom of the Barents Sea. The question was whether or not this type of large plant would fit into Speedy's ambition of becoming a one stop shop for their customers' every need. It didn't take Speedy long to decide that they didn't have the appetite for the technical nature of winch hire and we readily removed this option from the table.

Another major problem was our final-salary-based pension scheme, which had been in existence since the early 1970s. I'd set up the scheme originally to provide good pensions for our staff. The company and the employee each contributed 5% of salary into the central pot and the employee could expect a pension on retirement which was proportional to his or her length of service and final salary. The scheme had been fully funded for many years, so there was more than enough money in the pot to pay all the anticipated pensions. But then a series of adverse influences started to impinge on the health of all such pension schemes.

Firstly, Gordon Brown, when he was Chancellor of the Exchequer, removed the tax exemption on dividend income, which had previously been the norm for pension schemes. This massively affected the investment returns, on which we were reliant. Then successive actuarial charts showed that life expectancy was increasing, which meant that our pensioners could expect, on average, to collect their pensions for longer, so the pot would have to be even bigger. For a number of years in the 1990s, investment returns from the stock market were below the anticipated levels, which also negatively affected our funding.

Then we were required to inflation-proof the pension payments. This made further demands on the funds. We also had to equalise the benefits for men and women, which added to the problems. Despite the fact that we had recognised the problems and had closed the scheme in 1999, we still had a responsibility to pay the pensions that had accrued up to that time. Increased contributions from both employees and employer had made little impact on the deficit, which was now calculated to be over two million pounds. Not surprisingly, Speedy insisted that they would not take on responsibility for the pension scheme, which would remain as a problem for the shareholders.

Speedy's senior management changed half way through the protracted negotiations, with long-time CEO John Brown retiring and Andrew Simpson leaving them to join Peel Holdings. They were replaced by Steve Corcoran and Mike McGrath respectively. Eventually, after many months of hard negotiating by Ian and Matthew, a deal was made for Speedy to acquire the entire share capital of Lifting Gear Hire Ltd., which by then operated from thirty four branches in the UK for a total consideration of £13.5 million. The shareholders comprised Irene and me, together with our three children, Ian, Lorraine and Steven. The agreement excluded the five freehold properties at Atherton, Doncaster, Woolwich, Glasgow and Bristol. We formed a new business called Parkinson Property Partnership (PPP) to administer the properties, which were leased out to Speedy. The name of NIM Winches was changed to Rotrex Group and the suspended access maintenance business became Rotrex On Site.

It was necessary to gain the agreement of the Pensions Regulator, who could have blocked the deal if he felt that the pension scheme would be jeopardised. In the end, the shareholders had to pay over £1.0 million into the pension scheme to reduce the deficit and we had to pledge that future profits of Rotrex Group would be used to further reduce the deficit. We also had to pay a further £1.0 million into an escrow account, which was retained for five years as a guarantee that Rotrex would generate the profits to provide the promised contributions. Our lawyers, Eversheds, our professional advisers, PriceWaterhouseCoopers and our agents, Rickitt Mitchell, all took very hefty fees and we were faced with high levels of taxation. There were disputes with Speedy over the volume and value of our plant fleet, which also reduced the agreed consideration, so the final figure received by the shareholders was significantly less than we'd hoped or expected. Our consolation was that we retained Rotrex Group and our Dutch, German and US wholly owned Lifting Gear Hire businesses. This would prove to be hugely significant over the next few years.

Chapter 36 - Moorhouse's Brewery

I've covered the acquisition of Moorhouse's Brewery and the early problems in Chapter 19. The recovery from the first few disastrous years was massively helped by the Beer Orders legislation, which enabled us to offer our products into the pubs owned by the big six brewers and the very large chains of pubs which had been sold off by the big six as a result of this legislation.

Our first pub, The General Scarlett, had proved to be successful, not only as a retail outlet for our products but also as a profitable business in its own right, with a young married couple acting as managers. This success as a pub owner encouraged us to seek to expand that aspect of the business and, during the next two or three years, we added a further five pubs to our tied estate. The business was still being managed in its entirety by my brother-in-law, Malcolm MacDonald, who had done a great job in bringing Moorhouse's back from the brink of extinction. Malcolm had always had the ambition to retire early and health issues towards the end of the 1990s meant that it became difficult for him to continue this stressful job. I started the process of recruiting a successor and, from the many applicants, chose a man called Nigel, who had been a successful beer salesman for many years. Malcolm overlapped with Nigel for a few months before retiring to Spain with my sister Joan in 1999.

Our young, talented brewer, Robert Hill, had been producing exceptionally fine beer during the 1990s and we regularly won regional and national awards, mainly at CAMRA beer festivals. Robert was then head-hunted by The Orkney Brewery to be their head brewer. I was devastated when Robert handed in his notice and tried to dissuade him from moving with his wife and two children from the familiarity of Burnley to the isolation and 'foreignness' of the Orkneys. However, he was determined to take the offer and went on to continue to brew outstanding beer. He now runs his own small brewery, with the help of his two sons. Robert was replaced as head brewer by his assistant, Peter Goldsborough, who was as different from Robert as it was possible to be.

Peter drank lager as a matter of personal choice and didn't have a taste for our real ale products. This gave me some concern, as did his abrasive attitude. However, he proved that he could brew superb beer by meticulously following the methods and recipes originated by Robert and by having rigorous standards of hygiene and cleanliness. This culminated shortly after Nigel joined us by the winning of The Champion Beer of Britain Award in 2000. That was potentially of huge significance and gave us wide publicity on which we could surely build an intense sales and marketing campaign. The Award was presented in the newly opened Millennium Dome, now 02 Arena, and I flew to London from Portugal for the presentation.

Irene and I were in Portugal on a golfing holiday, with our friends the Garsides and the Slanes, but this was the biggest event in the Brewery's history and I badly wanted to share it with my Moorhouse's colleagues. Our brand that won the Award was Black Cat, a richly flavoured very dark beer with a low alcohol content of only 3.2%. It was the first time for over twenty years that a mild beer had been declared Champion Beer of Britain. Mild sales throughout the country represented only a small percentage of total beer sales and this was our product with the lowest volume of sales, so it proved difficult to exploit the Award commercially. The impact of the win turned out to be much less significant than we'd hoped and, after a few weeks of increased Black Cat sales, things returned to normal at the Brewery.

By 2001 it was becoming clear that Nigel was struggling to make the transition from being a sales representative to having responsibility for the management of the whole business and he readily agreed when I suggested that we should bring in someone else to take

Moorhouse's to the next level. Nigel had been chosen from a final short list of three candidates; I could recall that one of the other two had given a very good account of himself and had nearly been offered the job two years earlier. I still had the application details and my interview notes, which I retrieved and re-examined. The man in question was called David Grant and he lived in my old home town of Ramsbottom. When I called him, he readily agreed to see me in his local pub, The Shoulder of Mutton.

David was working in a senior but narrow capacity for Marstons and saw this as a rare opportunity to take full managerial responsibility for a complete brewing business. We agreed terms and he joined Moorhouse's as General Manager, with the promise of a Board appointment if things went well. During the next few years, David worked incredibly hard, throwing himself into the challenge of building the Moorhouse's brand into one which was recognised nationally. He was first to arrive in the morning and last to leave at night, but his relationship with our head brewer, Peter, was increasingly acrimonious.

We continued to win awards for the excellence of our products and, in 2005, exceeded my wildest hopes. This was the year of the bi-annual International Brewing and Bottling Awards and we had submitted samples in each of the three cask-conditioned (real ale) categories. The brands submitted were Premier Bitter 3.6% abv (my favourite), Pride of Pendle 4.1% abv and Pendle Witches Brew 5.0% abv. Over 180 other beers were also being judged from breweries all over the world. Premier Bitter won the Gold in its category and so did Pride of Pendle. It was almost unprecedented for the same brewery to win two gold medals but the biggest test was still to come. The three gold medalists, of which we had two, were judged against each other to determine the overall International Champion Beer. The announcement of the final results and the presentation of awards were made in the historic Guild Hall in London. The cask-conditioned category was considered the blue riband of the industry and we waited with bated breath for the announcement of the winner. I couldn't believe it when the Chairman of the Judges announced Pride of Pendle as the recipient of the ultimate prize. It was official, Moorhouse's Brewery (Burnley) Ltd. made the best beer in the world! The award was especially satisfying, not only because of the international standing of the competition but also because it was judged exclusively by our peers, the most respected and experience brewers in the industry.

David Grant and his sales team were able to capitalise on this success to the extent that turnover and profits at the Brewery grew satisfactorily. As I mentioned earlier, the Brewery was housed in a Victorian terraced row, with the Brewery in the middle with two small houses on one side and three on the other. With an eye on future space requirements, we'd been buying these terraced cottages as they became available and were hopeful of securing the final two imminently.

The main space requirement in a Brewery is taken up by fermentation vessels. The fermentation process takes five or six days to complete so at any given time a whole week's production is standing in the fermentation vessels. As sales grew, there were times when we didn't have enough fermentation vessels available and there was no room left to install more. Our plan was to break through the walls into the adjacent cottages to create the space for extra fermentation vessels to ease the production pressure.

Before we could implement this plan, though, we were shocked to receive a Compulsory Purchase Order (CPO) from Burnley Council for the three houses which we owned. The other two houses, which we didn't own, were also CPO'd. Much to my amazement and consternation, the Brewery building was not included in the CPO. The Council were in receipt of a European Grant for clearing the whole area, which was considered to be a slum. They were about to clear several streets of Victorian terraces but leave the dilapidated Brewery standing in the middle of the cleared area like a sore thumb. It was preposterous and, to add insult to injury, they only offered us a pittance for the three houses. I protested that these houses were commercial property to us and would have secured the future of the business on that site. The Council were adamant that they could only value them as small cottages and the compensation was calculated on that basis. Notwithstanding the fact that we'd refused their offer of compensation, they came and demolished the houses anyway one day, leaving the Brewery in the middle of a derelict site.

After a few months of further growth, it was clear that we couldn't continue in our present premises if we wished to continue to develop the business. It was increasingly looking as though we'd have to move to bigger premises, which might involve leaving Burnley. The Council didn't want that to happen and, in lieu of compensation for the CPO'd houses, offered us a large plot of the cleared land adjacent to our freehold property. This opened up an opportunity for which we weren't really prepared. Most businesses can grow incrementally. In our LGH company, for instance, we could buy new pieces of equipment or open another branch. Our brewing equipment consisted of a mash tun, a copper and about a dozen fermentation vessels together with ancillary equipment such as a boiler and hot and cold liquor tanks, with associated heat exchanger. We also had a grist mill to crush the malted barley. All of the vessels were compatible with a 25 barrel brew length, which was limiting our growth. If we could have gradually grown the brewing capacity to 30 barrels then 40 barrels then 60 barrels as sales increased, that would have been perfect, but unfortunately that was not a realistic option.

We were very optimistic for the future of Moorhouse's and, in 2008, decided to go for broke with a 100 barrel brewhouse. This meant that all the vessels used in the brewing process would have to be 100 barrel capacity and we'd need a much bigger building to house all the new equipment. David Grant liaised with builders, surveyors, brew plant manufacturers, planners, our bankers, Yorkshire Bank, and, of course, with our family shareholders. After much negotiation and hard work the plans were finalised and the finance was in place for me to be able to authorise the development of Britain's most modern brewery, involving an investment of £4.5 million.

In order not to interrupt production of beer at any time, the work was carried out in three distinct phases, which involved building the new brewhouse and commissioning the plant first, then knocking down the old brewery and finally building the administration offices and hospitality areas on the site of the newly demolished brewery. By 2011 work was completed and we now had the capacity to brew and ferment 1000 barrels of superb beer per week but the big question was - how long would it take for sales to grow to such an extent that, the investment would be justified?

I described in Chapter 19 the effects that legislation can have on the brewing industry. The Beer Orders had given us the opportunity to sell to the vast majority of the pubs in the UK, which had previously not been possible. A further dramatic piece of legislation occurred in 2002, when the then Chancellor of the Exchequer, Gordon Brown, introduced what was described as Progressive Beer Duty. This system of calculating beer duty which the brewers were required to pay on their production introduced a sliding scale. Small brewers would pay a smaller percentage of duty than the larger producers. It was recognised that small brewers need this cost benefit in order to survive against the massive international brewers, who enjoy benefits of large scale production and huge marketing budgets.

Initially, I very much welcomed this innovation and felt that Moorhouse's would greatly benefit, even though our production levels exceeded the minimum duty cut-off level. What I didn't anticipate was the incredible proliferation of micro-breweries fuelled by this significant cost advantage at the smaller end of the industry. Some of these new breweries made acceptable quality beer which they were able to sell to their local pubs at heavily discounted prices. I understand that there are now over 1,250 micro-breweries in the UK, all fighting for a share of a market which isn't growing. Against this background, Moorhouse's is faced with the task of doubling its sales in order to justify the greatly increased size of the brewing plant and it must achieve that whilst maintaining margins. As I write this in 2015, we have made great progress in growing sales but we still have a long way to go before the family shareholders are happy that their investment was worthwhile.

Chapter 37- More Health Issues

Although I 'retired' in 2005 I still take an active interest in all of our family's business interests which now comprise:-

In the UK
Rotrex Winches
Rotrex On-Site
Moorhouse's Brewery
Parkinson Property Partnership

In Holland
LGH Hijsmateeriel Verhuur BV

In Germany
LGH GmbH

In the USA
Lifting Gear Hire Corporation

My elder son, Ian, is Group Chairman and has grown very quickly into his new responsibilities. I'm happy to take a back seat and see the next generation take the businesses to new levels. It's a complex collection of businesses, operating in four different countries with three different currencies and covering several diverse sectors, but Ian has a firm grasp of the fundamental principles of each business and is confident in the management team who report to him.

This leaves me free to dabble in other interests and, in 2011, together with a close friend whom I'll call Tom for the purposes of this story, I invested in a speculative oil and gas exploration project in Texas. We were led to believe that there were about sixty investors in total, mainly British, some of whom were high profile sports stars. We received regular progress reports regarding the progress of our five or six oil well drillings. Initially, the reports, from independent surveyors, were extremely encouraging and we were easily persuaded to increase our initial investments. We were also invited to visit the site of the new development close to San Antonio. Although Tom and I had been introduced to this investment opportunity by someone we knew, and who had impeccable credentials, we were nervous that the whole proposal seemed too good to be true and we didn't trust the American principal of the scheme. He was called Wilson Rondini and he headed up Falcon Investments, who offered the chance to invest in all sorts of weird and wonderful schemes promising amazing rates of return. The chance to go to Texas and meet some other investors and see the operation in the flesh was too good to miss and in April 2012 Tom and I flew to San Antonio via Atlanta.

During the winter we'd spent a couple of months in Florida, partly in Orlando, with our children and grandchildren, and partly in Naples, in the company of friends. When we returned home in March I had some chest congestion and arranged to have a routine health check-up at the private Alexandra Hospital in Cheadle, Manchester. The doctor who prepared my report asked me if I was aware that I had a heart murmur. I hadn't been aware and, when I asked him what the implications were, he reassured me that there was no immediate concern but I should have an echocardiogram as soon as possible. This proved to be a lengthy exercise on the NHS and I had to wait about six weeks. As I'd already booked my flights to the US, my GP said that the heart murmur shouldn't cause me to alter my plans. In the event, I became very ill with severe breathing difficulty on the flight to Atlanta and even worse when we flew on to San Antonio. I could only take a cursory interest in the three day long proceedings of the investor group. I checked myself into a clinic in San Antonio, where they diagnosed that I was suffering from pneumonia and prescribed a course of antibiotics.

On my return to the UK, Irene was very concerned at my health and she and Lorraine took me to the Alexandra again, where I was referred to a cardiologist, Dr. Simon Horner, who, after administering an echocardiogram, diagnosed a prolapsed mitral valve in my heart. This meant that, as the heart pumped blood out into the body, the one-way mitral valve was failing to close properly, allowing much of the blood to be sucked back into my heart instead of circulating through the body. He told me that he'd admit me to the hospital immediately and arrange for me to have open heart surgery within a few days.

This was a massive shock, as I'd assumed that my breathing difficulties were caused by pneumonia and I'd soon be recovered. Dr. Horner explained that the mitral valve problem had been exacerbated by taking a long-haul flight. The prolonged exposure to lower atmospheric pressure in the cabin of the plane had caused a big build-up of fluid in my lungs. This caused me to suffer heart failure. On reflection, I realised that I'd been suffering similar, though not as severe, symptoms for years following long haul flights. I'd always blamed the airlines for providing dirty air in the cabins.

Dr. Horner visited me in my private room and explained that I could choose the surgeon who would perform the repair procedure to my valve. I was very much dependent on my cardiologist's advice, as I had no basis on which to make a decision, but I chose the younger option, Mr. Hassan, on the grounds that his hands were likely to be steadier and his eyes sharper than his older, more experienced colleague who was approaching retirement. The next few days were spent in getting me as fit as possible for the surgery and Mr. Hassan visited me every day to check on my progress.

On the night before the procedure was to be carried out, Mr. Hassan asked me if I had any last minute concerns or questions. I told him that I was calm and ready to face what was sure to be a big ordeal, but I also said that I didn't want to look back on this experience in a few months' time with any regrets of missed opportunities. I didn't know of anyone who had a photograph of their own heart so I asked him if it would be possible during the surgery for one of the nurses in the theatre to take a photograph, using my camera which I'd asked Irene to bring to the hospital for me, whilst I was 'opened up'. This seemed to amuse Mr. Hassan, as he'd never had such a request before, but he readily agreed. I'm so pleased that I thought to ask this, as I'm now the only person I know with a photograph of his own heart. Some people might think it gruesome or morbid but I think it's cool!

The surgery went extremely well and Mr. Hassan constructed five new 'chordae' from a very strong man-made fibre to replace the failed ligaments in my heart. As with all open heart surgery patients, my sternum had to be split down the middle and peeled back to allow the surgeon clear access to the chest cavity. The whole procedure took about six hours, during which time my heart was stopped and I was kept alive by means of a heart/lung machine which continued to supply my body with oxygenated blood. At the end, the sternal split was closed by applying sutures wrapped around the sternum through adjacent pairs of ribs.

It's usual to use wire sutures but in my case Mr. Hassan felt that the bone material of my sternum was a little on the soft side, so he thought it would be better to use a man-made fibre which wouldn't cut into the bone of the sternum. There followed gentle physiotherapy, consisting of walking 10 yards on day 1 then 20 yards on day 2, gradually building up the distance each day. After five days I was discharged from hospital with strict instructions to increase my walking distance each day - a target of one mile after a month and two miles after two months, at which point my sternal split should feel solid again.

The walking progress went very well and I was proud of the discipline which I maintained consistently. My iPhone helped tremendously with the Walkmeter App in measuring and timing my walks and recording all the data. I also enrolled in special heart patient physio classes at Royal Bolton Hospital. They were invaluable in building up strength and endurance, which had been seriously diminished for a time. Although I felt my fitness was improving, I was concerned that my sternum didn't seem to be as solid as I would have expected. It was now three months since the operation and my chest felt 'wobbly'. The two halves of the sternum would move relative to each other and it felt like my chest could burst open at any time.

I arranged to see Mr. Hassan to tell him of my concerns and he was amazed when he examined me. He told me that he'd never before had a failure of a sternal split joint and we arranged to have the procedure done again to effect a proper joining. This was done a few days later and this time wire was used but, as a double strand in order to reduce the cutting pressure on my bones. He told me after the operation that all but one of the fibre sutures had broken and my chest was being held together by a single thread. I then had to face a further three months of physio to try to recover my fitness once again. This was very disappointing after having gone through it all before and, at the age of 72, it wasn't easy. I consoled myself with the thought that I was fortunate my heart problem happened when it did. Thirty years earlier the mitral valve repair procedure wasn't available.

One of the consequences of my temporary incapacitation was that a planned house-hunting trip to Florida had to be postponed. During our two month holiday earlier in the year, in Orlando, we'd been invited to stay for three nights at the home of some Scottish friends, Gordon and Mary Morrison. Theirs was a beautiful house. located on a wonderful golf course in a gated community at Lake Nona. It was idyllic and before we left the Morrisons. I persuaded Irene to meet up with Kathy Williams, the real estate agent for Lake Nona who showed us a few properties which were for sale. We didn't do any deal at that time with Kathy, but arranged to return on a serious house-hunting trip in May.

The flights had to be cancelled, of course, and our dream of owning a house at Lake Nona had to be shelved. But not for long. We'd discussed our idea of buying a house in Florida with Ian, Lorraine and Steven and they'd become quite excited at the possibility of having an Orlando residence. As I was recuperating, they suggested to Irene and me that to wait for my full recovery would mean wasting another year. If we trusted their judgement they would be prepared to go to America and seek out the perfect property to suit the whole family. If they were successful, and a suitable house could be found fairly quickly, it would mean that Irene and I could spend that winter in Florida whilst I was convalescing, which would be perfect. So the three of them travelled to Florida that summer and found a wonderful house at Lake Nona. They concluded the complex negotiations, appointed a buyer's agent, arranged maintenance management, bought furniture where required and generally did a great job. The house is big enough for the whole family to visit us and we can also accommodate friends who care to spend time escaping the British winter. We've now spent the past three winters there and it gets better, as we've got to know our neighbours many of whom have now become friends.

Chapter 38 - The American Phenomenon

I described in Chapter 23 the start-up of our wholly owned American subsidiary, Lifting Gear Hire Corporation. On the one hand, this was a very exciting challenge, offering massive opportunity in the biggest economy in the world, but on the other hand, the sheer size of the country meant that our successful UK business model would have to be modified to a certain extent.

Branches in the UK were rarely more than fifty miles apart and it was relatively easy to pool resources of manpower, plant and transport, to offer an efficient and effective service to our customers. Also, the concept of hiring small items of relatively inexpensive lifting plant was readily accepted in the UK, but at this time was virtually unknown in the USA. Against this background, Pat Fiscelli worked hard at building up a customer base in Chicago. It was very slow at first, but Pat never lost his infectious enthusiasm and good humour, nor his confidence in the concept.

Gordon Worswick visited Chicago regularly to bolster Pat's efforts and between them they managed to establish a viable business within the first two or three years. They established a branch in Cleveland, Ohio and then another in St Louis, Missouri in a similar way to how I'd developed the UK business. However, this way of growing the business wasn't successful and the Cleveland branch was closed fairly quickly. The strategy was modified and the idea of operating warehouses throughout the country was introduced. A warehouse differed from a branch to the extent that there were no sales desk personnel or administrative staff and nor was there a branch manager. The warehouse was there merely to store and maintain equipment and to act as a base for regional distribution. All telephone calls from customers were routed through our Chicago head office, which processed all orders. Our sophisticated computer system meant that our Chicago based team knew the location and status of every piece of plant throughout the country and could confidently promise accurate delivery information to customers. This was to become increasingly important as the network of warehouses grew from coast to coast and from north to south.

In 1994, Gordon and Pat were flying back together to Chicago on a SouthWest Airlines flight from a business trip to St Louis. The drinks coasters on this airline incorporate a map of the USA and the two colleagues started to doodle on one of these coasters, imagining how future locations of LGH could be developed. They drew circles around fourteen of the major cities in the USA where they planned that LGH could possibly open warehouses at some stage in the future. Although this plan didn't exactly become the blueprint for our expansion in America, it helped Pat and Gordon to focus their efforts on opening new locations when cash-flow considerations allowed and the commercial opportunities were strong. Now, over twenty years after that fateful flight, we're about to open our twentieth location and the coaster is displayed in pride of place in a frame at our head office building in Chicago.

Although I received the monthly management reports and visited Chicago occasionally, I rarely became involved in the day-to-day decision making. However, I remember taking a call from Pat one day, when Gordon was on holiday. A potential customer in Ohio had the problem of lifting a very large bridge sufficiently to replace the bearings. For this he would require eight 1,000 ton hydraulic jacks, together with the appropriate pumps and hoses. Our biggest jacks at that time were 200 ton capacity and Pat had scoured the USA but found only three suitable jacks available for hire from different sources. So in order to meet the customer's requirement we would have to buy five new jacks at $25,000 each, with the promise of maybe only a couple of weeks hire revenue.

Cash flow, as ever, was tight and there was no guarantee that we'd ever get another order for this size of jack, but I felt that if we didn't accept the order then someone else would and we'd never again be considered as the leading hirers of lifting equipment in the USA. I authorised Pat to spend the $125,000 on five new huge jacks and, together with the three units he was able to rehire, the Ohio contract went ahead. In the event, Pat was able to negotiate a generous hire rate for these rare items and, as is usual, the job over-ran its anticipated time, so we were able to recover more than half of the capital cost on the first hire. We're still the only company who can offer so many large jacks and they've been out on hire several times since.

In any family controlled business, the problem of management succession planning is always prominent in our thinking and, by 2008, we had to consider Pat's forthcoming retirement, due in May 2009. Pat had been a very fit and active individual who would regularly be in the gym with his pals at 6.30 a.m. before turning up at the office. However, he had developed a liver problem which was proving to be very debilitating and because of this he was determined to retire at the age of sixty-five. Pat's son Tony, an engineering graduate, had worked in the business since the early days in a variety of roles and had been groomed to take over the chief executive's position when Pat retired. This worked out perfectly for all concerned and Tony's calmer and more measured conduct has proved to be well suited for taking the company forward from where we were in 2009, whereas Pat's qualities had been admirable for the start-up endeavours from 1990 onwards.

Irene and I, together with our two sons and Gordon Worswick, went to Chicago for Pat's retirement party. Pat and his wife Glori had become keen on ballroom dancing during the previous few years and plenty of their friends from the dancing club were also present. Pat made a big effort to be his usual jovial and energetic self, but it was clear that he was not well. The following day was a Monday and we all turned up at our Bridgeview offices to be told that Pat had been taken to hospital, having fallen into a coma during the night. After a few very anxious days, during which it was touch and go whether or not he would survive, he came out of the coma and doctors were able to stabilise his condition. A few weeks, later a donor was found with a perfectly matching new liver and Pat was able to have a transplant. The brave donor was Annette, Pat and Glori's daughter. Half of Annette's liver was transferred to Pat and both operations were perfectly successful. The liver is able to regenerate itself so both father and daughter now have fully functional complete livers. The miracles of modern medicine! Pat made a full recovery and, less than a year later, was able to join Irene and I together, with fifty guests, at Gleneagles in Scotland to celebrate my 70th birthday.

I remember going to a party at a friend's house in the 1970s where I met a solicitor and, after the usual small talk, he asked me what I did for a living. When I told him that I hired out lifting equipment he was incredulous and said, "Can one make a living doing that?" I wish I could show him our American business now, with its 98,000 sq. ft. facility in Chicago and nineteen other locations, generating over $50 million per annum turnover with almost 200 highly skilled and motivated staff.

Chapter 39 - Hobbies

I've always had a wide variety of interests and hobbies in addition to participating in several different sporting activities. The pursuit of these has allowed me to meet many interesting people with similar pastimes and I believe has kept me stimulated and motivated. I've never become particularly proficient in any of these activities, but just to try them has given me an extraordinary amount of satisfaction. In no particular order I can describe some of these hobbies as follows:-

Painting

During our many holidays in Menorca we would frequently see a particularly picturesque farmhouse which Lorraine claims that I often said that I'd love to be able to paint. She took me at my word and bought me a Christmas present in 1998 consisting of a variety of artists' equipment. There were acrylics, oils, watercolours, pastels, pencils, paper, brushes, palettes, an easel, art instruction books and videos. I had absolutely no artistic talent and had the distinction of being one of the only pupils at Clitheroe Grammar School to fail GCE Art. However, it would have been churlish not to give it a try after Lorraine had been so thoughtful and thorough.

Over the next few weeks, I worked my way through the different materials, followed the various instructional books and gradually improved my technique to such an extent that some of my efforts didn't get immediately consigned to the rubbish bin. I found oils to be fairly easy to use and forgiving to a certain extent, as it was possible to paint over any mistakes. However, they were messy and smelly with the constant addition of turpentine and linseed oil and I didn't get much satisfaction from this medium. For a time, I enjoyed using acrylics, which have a similar feel to oil paints without the smell. I tried oil pastels too, without much success. It was when I started regularly painting in watercolours that I became enthralled with this medium, which I believe is the most difficult and satisfying of all of the different painting techniques.

After trying one or two local painting classes, I finally found an instructor whose teaching and painting style exactly suited my needs. Nolan Abbott was a hippie 70 year old from Wigan with silver hair tied back in a ponytail and he played blues harmonica in a jazz band. He was a very talented watercolour artist and an excellent, good humoured teacher. His classes were held once a week in a church hall in Wigan, where the pupils were mainly retired professional ladies with a few men like myself. (When I say 'professional ladies' I mean teachers, secretaries etc.) The charge was £2 for two hours. After a year or so, my good friend Ken Fox, who was a talented technical drawer, also joined the class. Under Nolan's tutelage, we made great progress for several years and thoroughly enjoyed ourselves.

Unfortunately, Nolan's health forced him to give up teaching, leaving Ken and I without the disciplined structure of attending classes each week. This has meant that I've been less active with painting than was the case when Nolan was teaching. Each year in autumn it became my practice to paint a winter snow scene, which I then had printed as a Christmas card. After a few years of doing this I was contacted by David Bedford, who ran the Golfing Society for the Duke of Edinburgh's Award charity. I'd always sent a card to David and his wife, Pat, and David asked me to give him one of my paintings to be auctioned for the benefit of the charity at one of the golf events. I was mortified because I was convinced that it was unlikely that anyone would make a bid for one of my paintings, which would be highly embarrassing. In the end David persuaded me to let him have a painting of Ullswater in the Lake District, for which my friend David Smith, from Windermere, was generous enough to bid £500 in a fiercely contested auction. I was astounded and thrilled and now, every time I see David Smith, he tells me that he loves seeing my painting every morning at breakfast where it hangs in his morning room.

My love of watercolour painting was further stimulated when I saw a copy of Lancashire Life magazine in around 2002. The featured artist that month was a watercolourist from the village of Sabden, near Clitheroe. His work, reproduced in the magazine, completely blew me away. His paintings were very loose and impressionistic and achieved effects which I knew from my own experience were incredibly difficult to produce. His name was Trevor Lingard and the article informed the reader that his work could be bought at a gallery in the small Lancashire town of Whalley. I rang the gallery immediately and agreed to visit them the following day, when I bought two of Trevor's beautiful paintings. Luckily for me Trevor had stuck a label on the back of each painting giving his address and 'phone number. I wasted no time in contacting him and arranged to visit him at his house/studio.

Over the years, we have become firm friends and have spent painting holidays together in Menorca and Tuscany, together with Ken Fox. On one occasion, in Menorca, we had decided to paint the picturesque fishing village of Es Grau and had set up our easels in a quiet area overlooking the bay, a few hundred yards outside the village. Ken and Trevor were in front and I set up behind them so that I could include them in my scene. We were working away intently when a young woman climbed over the fence and went to talk to my two friends, who turned round and pointed at me. She approached me and explained that she and her colleague, who had by then appeared, were working for Spanish TV, creating a documentary about the tourism industry in Menorca. She asked if I could do an interview on camera and in Spanish!

My Spanish is good for ordering 'dos cervezas por favor' but not much more, but I agreed to give it a go provided that she spoke slowly and used simple terminology. I was able to tell her that we loved visiting the island for its tranquility and beautiful weather, together with astoundingly unspoilt countryside and excellent restaurants. Then she asked me a question of which I understood not a single word. I asked her to repeat the question and when I still didn't understand I just collapsed in a fit of laughter. She thanked me profusely for the few minutes she'd captured and said it would fit her programme perfectly. We were in a local bar a few nights later when, much to our surprise, the programme was on the TV in the bar, but thankfully they'd edited out my giddy fit.

Trevor took the plunge to become a full time professional artist a few years ago and his reputation has developed both nationally and internationally. He is undoubtedly one of the most talented British watercolourists and I have continued to add to my collection of his paintings which now number over twenty.

Magic

My introduction to the art of Magic came in a similar way to painting. I'd always enjoyed having little tricks with which to entertain the children and our younger son, Steve, interpreted this as a hankering to be a magician. One Christmas, around 2001, he sent a set of three video tapes from America which had been produced by an actor/magician called Larry Anderson. On each tape he demonstrated about a dozen magic tricks in front of a small group of young friends, then explained how the magic effect was achieved. He also showed how to prepare any gimmicks which might be needed and stressed the importance of diligent practice before presenting an effect to a live audience. On each tape there'd be three or four tricks which really impressed me and I thought, "I could do that".

I started slowly at first and chose one or two tricks for their impact and simplicity of performance then, after sufficient practice, tried them out on family and friends. The response was very satisfying and encouraged me to extend my repertoire over the next few months. When we stopped playing squash and badminton on Monday nights in 1995, my good friends David Slane, Ray Garside and John Holdbrook and I decided to continue to meet each Monday night for a few pints and a game of dominoes. Our numbers were supplemented by newer friends, Alan Greenhalgh and Andy Sanderson. This group formed the main sounding board for my magic effects and every Monday night I'd be asked to present a new trick. This sounds pretty easy but to do the research, find a new trick, prepare whatever gimmicks might be required and practice sufficiently to give a polished performance every Monday night proved increasingly difficult. However, it did force me to develop an extensive array of tricks and encouraged me to establish a distinct performance style.

It's said that the difference between a professional magician and an amateur is that the professional has only a few tricks which he performs incredibly well to a different audience every night, whereas an amateur has hundreds of tricks which he performs less well to the same audience every night. Having tried to satisfy my mates' appetite for new tricks every Monday night, I could see the truth in that saying. My brand of magic is called 'close-up' and is suitable for presenting to small groups sitting round a table rather than a stage presentation. A new group was formed called the Manchester Circle of Magicians, of which I was a very early member and which became one of the largest Magic Circles in the country. It was very interesting and informative to attend their regular monthly meetings and watch presentations by visiting world famous professional magicians, who would give instructional lectures.

Our local 41 Club (ex-Round Table members) contained quite a few talented musicians who gave a concert with a meal each December at the local golf club. One year they asked me to go round the tables performing magic in between the music acts and, although I was terrified, I agreed to give it a try. It was very exhilarating to perform in public to complete strangers and I gained a tremendous amount of satisfaction when I pulled off a tricky effect and saw the looks of astonishment on my audience's faces. The organisers must have had decent feed-back regarding my efforts because I was asked back every year after that

Notaphily

I've described briefly in Chapter 4 how I came to be interested in collecting bank notes, in particular old English bank notes. David Hindle wasn't to know at the time that showing me those £1 notes dating back to the First World War would spark a lifetime's interest in collecting old bank notes. My interest was further stimulated and sustained by the fact that within four miles of my home was the excellent shop of one of the country's best and most knowledgeable coin and note dealers, Brian Dawson who, along with his wife Veronica (Ronnie) and later their son Paul, would be of significant help to me in building my collection.

Whenever an auction featuring bank notes was to be held, usually in London at Sotheby's or Spink's, Brian would obtain a copy of the catalogue and we'd go through it together, assessing which notes on offer would fill a gap in my collection. I'd give him upper limits for my bidding strategy. Over a period of about forty years, Brian and Paul bought many notes on my behalf and my collection grew in a most satisfying way. We weren't always successful, of course. Although notaphily, as the hobby is called, is not as widespread as stamp collecting, there is keen competition from a number of wealthy collectors for the rarer specimens. One conspicuous hole in my collection was the absence of a £1,000 note. Although these had been issued by the Bank of England from 1725 up until 1943, they were very rare and opportunities to buy one occurred extremely infrequently. I remember being in London in the mid-1970s and called into the shop of Stanley Gibbons, the famous stamp dealers. They also stocked bank notes and I asked if I could see any interesting notes they might have in stock. I was amazed when they produced a £1,000 note with an asking price of £2,500. A stamp collector would have to pay many times that amount for a stamp with the same rarity as this £1,000 note.

I was desperate to buy the note, as I might never get the chance again, but my business was hungry for cash and I couldn't justify taking that amount of money for what was, after all, just a piece of paper. Reluctantly, I declined the deal and walked away from what would have been the jewel in my collection. I didn't hear of another such note being offered for sale for another twenty years, when Brian 'phoned me to tell me that Sotheby's were listing a £1,000 note in a forthcoming sale. We met to discuss tactics. By this time prices had hardened and the estimate for the star lot was £6 - 8,000. Brian assured me that if I was prepared to go to £10,000 then it would almost certainly be mine. I decided to accompany him to London for the auction, although I didn't sit with him. I was excited and full of anticipation that this rare and highly coveted note would finally be mine.

The auction proceeded smoothly until the bidding reached about £6,000, with Brian holding the winning bid. The hammer was about to fall when a new bidder came in, running it up to my agreed limit of £10,000. It was against us. Brian turned round to me and I signalled for him to keep going. When our bid of £12,000 was overtaken I instructed Brian to withdraw and I was left frustrated once more. Brian knew the successful bidder who was a dealer and we made arrangements to meet him later in his London office. He congratulated me on our spirited attack but said that there was no way that we could have been successful as he was acting on behalf of a client who had told him to buy the note with no limit set on the bidding. He told us that less than twenty £1,000 notes were known to be in private collections and his client owned twelve of them! The higher the price this note made, the more the value of his collection was enhanced proportionately.

Over the next few years I was eventually successful in buying several £1,000 notes, and other high denomination notes signed by different Chief Cashiers. The most notable addition to my collection came from another Sotheby's auction in the 1980s. During the Second World War, the economies of the European countries had been devastated whilst the USA enjoyed relative prosperity. To help their European cousins to recover after the war, the US government devised the Marshall Aid Plan, as a result of which funds were lent by America to the impoverished European countries. The UK received £8,000,000 of this aid as a loan and, as security, the Treasury printed eight £1,000,000 notes. In the event, the loan was repaid quite quickly and the eight notes were returned to the Treasury. Six of them were destroyed but, as a memento, the US and British Treasury Secretaries were each given a note with a hole punched through the signature of Lord Bridges. These two notes eventually found their way into the public domain and one of these was about to be offered for sale by Sotheby's.

Although the notes had never been legal currency, the sale of the highest denomination note ever printed in the UK attracted widespread media attention. The 1953 film *The Million Pound Note*, starring Gregory Peck, was remembered and bidding was expected to be keenly contested. I was unable to attend the auction but Brian and I had agreed that he could go to £40,000 to secure this iconic piece of history. That would represent the highest price ever paid at auction for a British note, but I felt that it was justified because (a) it was the largest value ever printed and had the iconic £1,000,000 denomination, (b) it was incredibly rare, being one of only two which existed, and (c) it was a document which formed part of an important part of world history. In the event I was delighted to secure it anonymously for £23,000.

There is a wider variety and larger quantity of Bank of England notes than most people realise. The notes bear the signature of the Chief Cashier and there were fifteen different Chief Cashiers, from Abraham Newland in 1778 to Leslie O'Brien in 1955. Notes were issued by the Bank in differing denominations, £5, £10, £20, £50, £100, £200, £500 and £1,000. Also, the Bank had regional offices in Manchester, Leeds, Hull, Liverpool, Birmingham, Newcastle, Plymouth and Bristol and other cities for much of the time. These regional offices issued notes with their own imprint so, when all of the combinations of different Chief Cashiers, denominations and regional offices are considered, there are a massive number of different collectible notes. Given the rarity of some of these, no collection could ever be considered to be complete. By 2008, my collection was valuable enough for my insurers to insist that it be kept in a bank vault, which denied me the pleasure of looking through my albums from time to time. None of my children or grandchildren showed any particular interest in my bank notes so I decided to sell the collection through a public auction at the specialist dealers, Spink of London.

The auction was held on 1st October 2008, with the impact of the international banking crisis at its height. I was tempted to cancel the sale because of the financial turmoil but the consensus opinion of the professionals was that the prices of rare collectibles would not be adversely affected and, in fact, there might be a move away from traditional stock market type investments into this type of alternative asset. In the event, Irene and I travelled down to London by train to be present at the auction. Spink had taken my collection some weeks earlier, photographed each item and produced a beautiful full colour sales catalogue showing upper and lower estimates for each note. The national daily newspapers had printed the story of the sale with great emphasis on the million pound note.

The catalogue had been distributed to known collectors all over the world and, as proceedings got under way, with telephone and on-line bidders in addition to those in the packed auction room, we were sitting on the edges of our seats. It was a bitter-sweet experience for me to see the fruits of almost fifty years avid collecting sold under my nose in under two hours of frenzied bidding. Hardly anything remained unsold and most items exceeded their estimates. The star of the show, of course, was the £1,000,000 Treasury Note which had been estimated to raise £35,000 to £40,000. The bidding for this was very keen and a new world record price was set at £85,000. It was incredibly exciting for Irene and myself and a very satisfactory final total of over half a million pounds was made.

Chapter 40 - In Search of Excellence

In 1982 a book was published which is reputed to have revolutionised business practices in the USA and elsewhere. It is called *In Search of Excellence* and was written by the McKinsey management consultant Tom Peters and his partner Bob Waterman. The book became an immediate best-seller in business circles and I bought a copy and devoured every word. The authors had set out to discover what common factors, if any, were shared by exceptionally successful businesses in a wide range of activities, from manufacturing to hotels, from supermarkets to restaurants. What was the magic ingredient which differentiated the massively successful companies from the rest? This was surely the fundamental question to which every serious businessman required the answer and it turned out to be surprisingly simple. The common denominator for all of these diverse companies was .... excellence.

This relatively simple concept seems obvious but Peters and Waterman found that the most successful ventures were excellent in everything they did. This meant not just their core activity of say, making automobiles, but in every other activity that supported the core. Design, planning, administration, finance, human resources, marketing, skills training and every other aspect of the business had to be given the highest priority to achieve the best possible level of excellence.

The book had a profound effect on my thinking, not necessarily because it was teaching me anything new, but because it reinforced what I was already trying to achieve in my rapidly growing business at that time in the early eighties. I bought several copies of the book and gave one to each of my senior management colleagues. This philosophy of continually striving for excellence was not just the preserve of senior management, though. It had to be endemic throughout the organisation in every department and at every level. I wanted everyone in the business to 'buy in' to the idea that anything less than excellent was not acceptable. This sounds so obvious that you'd expect every commercial enterprise to operate with such thinking in mind, but every day we experience examples of poor quality in manufacturing and standards of service.

Just as the characteristics of a human being are set at the moment of conception, I believe that the fundamental nature of a business is established very early in its life. And the nature of the business has to be determined by the owner or founder or partners. It will necessarily reflect their characteristics, so if you've recently established a business or are contemplating doing so soon, you need to give very careful thought, not just to the core activity of the business but to all of the peripheral areas which support the main revenue-generating activity. At the time that I started LGH in 1970 I'd never been on a management course or studied business administration. I'd never read a book on business management and just made decisions instinctively. But, whether through good luck or good management, the company structure and the founding principles by which the company's affairs were conducted stood the test of time and enabled the business to grow from its humble beginnings in the basement of my home into the international concern with over $60,000,000 in sales which it has now become.

The principles which I adopted in the very early days can be summed up as follows:-

Integrity

Always treat customers, staff, suppliers and professional advisors with honesty and fairness. You'll be rewarded with respect and trust from those around you.

Fallibility

You might be the boss and the owner of the business but that doesn't mean that you're infallible. You'll make hundreds of decisions in your business life and not all will be correct. Don't be afraid to admit that you're wrong when the occasion requires it. Others will see that as a sign of strength, not weakness.

Ability

You will require a wide range of qualities and skills to manage a successful business. I believe that it's more important to have an absence of weaknesses rather than an outstanding skill. For instance, if I'd been a highly skilled engineer I'd probably have spent a disproportionate amount of time dealing with technical issues rather than developing the business. Endeavour to identify your weakest talents and try to engage staff who are strong in those areas.

Staff

I preferred to think of my employees as 'staff' or 'colleagues' and that's how I always referred to them. Engage the highest quality staff which you can afford. Treat them well and with respect. Each member of staff has a contribution to make to the success or otherwise of your business. Don't hesitate to remind them how critically important their work is to the enterprise.

Empowerment

As your business grows in size and complexity it won't be possible for you to make all the decisions. You'll have to be prepared to delegate decision making increasingly to your colleagues. Be ready to accept that they won't always make the same decision that you would have made in the same circumstances. That's the price you have to pay for freeing up your precious time.

Passion

When your business is young and small it shouldn't be the most important thing in your life. It should be the ONLY thing. You have to eat, live and breathe every aspect of the business. If you're not passionate about it you can't expect anyone else to commit to your ideas.

Advantages

"Whatever is to the advantage of one side is to the disadvantage of the other." That is a quotation from Karl von Clausewitz, the great military strategist. It became a mantra for me as I realised that gaining an order from a customer in a competitive situation not only made my company stronger but, at the same time, made my competitor weaker. You work hard to generate enquiries. Don't let the order slip through your fingers.

Detail

"The devil is in the detail" - another favourite quotation which guided my philosophy. Keep checking that every aspect of your business is working as well as it's possible to do. Good enough is not an option.

Diary

Always keep a diary and meticulously note everything which you've arranged, agreed or promised. Review your notes continuously. Computers and Smartphones make this task easier.

What if?

Always look for potential risks to your business and make contingency plans to minimise the downside risk to your business in the event of detrimental outside events. The more obvious examples would be power cuts, petrol rationing, postal strike, computer failure etc.

Partners

In my main business ventures I always had and still have, sole control. Having a partner complicates and slows down the decision making process. If at all possible, my general rule would be to avoid having a partner.

Shareholders

It is not necessary to reward senior staff with shares in your business. Shares which are not traded on the stock market and do not pay a dividend are worthless until the business is sold. I'm a great believer in bonus schemes that include all staff at whatever level of seniority. If your company's doing well, let the staff know so that they can share the excitement of being part of a success story.

Your take

Especially in the early days, take only modest drawings for yourself from your company. Conserve cash in the business as much as possible to ensure that you can cope with the unexpected. Things go wrong from time to time and it's of no help at those times to have a fancy car in the garage.

Thinking

Indulge yourself in some thinking time. Stare into space. Try to envisage what your business could become in one, two or three years time. Dream a bit and then consider what you have to do to make your dreams come true.

If you're a small businessman or woman who wishes to be a big businessman or woman, follow these principles and I promise you'll succeed. It's not rocket science and it worked for me!

About the Author

Being born during the war of Lancastrian working class parents and subsequently only managing three 'O' level passes was not a promising start for businessman turned author Bill Parkinson.

After being sacked from his job in 1969, Bill started his own business hiring out lifting equipment. This company, Lifting Gear Hire Ltd, became the biggest such company in the world with locations not only in the UK but also in Holland, Germany and the USA. Along the way he has started, acquired and sold many businesses, some of which succeeded and others which didn't.

He is married with three children and four grandchildren and is a keen golfer. Despite his busy family and business commitments he still finds time to visit his local pub regularly to play dominoes and pool with his mates. His blog is at www.billparkinson.org/